RELIGIOUS STUDIES, THEOLOGICAL STUDIES AND THE UNIVERSITY-DIVINITY SCHOOL

Scholars Press

Studies in Theological Education

Christian Identity and Theological Education	Joseph C. Hough, Jr./ John B. Cobb, Jr.
Vision and Discernment: An Orientation in Theological Study	Charles M. Wood
The Arts in Theological Education: New Possibilities for Integration	Wilson Yates
Beyond Clericalism: The Congregation as a Focus for Theological Education	Joseph C. Hough, Jr./ Barbara G. Wheeler
The Education of the Practical Theologian: Responses to Joseph Hough and John Cobb's *Christian Identity and Theological Education*	Don S. Browning/ David Polk/ Ian S. Evison
Piety and Intellect: The Aims and Purposes of Ante-Bellum Theological Education	Glenn T. Miller
Religious Studies, Theological Studies and the University-Divinity School	Joseph Mitsuo Kitagawa

Religious Studies, Theological Studies and the University-Divinity School

Edited by
Joseph Mitsuo Kitagawa

Foreword by
Robert Wood Lynn

Scholars Press
Atlanta, Georgia

RELIGIOUS STUDIES, THEOLOGICAL STUDIES AND THE UNIVERSITY-DIVINITY SCHOOL

edited by
Joseph Mitsuo Kitagawa

© 1992
Scholars Press

Library of Congress Cataloging in Publication Data

Religious studies, theological studies, and the university-divinity
    School / edited by Joseph Mitsuo Kitagawa ; foreword by Robert Wood
    Lynn.
        p. cm. — (Scholars Press studies in theological education)
        ISBN 1-55540-559-2 (cloth). — ISBN 1-55540-560-6 (paper)
        1. Theology—Study and teaching—United States. 2. Universities
and colleges—United States—Religion. I. Kitagawa, Joseph Mitsuo,
1915- . II. Series.
BV4030.R45   1992
207.1'1—dc20   92-23083
                                                    CIP

Printed in the United States of America
on acid-free paper

Dedicated to
The Unfulfilled Vision of
William Rainey Harper

Contents

Preface ix

Foreword
    Robert Wood Lynn xiii

Introduction
    Joseph Mitsuo Kitagawa 1

The Marginalization of Theology in the University
    Joseph C. Hough, Jr. 37

UBI THEOLOGIA, IBI ECCLESIA? Schleiermacher,
Troeltsch, and the Prospect for an Academic Theology
    B.A. Gerrish 69

Three Revolutions in Theology and Theological Education
    Glenn T. Miller 95

The Study of Religion and the Rise of the American University
    Conrad Cherry 115

A Common Ancestor: Theology and Religious Studies
    Charles H. Long 137

Between Church and Academy:
The Dilemma of American Catholic Theology
    William C. Spohn, S.J. 151

Theological Consortia: The Creative
Space Between Church and University
    Judith A. Berling 171

Biographical Notes 197

Editor's Preface

JOSEPH MITSUO KITAGAWA

The aim of this volume is to reflect on the nature, perspective, and objective of the "university-divinity school." It is not to explore the relevance of theological education or religious studies in general. Excellent studies on these subjects are readily available. The "university-divinity school" is a present enigma to most outsiders as well as to many insiders. Our discussion will touch upon the historical and modern features of the institutions of higher learning in Europe and elsewhere, but our primary concern is with the contemporary university in North America, especially in the United States. Since we are concerned basically with the subject matters of theology and religion, we are compelled to refer both to theological studies, which are carried on in free-standing denominational or interdenominational seminaries and to non-theological, religious studies programs of the American college or university. Our purpose is to delineate the proper and adequate relationships between the university-divinity school and other significant institutions which share many concerns in common.

In today's society, most people take it for granted that they know what the university is all about. A fair number of people believe that the nomenclature of the divinity school is nothing but a synonym for the theological seminary, that is, a training school for ordained minsters and other religious leaders. As such, it is thought to be a scholarly arm and an academic echo chamber for religious groups and communities. To them it is problematic to envision the existence of the divinity school as a part of the university which ideally stands for unbiased objectivity, neutrality and universality. Many people realize through historical reference why and how the university-divinity school came into existence, but they question the wisdom and validity of such an institution for the present and future. Today, the university-divinity school is bound to raise serious intellectual, academic, religious, and theological questions.

Giving serious thought to the nature and task of the university-divinity school in the contemporary world is one of the several related projects which have been inspired by Robert Wood Lynn, for many years vice-president in charge of religion for the Lilly Endowment. Dr. Lynn has for some time been deeply disturbed by the increasing unclarity of the unique character of the university-divinity school. An added issue is its relationship, on the one hand, to *theological studies* of free-standing seminaries, and on the other, to the mushrooming programs of *religious studies* in the college and the university. Both of these currently exhibit impressive vigor and zest. The writer, who in much more modest ways shares similar concerns, considers it a great privilege to have received subsidy from the Lilly Endowment for a year and a half of concentrated research on this problem.

We agreed that the best outcome of our research project would be to encourage other colleagues and friends to carry on meaningful discussions on this intricate issue however inadequate our current thinking on the subject may be. We are very grateful to the Lilly Endowment for providing "consultants" and "local advisors" to keep the project from going too far astray, and also for enabling Joseph C. Hough (formerly Dean of the School of Theology, Claremont, now Dean of the Divinity School of Vanderbilt University) and Glenn T. Miller (author of the recently published *Piety and Intellect: The Aims and Purposes of Antebellum Theological Education*) to enrich our volume with their contributions. Our project was significantly aided by "local advisors"—our colleagues at the University of Chicago, Anne E. Carr, W. Clark Gilpin, and Robin W. Lovin, who cheerfully read voluminous papers and offered insightful comments and advice.

Undoubtedly the real backbone of the project was the "consultants" (listed below). They not only exchanged stimulating papers among themselves but also carried on, with the helpful participation of Robert Lynn, Joseph Hough, and Glenn Miller, perceptive, multi-dimensional—and often very heated—discussions. We are greatly indebted to them for their contribution of articles in this volume. (It is a matter of regret that we are deprived of James Hennesey's contribution because of ill health, and that Stanley Lusby could not complete his article on time.)

Judith A. Berling Dean
  Graduate Theological Union, Berkeley, California

Conrad Cherry
  Director, Project on Religion and American Culture
  — Indiana & Purdue Universities, Indianapolis, Indiana

Brian A. Gerrish
  John Nuveen Professor of Theology, The Divinity School
  of the University of Chicago, Chicago, Illinois

*James Hennesey, S.J
  (Formerly President, Jesuit School of Theology at Chicago);
  now at Canasius College, Buffalo, New York

Charles H. Long
  Jeanette K. Watson Professor of History of Religions,
  Department of Religion, Syracuse University, Syracuse, New York

F. Stanley Lusby Professor of Religion
  Department of Religious Studies, University
  of Tennessee, Knoxville, Tennessee

William C. Spohn, S.J.
  Associate Professor of Theological Ethics at the Jesuit School
  of Theology and Graduate Theological Union, Berkeley, California

We are delighted that Robert Lynn, now retired from the Lilly Endowment, has agreed to add a brief "Foreword" to this volume. Obviously, without his untiring support, together with the cooperation of Franklin I. Gamwell, Dean of the Divinity School of the University of Chicago who hosted our Project, this volume would not have come into being. It is also my pleasant duty to acknowledge profound gratitude to my able research assistants, Jeffrey Kripal and Karen Pechilis, who have been willing to shoulder heavy editorial responsibilities because of my poor health.

Readers will readily see that no one (including the Lilly Endowment and the editor) has imposed any strictures or common framework on the essays included in this volume. None of the contributors feels that she or he has found new answers to solve over-night the tangled issues involved in the university-divinity school, but all felt it necessary to raise issues and questions for further discussions.

Let me conclude this Preface with an anecdote. Once John T. Wilson, former provost and president of the University of Chicago (who guided me during my deanship of its Divinity School), pointed out an unusual habit of some of the trustees, faculty, and students at Chicago. They referred to the first president as "President Harper" or "Mr. Harper," as though he were alive, still working somewhere on the campus. I must confess I am one of those who almost intuitively follow this habit. How often, as I struggled with the problems of the Divinity School, did I reflect on the policies and objectives advocated by President Harper! And I learned as much from his failures as from his rather conspicuous successes. Like other great university presidents of his time, he was sensitive to cultural and social realities which shaped the American private, graduate university. More than most other university presidents, however, he had a unique harmony with the religious (probably neither pious nor ecclesiastical) underpinning of higher education. He was persuaded that the religiously-inspired university should and could criticize, purify, and reform empirical religious traditions. He was convinced that university-oriented religious inquiry should be suffciently alert in questioning the adequacy of science and rationality (and other "sacred cows" of the modern university) as the sole resources for the discovery of and search for truth. Throughout his life, he tirelessly wrote and lectured on the imperative for religious vision, scrutinized to be sure by the critical inquiries of the university, to guide and transform our national and global social, cultural, and political orders. Most ironically and regretfully, his own personal commitment to biblical research often disguised his larger and deeper "religious vision" (in the broad sense of the term).

He left an abiding legacy of genuine religious concern to those of us who struggle with the question of proper relationships between religion and higher education in our time. Since we will soon observe the centenary of the university which he was instrumental in establishing in 1892, it might be appropriate for us to dedicate this volume as a token of gratitude to and appreciation of President Harper's unfulfilled educational and religious vision.

J.M.K.

Foreword

ROBERT WOOD LYNN

During the 1980s, a few scholars in American divinity schools and seminaries led the way towards rediscovering an important task that had been almost forgotten in the preceding decade and only intermittently remembered in the previous years of the twentieth century—the development of a critical literature about theological education. In 1980, theological faculty members or administrators in search of help in understanding their responsibilities would have found the available material on this subject thin, uneven, and for the most part, unilluminating. By far the best contributions to this body of material could be found in the multi-volume reports of gifted theologians who assessed the health of the enterprise in their times. So, for instance, the work of William Adams Brown of Union Theological Seminary (NYC) and his colleagues in the 1930s or the later reflections of H. Richard Niebuhr, Daniel Day Williams, and James M. Gustafson in the 1950s remained genuinely instructive and helpful. Although the authors of the "Niebuhr-Williams-Gustafson report" offered their findings as an invitation to further critical work on the "aims and purposes of theological education," their successors in the 1960s and 1970s largely ignored that topic and thereby missed the chance to build upon the work of H. Richard Niebuhr and associates.

The first sign of renewal of that conversation came in 1983 with the publication of *Theologia: The Fragmentation and Unity of Theological Education*[1], the pioneering work of Edward Farley of Vanderbilt Divinity

---

[1] Edward Farley, *Theologia: The Fragmentation and Unity of Theological Education* (Philadelphia: Fortress Press, 1983).

School. That small volume signalled the beginning of an exchange of views among a small cluster of scholars about the fundamental problems and purposes of American theological education. Two years later, to cite just one example, two professors from the Claremont School of Theology, Joseph C. Hough and John B. Cobb[2], as well as Charles M. Wood[3] of the Perkins School of Theology at Southern Methodist University brought other perspectives to bear upon the common problems facing seminary and divinity school leaders. By the end of the decade, W. Clark Gilpin of the University of Chicago could point to a "notable series of articles and monographs"[4] that had appeared in the span of just a few years.

Just as Professor Farley's first book opened the way toward discussion and debate in the 1980s, so his sequel volume—*The Fragility of Knowledge: Theological Education in the Church and University*[5]—gave a foretaste of the issues that might surface in the current decade. Among other suggestions, he called for a decisive turn in the conversation about theological education. The time has come, he implied, for a fresh appraisal of the place of theological studies in the contemporary university.

The work of Joseph M. Kitagawa and his colleagues in this volume will be an indispensable companion to anyone caring to join in this second round of discussion. There is nothing quite like this book in the available literature on American theological education.

An Identity Crisis

It is a curious fact that none of the major contributors to the previous body of writing had much to say about the university theological school, even though the principal authors of the surveys in the 1930s and 1950s were members of a divinity school faculty or else a university-related seminary. In their efforts to portray the bewildering diversity of American seminary life, they seldom focused on the particular work of

---

[2] Joseph C. Hough and John B. Cobb, *Christian Identity and Theological Education* (Chico, CA: Scholars Press, 1985).

[3] Charles M. Wood, *Vision and Discernment: An Orientation to Theological Study* (Atlanta: Scholars Press, 1985).

[4] W. Clark Gilpin, "Basic Issues in Theological Education: A Selected Bibliography, 1980-1988," *Theological Education* 25, no. 2 (Spring, 1989), p. 115. It should be noted that many of the entries in Gilpin's selection came from the pages of the journal, Theological Education. Indeed, the marked improvement in the quality of that publication in the course of the decade reflected the expanding conversation about "basic issues" in North American theological education.

[5] Edward Farley, *The Fragility of Knowledge: Theological Education in the Church and the University* (Philadelphia: Fortress Press, 1988).

this type of institution. In the early 1930s, for example, William Adams Brown could look back upon the first third of the twentieth century as a period in which the university schools had taken the lead in educating future seminary leaders and in setting the academic standards for most American theological schools. Therefore he took for granted the existence of this pace-setting institution and assumed it would continue to flourish in the future.

Today, however, that kind of assurance is no longer so easy. Ever since the 1960s, the university schools have faced increasing pressure on two fronts. The rapidly-expanding programs of religious studies in colleges and universities have offered tough intellectual challenges and competition for promising scholars in the study of religion. On the other side, some free-standing seminaries have become increasingly confident that they could match the divinity schools as centers of scholarship and then surpass them in providing first-rate professional education. The result, as the contributors to this book make abundantly clear, is an identity crisis of major proportions.

I know of no better description of that identity problem than the one embedded in Professor Kitagawa's introductory essay. His discriminating analysis helps the reader sort out the variety of theological institutions which claim some kind of relation to a university. The climax of the argument comes in his effort to distinguish between "university-oriented" and "church-oriented" divinity schools. That distinction should provoke some lively discussion and debate in diverse quarters. Joseph Kitagawa clearly hopes that a few American divinity schools will become genuinely "university-oriented" in perspective. (An aside: it is not clear, at least to this reader, whether he believes that *any* present-day school can make a legitimate claim to be "university-related.")

Yet those of us who would applaud such a move will encounter considerable skepticism in different quarters. Some critics will doubtless ask questions along the following lines. To wit: what constituency—either within or without the university—will provide support over an extended period of time to a divinity school that is serious about being "university-oriented"? While the interpretation of the divinity school as one among several university-based *professional* schools is now well-worn and finally limited in its illuminating power,[6] it is still familiar enough and seemingly plausible to stir modest response from some individuals. An argu-

---

[6] For a thoughtful criticism of the time and energy lavished upon the "professional model of ministry" in both seminaries and divinity schools, see Glenn T. Miller, "Three Revolutions in Theology and Theological Education," see below p. 116.

ment of similar popular appeal on behalf of a "university-related" divinity school has yet to be mounted.

Whatever the outcome of his suggestions about the future work of an authentic "university-related" divinity school, Mr. Kitagawa has already made his most important point. He is surely right in pressing the current divinity schools to be clear about their distinctive work not only within the universities but also in contrast to religious studies programs and other kinds of theological institutions.

Most of his collaborators in this volume arrive at the same conclusion, each in his or her own fashion. Hence, they welcome the question, stated ever so bluntly by Joseph C. Hough—"Do theological studies have a home in the modern secular university?"[7] Significantly enough, Dean Hough's own response to that query implies doubts about the usual invocation of the university's responsibility to provide "excellent leadership in all of the various professions,"[8] including the ministry. His rejoinder to that standard bit of conventional wisdom is worth pondering, especially since it comes from the dean of a major university divinity school. "It is, of course, not self-evident that only university divinity schools are capable of ensuring the highest standards of competence and learning in the ministry."[9] He prefers an alternative argument that is more modest: "It is rather the fact that the faculty of the university schools continue to be the chief educators of the leadership of all theological education, particularly those who teach in divinity schools and seminaries."[10]

Some of the other essayists in the book apparently agree with this conclusion, though one registers a thoughtful *caveat* about the occasional results. The carefully stated worry of William C. Spohn, S.J., should not go unheeded: "Although Catholic higher education has benefitted considerably from the graduates of the major United States university-related divinity schools who increasingly staff its department of religious studies, those divinity schools have not infrequently left such graduates unequipped for the church context in which they will do theology."[11] I suspect that the leaders of Protestant free-standing seminaries would report much the same concern. If, in fact, the divinity schools do pin their

---

[7] Joseph C. Hough, Jr., "The Marginalization of Theology in the University," see below, p. 64.
[8] Ibid.
[9] Ibid.
[10] Ibid., p. 65.
[11] William C. Spohn, "Between Church and Academy: The Dilemma of American Catholic Theology," see below, p. 170.

hopes for the future on being the "chief educators of the leadership of all theological education," they might well attend to these reports.

In sum, the current dreams and faculties of university divinity schools—whether "church-oriented" or "university-oriented"—are up against formidable problems in clarifying and re-defining the fundamental identity of their institutions. Significantly enough, they share that challenge with the other two major "actors" in this small sector of American higher education, the college and university-based programs in "religious studies" and the "free-standing" seminaries. Informed observers of contemporary religious studies departments believe that many of these programs remain mired in the intellectual confusion of a new and still insecure academic guild. In this book, for instance, Professors Kitagawa and Long point in different ways to a hidden identity crisis that lurks beneath the surface of the religious studies enterprise.

Likewise the free-standing seminaries are no strangers to this syndrome. As hybrid institutions responsive to the competing and sometimes conflicting claims of the church and academy, these schools have often found it hard to arrive at a *principled* understanding of the appropriate balance between those two loyalties. In recent years, a fair number of free-standing schools have felt the pressures growing from both quarters. While some denominations press their seminaries to become more "accountable" to the church, scholarly critics question the intellectual integrity of studying only one religion as an academic enterprise. These contrary forces are slowly pushing the free-standing schools toward recognizing, however begrudgingly, the unsettling depths of their own identity problems.

Who will take the lead in acknowledging the seriousness of these three, somewhat inter-related, crises in institutional identity? My own guess is that the university divinity school leaders are the most likely hosts and intellectual *provocateurs* for launching this conversation. For the time being at least, the divinity schools constitute a "bridge" between the burgeoning empire of "religious studies" and the smaller world of the free-standing seminaries. If they possess the requisite historical imagination and clarity of mind and spirit, the divinity school faculties could make a crucial contribution to the future of North American studies of religion. This work constitutes, in effect, an invitation for divinity school leaders to discern the larger opportunity before them.

Spohn has nicely stated the *double jeopardy* involved in any failure to live creatively with those tensions.

Likewise, Judith A. Berling's essay points to another connection with Harper's legacy. Her timely portrait of the contemporary theological consortia rescues this subject from both the excessive enthusiasm of its advocates (especially in the 1960s) and the neglect it has suffered in more recent years. More important, Dean Berling's candid account of the "complex and chaotic"[15] nature of such consortial enterprises as the Graduate Theological Union (GTU) in Berkeley re-enforces the credibility of her argument for these institutions as occupying a potentially "creative space" between church and university. She also makes it clear that the GTU has probably gained considerably from the absence of a university divinity school as a partner in the Union—a turn of events, obviously enough, which William Rainey Harper did not anticipate. Can a theological consortium flourish if it includes a major divinity school? And if "[t]he moment is ripe for theological scholars once again to exert some leadership in defining the research agenda of the university,"[16] will those scholars have the confidence and competence necessary to take advantage of that occasion? I hope those questions will be asked in the days ahead, when more theological schools and universities begin to discover for themselves that "creative space between church and university."

Now I come to the third and most controversial of the three Harper affirmations. His vision of the modern university as a free and open "city on a hill" strikes a fair number of contemporaries as a relic left over from a vanished past. What once appeared grand and hopeful now seems merely grandiose. I would guess that Conrad Cherry might be among the critics, even though he does not mention Harper by name or Harper enthusiasts when he warns against "anachronistic reform movements which attempt to 'restore' an institution...to its 'unifying ideal.'"[17] In his clear and forceful essay, he stands astride the path of anyone who is tempted to return to earlier unitary visions of the university, whether it be the ideal of "liberal culture," "pure research" or of "public service"[18]—or in the case of Harper, the educational "city on a hill." Professor Cherry urges us, instead, to come to terms with the "twin

---

[15] Judith A. Berling, "Theological Consortia: The Creative Space between Church and University," see below, p. 184.
[16] Ibid., p. 194.
[17] Conrad Cherry, "The Study of Religion and the Rise of the American University," see below, p. 115.
[18] Ibid., p. 120.

movements of professionalization and specialization,"[19] forces that have irrevocably shaped the destiny of the contemporary university. Its "stubborn refusal to be governed by any one ideal,"[20] he concludes, makes the university impervious to the ambitious designs of the Harpers of this world.

His reminders about the dangers of nostalgia are salutary and well-taken, particularly in a period when we keenly feel the absence of powerful regulative ideals. The late A. Bartlett Giamatti, Yale's president for eight years before he moved on to the greener pastures of baseball, worried about the way in which leaders of American higher education had unwittingly created a "vacuum of definition"[21] about the nature of their common enterprise. Living in the strange emptiness of that "vacuum," we are all the more drawn to the presumed comforts of definitions which come out of an imperfectly remembered past.

But while appreciating these warnings against escapist diversions, I can still imagine that somewhere in the future, a group of divinity school and university leaders will once again be convinced of the need for a new religious vision of American higher education. If perchance they do turn in that direction, they will find the "unfulfilled vision" of William Rainey Harper—and therefore this book as a source of insight into his work—helpful in their quest.

A Turning Point

The larger significance of this series of essays lies both in its appearance at exactly the right time and also in its power to shed light upon this particular time in history. If the book had been published twenty-five years ago or so, it might well have aroused little interest, except perhaps for an occasional puzzled retort—"Why write anything on that subject?" In other words, the existence of the university divinity school in 1965 was not yet widely recognized as problematic. A quarter of a century later, the editor of this volume and his collaborators write out of a deepening awareness that the university divinity schools have arrived at a major turning point in their common history.

In the luxury of retrospective wisdom, one can look back and see why the divinity school seemed to be so "natural" a part of the university scene in New Haven, or Nashville or Chicago. In this connection,

---

[19] Ibid., p. 115.
[20] Ibid., p. 134.
[21] A. Bartlett Giamatti, *A Free and Ordered Space: The Real World of the University* (New York: W.W. Norton and Company, 1988), p. 26.

Professor Kitagawa is fond of quoting the words of Jacob Neusner of the University of South Florida: "It was the Protestant vision which shaped American university perspectives until the most recent past...I think...that the history of all forms of study in secular American universities can be written in terms of the history of *cultural, if not religious Protestantism.*"[22] If that daring thesis holds up under the closer inspection of inquiring historians, it will explain much about why the divinity school has remained so largely exempt from critical scrutiny.

Whatever the final verdict on that particular interpretation, such assumptions and habits of thinking no longer help in making sense of the *current* scene in New Haven, Nashville, or Chicago. When did this change take place? In his essay in this book, Charles H. Long points to the years between the publication of Paul Tillich's *The Protestant Era* in 1948 and today. "Now at the beginning of the last decade of the twentieth century," he writes, "it is clear beyond the shadow of a doubt that we are at the end of the Protestant era."[23]

What Tillich wrote in that concluding chapter, "The End of the Protestant Era?" has turned out to be strangely perceptive, although when it appeared it perplexed many of us. At least I can well remember my own confusion at the time (the late 1940s) about the apparent contradiction between Tillich's rather lugubrious and murky intuitions and the booming religious prosperity of post-war American Protestantism. When questioned about this jarring incongruity, one of my mentors at Yale Divinity School offered assurance that Tillich's interpretation applied to Europe, but probably not to the U.S.A. A recent re-reading of the essay helps me understand that response: Tillich did, in fact, orient his analysis toward the European experience—central Europe, to be exact. Even so, the advent of that piece marked the beginning of a transitional era in which "mainstream" Protestant in this country would gradually (and often reluctantly) come to understand the import of Tillich's work. In retracing the changing conceptions of "the end of the Protestant era" throughout the last four decades, Professor Long has convincingly demonstrated the magnitude of this period as a major turning point in the history of the study of religion and theology in America.

---

[22] Cited by Joseph M. Kitagawa in an unpublished paper, "Some Remarks on the Divinity School of the University of Chicago," p. 5 ms.
[23] Charles H. Long, "A Common Ancestor: Theology and Religious Studies," see below, p. 146.

The Long essay should be read in tandem with the chapters of Glenn T. Miller[24] and Joseph C. Hough, Jr. Dean Hough locates the story of the past forty years as one chapter in a longer history of "marginalization" that stretches over the sweep of centuries. His interpretative point is akin to the conclusions reached in a fine book edited by William R. Hutchison of Harvard University.[25] Professor Hutchison suggests that anyone intent upon comprehending the "decline" of the Protestant establishment since the 1960s should place the events of the last quarter of a century in the context of trends that were evident in early twentieth century America. So, for example, both interpreters point to the presence of William Adams Brown as a leader of an "establishment" already in considerable difficulty. Here, in brief, is a story that has been long in the making.

Another story long in the making is told in B.A. Gerrish's well-wrought essay about the "prospect for an academic theology." At the outset of this work, Professor Gerrish acknowledges the forces of the changes described earlier in the Hough and Long chapters. "It goes without saying," he notes," that the place of theology in the modern university can be defended only where its abdication as queen of the sciences is presupposed."[26] Within that context, he points to the possibility of an academic theology as a way beyond the unacceptable options currently available—"either a bloodless religion of reason that fits comfortably into the academy, or else a frankly Christian theology that awakens the suspicion of a divided loyalty."[27] His deft reconstruction of an immensely complicated history and his gentle pleas for a "tradition of learning" that is something more than a "cold autopsy on a dead body"[28] comprise a splendid addition to the literature on this subject.

In summary, the volume as a whole will enrich the thought of a wide range of readers—whether in divinity schools, university-related theological schools, free-standing seminaries, or those in departments of religious studies in colleges and universities—or anyone else ready to study it with the care it deserves. Of all these possible audiences, how-

---

[24] In this connection I should also mention Glenn T. Miller's recently published book, *Piety and Intellect: The Aims and Purposes of Theological Education in Antebellum America* (Atlanta: Scholars Press, 1990). Mr. Miller provides the first full-length treatment of the early history of the Protestant seminary in America. That account will help the reader understand the historical context within which the story told by Charles Long makes even greater sense.

[25] *Between the Times: The Travail of the Protestant Establishment in America, 1900-1960*, ed. William R. Hutchison (Cambridge: Cambridge University Press, 1989).

[26] B.A. Gerrish, "Ubi Theologia, Ibi Ecclesia? Schleiermacher, Troeltsch, and the Prospect for An Academic Theology," see below, p. 71.

[27] Ibid., p. 74.

[28] Ibid., p. 93.

ever, the university divinity school faculties have the most to gain in accepting this book as a point of departure for sustained conversation and study. It will provide a way of advancing into the thicket of problems that will confront them on any foreseeable path into the future.

And of all these challenges that lie ahead, the most important one—in my judgment—is the question to which Joseph Kitagawa has devoted so much of his life as a teacher and scholar: How can we learn to "criticize and restrain the absolutizing tendency of cultural ethnocentrism?"[29] Any progress made on that front will open up the promise of a new chapter of service in the honorable history of the university divinity schools.

---

[29] Joseph Mitsuo Kitagawa, "Introduction," see below, p. 34.

Introduction

JOSEPH MITSUO KITAGAWA

There are many ways to introduce the subject of the university-divinity school. I came to be concerned with this subject when I was asked to assume the Deanship of the Divinity School of the University of Chicago in 1970. It was then that I received a series of letters denouncing the Divinity School as a betrayer of the Christian religion and a sinkhole of hell. Soon I learned that previous deans had the honor of receiving such epistles. These letters made me curious about the background of the Divinity School and led to a considerable amount of reading on the subject of the university-divinity school.

I. *The Ambiguous Identity of The University-Divinity School*

Prior to assuming the Deanship, I asked a number of people—inside and outside the university, inside and outside religious communities, ordained ministers and laity, atheists, agnostics and believers, scholars of various disciplines, and friends in various parts of North America, Europe and Asia—what they considered the identity of the university-divinity school to be, and in what sense they thought it was going to be a viable institution in the United States in its third century. Some of them knew the past accomplishments of the university-divinity school. Many thought that the university-divinity school historically had provided a tangible model and realistic standard for what is now called "free-standing (usually denominational) seminaries." In recent decades, these have become academically sophisticated "theological colleges," emulating in part continental university theological studies as well as the university-divinity school in North America.

Many of the people with whom I spoke were very uncertain about the present or future relevance of the divinity school. About half of my friends felt that the university-divinity school is just another free-standing seminary (more often than not non- or inter-denominational in character) that, for historical reasons, happens to be situated on a university campus. Lamenting the confused state of the university-divinity school in our times, some of them even consoled me, saying that the university-divinity school had nurtured many outstanding free-standing seminaries. This, they said, was sufficient reason to be proud, despite the fact that the future of theological education and scholarship to them appeared to be clearly in the hands of the free-standing seminary which has now sufficiently matured to shoulder such responsibilities.

I was equally fascinated by another view held by a considerable number, especially those in general academic circles. They were persuaded that the term "divinity" is nothing but a dated nomenclature for the more modern "religious studies" departments that have become integral parts of North American state and private colleges and universities since the end of World War II, and especially since 1967. I readily recognized that this impression was not altogether groundless. Many men and women who now teach in religious studies were trained in the university-divinity school. Moreover, the objectives, scopes, styles, and methods of the university-divinity schools and those of the religious studies departments in colleges and universities have much in common. However, there are some formidable differences between the "religious studies" programs and the university-divinity schools, just as there are some basic differences between the university-divinity school and the free-standing seminary.

Part of this ambiguity can be attributed to the variety of university-divinity schools. While some divinity schools affiliated with church-sponsored colleges or universities are justly classified as university-divinity schools, they are in many ways not very different from the free-standing seminaries of their respective denominations in terms of financial subsidies and administrative styles. Many of their faculty members serve on denominational committees, and their students have direct access to their denominations' operative structures, including procedures for ordination and job placement. At the other extreme, there are "clusters" of free-standing seminaries, which as clusters are often affiliated in varying degrees with universities. Although none of these free-standing seminaries or clusters claims to be a university-divinity school, one cannot overlook the existence in each of some degree of university affiliation. Even the university-divinity schools in the narrow sense betray various kinds of differences among them, including historical backgrounds, tuition structure, faculty appointments, and styles of student activities.

II. Three Types of American Institutions for Theological/Religious Studies

Among numerous institutions that are directly or remotely concerned with theological/religious studies, for the purpose of this study, three broad types of institutions are depicted:

A. Free-standing (usually denominational) seminaries. Granted that a wide range of institutional styles and scholarly standards are represented in this category, all of them have one thing in common—that is, their dedication to one religion (Christianity or Judaism for the most part) not only as an important tradition to be studied, but as the most viable living faith to be advocated. Nevertheless, as hinted before, there is an almost infinite variety of institutions within this one broad category. While some of the free-standing seminaries are not much different from informal preacher training schools or Bible seminaries, some seminaries have become *de facto* "theological colleges," very sophisticated academic institutions devoted to "theological studies." (This trend has been accelerated by the concerns for accreditation and high scholarly faculty credentials, promoted especially the Association of Theological Schools in the United States and Canada). Also, as noted above, a number of free-standing seminaries now have some kind of university affiliation, often through "cluster" arrangements with other seminaries.

B. University-divinity schools. These are quite dissimilar in their relationships with their universities. Those divinity schools that are affiliated or related to church-owned or church-sponsored universities are in some ways closer to the free-standing seminaries of their respective denominations in ethos, objectives and styles. Those divinity schools that belong to or are affiliated with non-church-related universities seem to have much in common with the so-called "religious studies" programs of public universities, though the differences between these two programs are also substantial and should not be overlooked.

The university-divinity school appears differently to different people depending on the perspective from which it is viewed. Today many faculty members of free-standing seminaries presume that what they are doing is not any different from the theological/religious studies carried on in the university-divinity schools and hope that what they do as scholars will enhance the cause of the denominations that sponsor and support their seminaries. Since there is a far greater number of free-standing seminaries than university-divinity schools, many of these seminary scholar-teachers assume that theology covers the same scope in free-standing seminaries as it does in the universities. They are often not attentive to the fact that university-divinity schools might have different aims and perspectives concerning theological/religious studies. There are also faculty members of university-divinity schools who equate the tasks of their institutions with those of the free-standing seminaries, promoting, for example, more spiritual formation for future religious leaders or more diversified ministerial training programs within the curriculum of university-divinity schools.

On the other hand, many scholar-teachers of religious studies in various colleges and universities often jump to the conclusion that what goes on in the university-divinity schools is substantially the same kind of religious studies that they do. Many of them, however, acknowledge that university colleagues are probably more concerned than they are with the religious, theological "meaning" of religions. There are some faculty members in university-divinity schools who are restless, perhaps because of their rebellion against their own religious upbringing and/or what they regard as the "pettiness" of religious-philosophical symbols attached to their institutions. Many of them would prefer to replace their schools' inherited curricula with non-theological programs like religious studies programs of the colleges and universities. It is their hope to improve the current program of their schools with a heavier concentration on sociological, psychological, cultural, and anthropological analyses of the religions of the world. In their eagerness to introduce the subjects of world religions, they wish to de-emphasize courses on Judaism and Christianity, and some of them hope to do away with offerings on religious praxis.

C. Department of Religion/Religious Studies. These departments are often established within the arts and science faculties of state as well as private colleges and universities. Although there are inevitable differences in scope, objectives, and standards between undergraduate and graduate programs of religious studies,[1] they share similar concerns for the objective study of religion and religions (including Judaism,

---

[1] See J.M. Kitagawa, *The History of Religions: Understanding Human Experience* (Atlanta: Scholars Press, 1988), pp. 146-150.

Christianity, and other religious traditions) in contradistinction to the scholarly commitment of free-standing seminaries to study "one religion" which claims ultimacy (since advocacy is a natural component of such a theological approach). The main concern here is with the perspectives of religious studies in general in contradistinction to those of theological/religious studies both in the free-standing seminaries and university-divinity schools. Understandably, in some institutions of higher learning, e.g., Duke, Emory, and Southern Methodist, there are both divinity schools and departments of religious studies coexisting side by side as independent academic units.

Until recently, religion as a formal subject was not taught in American state colleges and universities, although many courses inevitably discussed the religious aspects and implications of human experience and culture. Several state universities have had so-called schools of religion, either on or adjacent to campuses, with salaries of faculty members paid mostly by sponsoring religious groups but with their courses usually accredited by the universities. After World War II, with the Supreme Court decision that objective study *about* religion was not in conflict with government neutrality with respect to religion, programs of religious studies mushroomed in colleges and universities. The justices stressed the distinction between the inculcation of specific religious beliefs and habits and the objective study of religion. The justices did not have to define what they meant by objective study, but those who were responsible for religious studies were keenly aware of the elasticity of objective study in reference to religion(s).

Many agreed that religious studies precluded religious advocacy or proselytizing, and no one was about to light candles or sing hymns in the classroom. Some people cogently argued that religious studies should not touch religious doctrines but rather stick to psychological, sociological, and cultural analyses of religion and religions. Others insisted equally cogently that to teach a religion, even objectively, one must go beyond offering information about the external aspects of a religion and evoke participation on the part of students in its sacred texts and their truth claims.

The meaning of "objective study" is still an open question, and this undoubtedly explains in part the contemporary disarray of religious studies programs. Meanwhile, concerned parents, religious leaders, and politicians have expressed their diverse opinions on the subject. There has been a persistent fear that a predominantly cognitive approach, with a heavy dependence on philosophical and/or various social-scientific methodologies, might rob religion of its "faith" and "piety" elements, that religious studies would not only explain religious phenomena but explain away religion altogether, effectively producing generations of intellectually well-informed but spiritually insensitive "agnostics." Over the years, however, religious studies programs in colleges and universities generally have been accepted in North America. A pragmatic agreement has developed, not about the meaning of *objectivity*, but about the *scope* of religious studies, based on the convergence of historical, political and common-sense factors, so that today religious studies stress the following three foci: (i) historical and contemporary analyses of Western, with special reference to the American, religious-cultural traditions; (ii) studies of major "world religions," based on the conviction that there are religious aspects to all human cultural traditions and that any intelligent study of religion in our pluralistic age must involve comparative approaches to diverse religions rather than viewing all the religious/cultural traditions of the human race from a particular, provincial religion's perspective; and (iii) the counteracting and overcoming of the public's habit of misunderstanding or overlooking not so apparent religious realities, often buried under social, economic, or political factors both historically and in the contemporary world. This includes various issues with which religion(s) deal, from individual, spiritual issues to social, cultural, economic, and political problems.

For all their lofty ideals, the programs of religious studies have had to deal with a rather extreme shortage of qualified teachers. The fact that most departments of religious studies have settled on hiring "experts" (with PH.D.s in most cases) in all too narrow specialized subjects has not solved this crucial problem. Indeed, it might have added further complications. There are at least two main reasons—one pragmatic and one theoretical—for this development. Pragmatically, architects of religious studies have had to convince the university faculty of the scholarly respectability of religious studies as well as to acquire appropriation of funds for their study. They have felt that hiring experts with graduate degrees is the easiest and best way to meet these practical needs. Theoretically, many of the pioneers of religious studies, following the bad examples of scientific and theological studies in the West, have adopted the model of the "machine" rather than the "picture" in approaching religion. They have thought it important to dissect this machine-like phenomenon called *religion* into a series of parts and compartments, each one requiring technical knowledge, e.g., languages, chronologies, and familiarity with the theoretical, practical, and sociological dimensions of religion. The lamentable fact is that a group of experts on disparate dimensions of religion do not create coherent programs of religious studies any more than a group of competent players of different instruments do not automatically create a coherent orchestra. Moreover, all the methodologies that these scholars are anxious to apply to non-Western religious/cultural traditions are very Western provincial methods rooted in the circular and self-authenticating Western convention of analyzing the texture of human experience. Thus, as hinted above already, what many programs of religious studies in North American colleges and universities provide today, despite their claims of "objectivity," "neutrality" and "universality," is a very West-centric approach to world religions and cultures, even given its relative freedom from the "religious ethnocentrism" that affected much of the earlier theological approaches to non-Western religions.

At any rate, this lack of a clear self-understanding of the objective, scope, perspective, and methodology of religious studies sometimes misleads people into assuming that almost any approach to religion—psychological, sociological, ethical, philosophical, even "semi-theological—is tolerated in religious studies, as long as it avoids such non-academic religious features as faith, piety and "truth claims." In addition to very negative reactions to the subjective affirmation of truth claims implicit in Christian or Jewish theological studies on the part of many who teach religious studies, these teachers' interpretations of non-Christian and non-Jewish religions are often mixed with their own brands of positive or negative subjective affirmations.

III. *The American Cultural-Religious Ethos*

The three basic types of programs we have identified—1) the free-standing seminary, 2) the university-divinity school, and 3) the department of religious studies of the college or university, suffer today from having "fuzzy edges" concerning their respective theoretical models, organizing principles, and practical implementation.

In this connection, there are analogies that exist between three Asiatic peoples (the Chinese, the Koreans and the Japanese) and these three American theological/religious programs. In the former, peoples of each group are convinced of their own "uniqueness," but there are enough similarities among them so as to deceive outsiders, who as a result often mistake one group for another. In the latter case, each program is supposed to be unique, but there is so much confusion concerning the identity of each on the part of its trustees, administrators, faculty members, and students as well as of outsiders that sometimes it is very difficult to know the exact nature of each program and to differentiate one from the other.

It may be too arbitrary to discuss the confusing contemporary state as well as the future outlook of theological/religious studies in America in terms of three broad categories of programs and institutions. I do not claim that such an approach is novel or the most expedient. However, it may have some merit in helping to break out of the usual cycle of interminable discussions of theological vs. religious studies or universities vs. seminaries. It will also allow those who are particularly concerned with the nature, perspective and objective of the university-divinity school to think through its unique way of going about theological and religious reflection, different from that of the free-standing seminaries and from the programs of religious studies of the colleges and universities.

One reason we cannot satisfactorily articulate the distinct features of the free-standing seminaries, university-divinity schools, and departments of religious studies is that all three are products of the same American experience, and thus all betray similar earmarks of the American ethos. This fact becomes apparent when one compares the experience of colonial America with that of medieval Europe. The *Corpus Christianum*, of course, refers to the medieval European form of religious/cultural/social/political synthesis which was given cosmic legitimation by Christianity, the religion of the Roman empire from the time of emperors Constantine (d. A.D. 337) and Theodosius (d. 395). Internally, medieval Europe depended heavily on three well-known pivotal institutions—(i) the church (*sacerdotium*), (ii) the state (*imperium*) and the university (*studium*)—understood by Europeans as three *competing, rival institutions*. Indeed, there was constant bickering among them. For example, conflicts between the papacy, the symbol of the *sacerdotium*, and the emperor, the embodiment of the *imperium*, are legendary. Also, when Martin Luther and other Reformers dared to act on the conviction that what they had learned at the university (*studium*) had valid truth claims, even though it was a different kind of truth from that which was taught by the church (*sacerdotium*), Rome responded by claiming a monopoly on the teaching authority (*magisterium*) regarding truth, faith, and morals. The university (*studium*) quickly sided with the *imperium*, then contributing to the rising nationalism. It was this not-so-holy alliance between nationalism (initially that of Spain and Portugal, but later of other European nations) and more internationally oriented church bodies that propelled both the Christian world mission and European colonialism.

IV. Ecclesiastical Tradition, Religion of the Republic, and Cultural Religion in America

It was in the U.S., one of the major showpieces of European colonialism, that people approached 1) the political order (the sphere of the *imperium* in medieval Europe), 2) religion (*sacerdotium*), and 3) culture/education (*studium*) not as competing rival features, but as distinct but mutually dependent dimensions of corporate life all of which received "cosmic legitimation" from Providence. The pioneers of America and the medieval Europeans shared a similar passion for a totalistic synthesis of all facets of life in the traditional Western drive toward "unity in diversity,"[2] but they perceived the structure of this synthesis following very different paradigms. For example, medieval Europeans took a hierarchical model of the synthesis for granted. It was their understanding that all important things in life, whether political power, religious grace, or cultural virtue, were gifts given from above. Early Americans saw the necessity of balancing the "upward movement" of political life ("government by the people ..."), the "downward movement" of religion, and the horizontal thrusts of culture/education in order to enhance the three necessities of life—morality in political life, piety in religion and knowledge/rationality in the cultural sphere.

A. Ecclesiastical Tradition and Religion of the Republic. Although early Americans were not sophisticated political thinkers and ideologues, they nevertheless were convinced that the hierarchical, downward system of political order which depended on kings and aristocrats had to be rejected. Instead they chose an egalitarian, democratic, republican model, a paradigm they felt had been given to them by the Almighty ("In God—and not in kings—we trust..."). In this connection, however, their simplistic and dogmatic convictions in "progress," as they interpreted its meaning in the Jewish and Christian scriptures, tended to degenerate into, and often blindly supported, the complacent notion of Manifest Destiny. Undoubtedly, this notion of "inevitable progress" served as the spiritual engine of the westward movement and in the course of time drove the cause of economic and colonial expansionism across the Pacific Ocean.

---

[2] See William S. Haas, *The Destiny of the Mind: East and West* (London: Faber & Faber, 1965).

"Religion" (which had inherited the medieval tradition of the *sacerdotium*) responded very sensitively to this new American experiment by evolving three overlapping but separable features: 1) an ecclesiastical religious tradition, consisting predominantly of Protestant churches but with Roman Catholic and Jewish presences visible as well; 2) a "religion of the republic"; and 3) a cultural religion (sometimes called "Cultural Protestantism," which until recently served as the underlying foundation of American culture). The early American religious/cultural/social/political synthesis was believed to receive its "cosmic legitimation" from this "tri-partite American religion." Many are apt to misunderstand the early American situation and jump to the conclusion that 1) the ecclesiastical tradition alone, without either 2) the "religion of the republic" or 3) the "cultural religion," dominated the early American scene. Such a mistake is understandable. The early colonists, who had been strongly influenced by the northern and western European Protestant traditions, often carelessly and naively equated "religion" with Protestantism, even though in reality they considered the ecclesiastical tradition a "spiritual commonwealth" within the larger national commonwealth that was to be guided by the religio-political thrust—in Sidney E. Mead's expression, "The Nation with the Soul of a Church,"[3] or "cultural Protestantism," in Jacob Neusner's phraseology.[4]

A striking feature of the early American "ecclesiastical tradition" was its spawning of a novel Christian institutional form, later called the "denominational type" by sociologists, which effectively swallowed church polities (classified as "church" and "sect" types in Europe by Ernst Troeltsch).[5] This happened in spite of the fact that some groups continued their "church-type" theological orientations. It was the "religion of the republic," with its explicit and implicit support of the "cultural religion," that brought about "religious liberty" and "government neutrality with respect to ecclesiastical religion," although there was undoubtedly much foot-dragging on the part of ecclesiastical groups with regard to such notions as "religious liberty" and the "separation of church and state." As to "cultural religion," or "cultural

---

[3] Of Sidney E. Mead's many writings, see especially *The Nation with the Soul of a Church* (New York: Harper & Row, 1975), *The Lively Experiment: The Shaping of Christianity in America* (New York: Harper & Row, 1963).

[4] Jacob Neusner, "Judaism in the History of Religions," *History and Theory*, Supplement 8: *On Methods in the History of Religions*, ed. James S. Helfer (Middlebury: Middlebury College, 1968), p. 37.

[5] See Joachim Wach, "Church, Denomination and Sect," in his *Types of Religious Experience: Christian and Non-Christian* (Chicago: The University of Chicago Press, 1951), pp. 187-208.

Protestantism" in Neusner's phrase, it served as the invisible *Geist* of American culture. The combination of the "religion of the republic" and "cultural religion" is what sociologists usually refer to as American "civil religion" in order to differentiate ecclesiastical and non-ecclesiastical religious traditions.

B. Cultural Experience and Cultural Religion. One of the salient features of early American education and culture (a distant heir of the medieval *studium*) was its inauguration of an "educational revolution," a matter of global significance, almost as important as the French Revolution and the Industrial Revolution. It was American culture under the inspiration of its Cultural Religion (Protestantism) that introduced the "one-tier" system as a normative practice in education. The "two-tier" system common in Europe and elsewhere sent only a select group of youngsters to preparatory schools for institutions of higher learning, while the majority of children were given practical education for trades and professions. Invariably, early Americans, especially Protestants deeply concerned as they were with the ecclesiastical, political, and cultural dimensions of life, were ardent supporters of various types of education. The latter included public school systems, private colleges and later universities, land-grant colleges, and theological seminaries. These early Americans adopted "education" and "corporate life" as new vocabulary for their world views. Understandably, the American cultural experience had a tremendous impact on the development of the three kinds of educational institutions that especially concern us in this volume, namely, (a) public and private colleges and universities (b) seminaries and theological colleges, and (c) graduate research universities.

The public schools, including state colleges and universities, exist for the training of citizens for the common life in social, economic and cultural dimensions of the American national community.[6] Although these institutions are concerned with the ever-changing ethos of a pluralistic world community, they also are keenly aware that they are an arm of the American social community which supports them more often than not with tax money. Thus they feel compelled to be more sensitive in responding to the needs and demands of the supporting community. It is to the credit of many American community leaders that they have recognized the importance not only of the more practical courses but also

---

[6] See, for example, Burton R. Clark, *Educating the Expert Society* (San Francisco: Chandler, 1962).

of subject matter which does not have instant relevance, e.g., history, literature, and the fine arts. Until after World War II, many community leaders were unduly sensitive to the legal implications of teaching "religion" in public institutions. They feared for the integrity of the principle of the separation of Church and State enunciated in the First Amendment to the Federal Constitution. Fortunately, with the Supreme Court decision that the objective study of religion does not conflict with government neutrality with respect to religion, departments of religious studies in colleges and universities began to mushroom in various parts of the country.

The impact the American cultural experience had on *seminary* education was decisive but subtle and elusive. Early America inherited a heavy dose of European Protestant Christianity along with a mixed bag of various social and cultural features—nationalism, mercantilism, scientism, utopianism, and agnosticism among others. Contrary to some peoples' idealized conjectures, colonial America was far from being a spiritually charged society guided by the Ten Commandments and so presented a real challenge to ecclesiastical leaders. As might be expected, education conscious Protestants readily saw the importance of ministerial education. Deprived of European types of institutions for higher learning and clergy training, some of the learned and experienced ministers began informal theological training for future ministers with three main foci— (i) evangelism, (ii) pastoral training, and (iii) the scholarship and learning necessary for (i) and (ii), particularly biblical studies. This early emphasis on the salvation of individual souls foreshadowed American revivalism—the stock in trade of American Protestantism—with the implication that regenerated men and women, inspired by Christian faith and morals, would work toward the establishment of a "Christian America," as well as the "Christianization of the whole world."[7] Their concern with individuals dove-tailed amazingly well with the other side of their concern, i.e., education.

Although we look back and differentiate sharply between educated "ecclesiastical Protestants" and "cultural Protestants" in early America, many of them were in reality both simultaneously. Not all of them, however, espoused the cause of the religion of the republic, especially its stance on the separation of Church and State. Both as educated Protestants and cultural Protestants, many Americans not only promoted the public school system but also supported private schools and colleges,

---

[7] Robert T. Handy, *A Christian America: Protestant and Historical Realities* 2nd ed. (New York: Oxford, 1971).

some of which eventually became universities, and theological seminaries. They were the heirs of both Protestant Christianity and the Enlightenment. Just as many non-religious college teachers were eager to study at various European universities, many seminary teachers were anxious to study under learned European scholars, most of whom were on the faculties of the universities. Almost unconsciously, some of the seminary professors inhaled the European university ethos.

This fact accounts for the confusing coexistence of two related but different institutions among American seminaries. First, there are seminaries dedicated primarily to the training of clerical and other church leaders. Second, there are other institutions that, under the spell of European theological studies, have grown into a sort of "theological college" but which serve as seminaries for denominational ministerial education as well. This creates an unfair contrast. Professors in divinity schools of graduate universities can apply religious and theological insights to the cooperative inquiry of the "university communities," whereas professors of even the *de facto* theological colleges—actually supported as seminaries by respective denominations—cannot expect their ecclesiastical communities always to be receptive to the values and standards of their scholarly research like the European or American universities. Accordingly, we see today the curious phenomenon of seminary professors who, although they are not engaged in scholarly research in the context of a broader multi-departmental university, possess greater specialized learning than required for the purpose of ministerial training in the seminary. This may account partially for the fact that so many seminary professors eagerly participate in the American Academy of Religion and other societies, despite the fact that these organizations have nothing to do with ministerial education.

Numerous books and articles have been written on the subject of American universities. It is fair to state that it is confusing to lump so many different kinds of institutions into a single category called the "university." At the risk of oversimplification, I will differentiate three types of universities which will be pertinent for this discussion. They are:

(1) State universities (which have something in common with the *imperium*-supported European universities).

(2) Religiously oriented, that is, church owned, supported or affiliated universities (which have affinities with the *sacerdotium*-inspired European universities).

(3) Private, graduate universities (at least in principle independent of the state or the church, presumably a unique product of American culture, even though many of them were church-affiliated institutions at one time).

The distinctions to be made in defining these three types of institutions today are murky.[8] Space does not allow us to dwell on the distinctions between the undergraduate college and graduate university in religious studies at this juncture.

C. The Religious Studies Program and the Free-standing Seminary. Although our institutions of higher learning—dedicated to research, teaching, and discovery of new knowledge—are products of provincial American culture and society, most of them seem to be well aware not only of American but also global religious and non-religious developments. Therefore, religious studies programs of the college and the university deal with "religions" ideally from the perspective of the "whole" religious experience of humankind together with related theoretical issues.[9] Their emphasis is to study all religious traditions from outside. There are notable exceptions. Centers for Jewish, Islamic, Hindu, and Buddhist studies are concerned with some aspects of the insider's perception of their respective traditions.

In sharp contrast to the emphasis of the religious studies program of the college and the university, free-standing (Jewish or Christian) seminaries must concentrate on one religion (Judaism or Christianity) and view even the whole of the religious experience of humankind through the window of that one religion. Although many seminary scholars, especially those in the *de facto* theological colleges, utilize all kinds of critical methods and sophisticated sociological, psychological, anthropological, and philosophical concepts, theories, and rhetorics, in the end these resources are utilized to enhance the relevance of either Judaism or Christianity. All free-standing seminaries are expected to train clerical and other religious leaders, and they have to explore and explicate the crucial significance of one religion above all others.

---

[8] For my discussion of the theological/religious studies in the university, however, I am using "private, graduate University" as an implicit paradigm, although much of what I say may be also applicable—though with some constraints due to the affiliation to the state or the church—to the two other categories of universities as well.

[9] See Gregory Alles and J.M. Kitagawa, "Afterward: The Dialectic of the Parts and the Whole," in J.M. Kitagawa, ed., *The History of Religious: Retrospect and Prospect* (New York: MacMillan, 1985), pp. 145-181.

D. The "Church-oriented" and the "University-oriented" University-Divinity Schools. Are there some unique perspectives, objectives and approaches of the university-divinity school, if they are indeed different from those of the religious studies program of the college and the university as well as those of the free-standing seminaries? There are definitely differences, but there does not seem to be any unanimity among university-divinity schools at this moment. For the sake of argument and further discussions for the present and future, two different perspectives are suggested, (a) "church-oriented" and (b) "university-oriented" approaches to theological/religious studies within the category of the university-divinity school.

The "church-oriented" university-divinity schools have much in common with free-standing seminaries regarding the premise about viewing religious experience of the whole human race through the window of one particular religion (Judaism or Christianity at the moment, but probably other traditions will soon demand equal rights on this score).[10] It follows that various critical methods and modern scholarly resources will have to enrich the significance of that one religion, even though in principle the "church-oriented" university-divinity schools have nothing against critical approaches to various religions, including their own primary traditions. Many "church-oriented" university-divinity schools accept the intellectual challenges of their non-divinity colleagues, departments, and professional schools of their universities, and they are determined to bring the Jewish or Christian religious insights into the cooperative inquiries of their universities.[11] They may not be as effective as the free-standing seminaries in the actual training of clerical and other religious leaders, but they have important, "mediating" intellectual roles between the university and their particular religious communities. This is especially true if the university in question is church-related.

In contrast to the "church-oriented" institutions, the "university-oriented" university-divinity school, in principle, has greater affinity with the religious studies programs of the college and university in approaching the religious experience of the world from the perspective of the "whole." In contrast to most religious studies programs which soft-pedal

---

[10] In this connection, the application of the Unification Church's seminary to join the Association of Theological Schools in the United States and Canada presents an interesting program.

[11] See Jim Waits, "Church and School: Promises to Keep," *Occasional Papers*, No. 81, November 13, 1989, issued by the United Methodist Board of Higher Education and Ministry.

the internal texture of religions and the perspective of the "whole," the "university-oriented" university-divinity school is persuaded that an adequate understanding of any religion requires both the insiders' perception and the outsiders' critical assessment of that religion as well as the perspective of the "whole" in the study of religious experience of the human race. It is at this point where the university-oriented university-divinity school takes seriously the insiders' accounts of, say, Judaism or Christianity, for academic reasons and not because the university-divinity school is another free-standing seminary historically or accidentally situated on the university campus. Needless to say, the "university-oriented" divinity school does not consider the training of ordained ministers as its primary mission, although its curriculum is open to any prospective church leaders, including ordained ministers. One of the crucial tasks of the "university-oriented" university-divinity school is to reassess the historical phases of Christianity's compromise with nationalistic orientations in Europe, starting with the Constantinian schema and ending with what many people regard as Christianity's "Babylonian captivity" in which Christianity became a feature—albeit an important one—of the Western civilization that had come to regard itself as a religion of secularized salvation. Such reassessment should be accompanied by a keen awareness of non-Western and non-Christian perceptions of reality, human experiences, the world, and other factors which cannot be ignored in the contemporary global community of religious and cultural pluralism.

V. *Elementary Grammars for Theological/Religious Studies*

By grammars for theological/religious studies, I refer to two related sets of "two-sidedness"—that is, (1) our thinking, and (2) religion itself.

A. Autobiographical and Biographical Modes. The first set of two-sidedness becomes evident in auto-biographical and biographical modes of thinking which all human beings share. Certainly, one knows himself or herself better than others in a basic sense, hence the importance of the autobiographical genre. Much of what we call faith or religious statements is often based on an autobiographical internal language, looking at the religious experience of one's own community from within. From an autobiographical perspective, van der Leeuw was perfectly right when he said:

> ..."community" is something not manufactured, but given; it depends not upon sentiment or feeling, but on the Unconscious. It needs to be founded

upon no conviction, since it is self-evident; we do not become members of it, but "belong to it."[12]

Lamentably, many people are exposed primarily to autobiographical religious statements and therefore conclude erroneously that all religious propositions, enunciations, or descriptions must be solely autobiographical. They seem not to realize that there is also a "biographical" approach to religion(s) which looks at it from outside, and which is crucially important particularly in the programs of religious studies in the college or the university.

Following the examples of politicians and movie stars who write their autobiographies with the help of "biographical sensitivities" of ghost writers, some hold to the misguided hope of collapsing the autobiographical and biographical perspectives. Like it or not, there are qualitative, insurmountable, and inviolable differences between these two modes of apprehension of reality, human experience, and the world.

B. Inner and Outer Meanings of Religions. Related to the first set of two-sidedness is the second set, namely, the two-sidedness of what we call "religion," or two dimensions of religion itself, which invariably all religious traditions are bound to share. Someone has said (I believe Hamilton A.R. Gibb), to outsiders Islam is a religion of Muslims while to Muslims it is a religion of truth. Similar observations can be made about all other religions. The most obvious example of this two-sidedness is seen in Judaism, Christianity, and Islam, which hold "monotheism" as the core of inner meanings of their religions, while acknowledging *de facto* "monolatry" (belief in one supreme deity for one's own tradition, but recognizing similar affirmations of one supreme deity on the part of other religious traditions) as the outer meaning of their respective religions. This holds even in the case when tolerance is only grudgingly granted due to practical necessity as in the case of the American practice of religious liberty.

One's autobiographical understanding of one's own religious tradition is colored more often than not by the inner meaning of one's religious tradition, which together constitute the self-authenticating, circular logic of that religion. Historically, when one particular religion remains as a dominant tradition for any length of time in certain areas, adherents of that dominant tradition are easily mesmerized to conclude that their autobiographical understanding of the inner meaning of their

---

[12] G. van der Leeuw, *Religion in Essence and Manifestation: A Study in Phenomenology*, trans. J.E. Turner (London: G. Allen & Unwin, 1938), pp. 242-243.

religion, legitimized by the self-authenticating circular principle implicit in that tradition, has unquestionable objective and universal validity. They do not realize that outsiders, who because they cannot share the insiders' autobiographical affirmation of the inner meaning of that religion, usually have no choice except to understand that religion by interpreting its outer meaning, and thus do not accept the insiders' assertions of the dominant religious tradition being unbiased, objective, and universal.

One would like to believe that a person is aware of having both autobio-graphical and biographical modes of perception. One would also think that a person recognizes two dimensions (inner and outer) of every tradition—be it linguistic, cultural, or religious. But that is not the case, especially when one particular tradition dominates all others, because it is easy for its adherents to lose sensitivity for the biographical perspective and outer meaning of their religion.

Christians in Europe participated in this type of dynamic after their religion became the state faith in the fourth century. Earlier, when Christianity was one of many traditions in the Mediterranean world, Christian tradition was cognizant of its inner (monotheistic) as well as outer (monolatristic) traditions. Thus, no less than the Apostle Paul affirmed such a double religious orientation as illustrated by his statement (I Cor. 8:5-6) "...although there may be so-called gods in heaven or on earth—as indeed there are many "gods" and many "lords"—yet for us there is one God...and one Lord, Jesus Christ..." After the time of Constantine and Theodosius in the fourth century when Christianity became the dominant tradition in the Empire, adherents of Christian religion gradually began to feel that others must accept their autobiographical affirmation of the inner meaning of Christianity as the eternal and universal truth. Understandably the self-confidence of the Christian community was such that, in the words of Peter Brown:

> ...[it] reflects the attitude of a group confident of its powers to absorb the world without losing its identity...It is a group no longer committed to defend itself against society; but rather, poised, ready to fulfil what it considered its historic mission, to dominate, to absorb, to lead a whole Empire. *'Ask Me, and I shall give the uttermost parts of the earth as Thy possession.'*[13]

---

[13] Peter Brown, *Augustine of Hippo: A Biography* (Berkeley: University of California Press, 1969), p. 214.

VI. *"Religion"* vs. *"Religious-Cultural-Social-Political" Synthesis*

Those of us who study the various aspects of religion have reasons to worry about the elusive meaning, status, and identity of the notion of "religion," itself. Although this term has been defined variously as power, belief in spiritual reality, piety, ultimate concern, experience of the Holy, and in numerous other ways, our intellectual honesty compels us to agree with Mircea Eliade's considered opinion that "it is unfortunate that we do not have at our disposal a more precise word than 'religion'..."[14] Unfortunately, we have not discovered a better notion to replace this ambiguous term. It is not only ambiguous but is sometimes outright misleading and thus not applicable in a great many cases. For example, a perceptive Islamicist, Bernard Lewis, stated recently:

> When we in the Western world, nurtured in the Western tradition, use the words "Islam" and "Islamic," we tend to make a natural error and assume that religion means the same for Muslims as it has meant in the Western world...that is to say, a section or compartment of life reserved for certain matters, and separate, or at least separable, from other compartments of life designed to hold other matters... [But] in classical Islam there was no distinction between church and state...[15]

Religious traditions of the world, like Islam, do not share the usual Western notion of "religion" as a separate or separable human activity. Rather, as I once stated elsewhere:

> ...it is a peculiar Western convention to divide human experience into such pigeonholes as religion, philosophy, ethics, aesthetics, culture, society, etc. Obviously, this type of convention—[useful though it may be in the Western world]—is a very provincial usage, even though many Westerners still assume that such a provincial Western mode has universal validity, partly because they are not aware of other, that is, non-Western ways of dividing human experience. Actually people everywhere live and breathe in their own respective "seamless whole"—what [to Westerners] look like syntheses of religion, culture, and the social and political orders, to use the Western convention of divided categories.[16]

Because what is called "religion" in the West is of such multi-dimensional and yet ambiguous nature, it cannot be easily defined to satisfy various peoples. It may very well be that, instead of trying to get at reli-

---

[14] Mircea Eliade, *The Quest: History and Meaning in Religion* (Chicago: The University of Chicago Press, 1969), Preface.
[15] Bernard Lewis, *The Political Language of Islam*, (Chicago: The University of Chicago Press, 1988), p. 2.
[16] J.M. Kitagawa, "Religious Visions of the Unity of Mankind," *Crossroads*, June 1988, p. 10.

gion as such, we might more profitably attempt to understand the intricate and many-layered relationships between what is called "religion" and the rather wide-spread patterns of the "religious-cultural-social-political syntheses," which have been known to exist in various stages of history in many parts of the world. Otherwise, religious idioms and logics alone, without taking into account the non-religious dimensions of life, may prove to be too confusing and misleading. For example, according to religious rhetorics, most traditions acknowledge some sort of supramundane references, be they personalistic in perception as in Judaism, Christianity, or Islam, or non-personalistic as in Buddhism. But religious rhetorics do not always tell us how actually and historically most religions have survived—despite their doctrinal affirmation of supramundane realities—as *de facto* this-worldly traditions, e.g., Buddhism and Christianity.

It is well known that Buddhism, which began as a humble religion of mendicants in Northeast India in the sixth or fifth century, B.C., became the religion of the Indian Empire under King Asoka in the third century B.C. Although Asoka personally affirmed the *marga* (path) toward suprahistorical *nirvana* in terms of the "Three Treasures," *Buddha, Dharma* (Buddha's teaching or law), and *Samgha*, (the Buddhist community), Buddhism from his time onward prospered as a this-worldly religious tradition, based on the "immanental triad" (Buddha as guide in the saving path in this phenomenal existence to both clergy and laity; Buddhist-inspired but pan-Indian ethics now known as dharma, and Buddhist-based social and political order with a Buddhist king at its apex).[17]

The immanentalization of Christianity was just as dramatic. Christianity, born in the Jewish fold, came into existence in a little-known corner of the Roman Empire as a community of faith *in* this world but not *of* this world and expected its adherents to belong to the heavenly realm. According to Biblical tradition, in this world the faithful were nothing but "aliens and exiles," to use the expression of I Peter (2:11). While the followers of Christ lived in the earthly kingdom, they knew that the loyalty to God which was most decisive for them was different from loyalty to Caesar. After the fourth century A.D., when the successive policies of the emperors Constantine and Theodosius made Christianity the religion of the Roman Empire, loyalty to Caesar became loyalty to God. From that time until today, all branches of Christianity survived as

---

[17] J.M. Kitagawa, "Buddhism and Social Change—An Historical Perspective," Somaratna Balasooria, Andre Bareau, *et al.*, ed., *Buddhist Studies in Honor of Walpola Rahula*, (London: Gordon Frazer; Sri Lanka: Vivamsa, 1980), pp. 84-102.

de facto this-worldly religion with the earthly church, papacy, Caeseropapian emperors or church councils, determining the divine will on behalf of the deity who became in effect *deus otiosus*. Like Buddhism and Christianity, most other religions also behaved as this-worldly religions in spite of some of their theoretical or doctrinal affirmation of the supra-mundane and supra-historical realities.

As far as can be ascertained historically, the relationships of most "religions" (in the Western sense) and the "religious-cultural-social-political syntheses" in various parts of the world have been multi-dimensional. In many cases, religions constitute explicitly ecclesiastical or spiritual traditions; they inspire cultural as well as social and political orders; and they serve as invisible glues of disparate elements of life and the world. As agents of metaphysical intuition, religions define the kinds and levels of reality, including what we, for lack of a better term, call "ultimate reality." Usually, religions transfer their formulas of double ("inner" and "outer") meanings to the "religious-cultural-social-political syntheses." Thereby insiders within the respective syntheses tend to assume "autobiographically" the religiously-based self-authenticating circular logic of their syntheses as the self-evident universal truth, regardless of outsiders' "biographical" and usually more critical assessment of the coherence of their syntheses. Above all, religions provide "cosmic legitimation" to their respective religious-cultural-social-political synthesis. In today's world, and in the years ahead, any serious program of religious/theological studies, be it non-theological religious studies of the college and the university, or those of free-standing seminaries, as well as those of the university-divinity schools both "church-oriented" and "university-oriented," should take with utmost seriousness the study of the relationships between "religion(s)" and the "religious-cultural-social-political syntheses" from their own different perspectives.

VII. *Religious Studies and Theological Studies of the Free Standing Seminary.*

In order to emphasize and clarify the task of the university-divinity school, let me first touch upon my personal view of the tasks of the program of the non-theological "religious studies" of the college and the university and "theological studies" of the free-standing seminary.

The primary objective of religious studies in the undergraduate college might be succinctly summarized as providing intellectual stimulation, guidance, resources, and "understanding" (*verstehen*) to college students for their growth as intelligent citizens of the republic. At the risk of oversimplification, American college programs of religious studies now and in the years to come might include among other things courses on: (1) general features of religion(s) as well as the relationships between "religion" and the "religious-cultural-social-political synthesis;" (2) exemplary—not exhaustive because of time constraint—phases of historical development of religions and various "syntheses" in the West; (3) the discussion of the gradual dissolution of the *corpus Christianum* (the Medieval Christian church inspired religious-cultural-social-political synthesis) under the impact of Renaissance, Reformation, Enlightenment, American, French, and Industrial revolutions, and the rise of scientific thinking, leading up to the disintegration of the residual coherence of the Western synthesis, epitomized by World War I; (4) development of the uniquely American pattern of the "religious-cultural-social-political synthesis," including the contemporary problem of "rainbowization" due to the self-conscious awakening of native, African-, Latin-, and Asian-Americans; and (5) "religious" problems of the emerging world, Western and non-Western, especially the necessity of the religious and cultural encounters on the global level.

By necessity, college programs of religious studies cannot require the depth research utilizing foreign languages, and instructors are compelled to use cliches as a teaching device knowing very well that those cliches should be abandoned when the students mature intellectually. Ironically, it is not very easy for college faculty members, trained as most of them are as experts in narrow specialized areas, to teach courses on religious traditions broadly and in "hermeneutical mode." Their difficulties are magnified in reference to Christianity and Judaism, the two traditions which had exerted decisive influences in the West.

The programs of religious studies on the graduate university level, however, should go beyond the *"verstehen* model" objective of the undergraduate program. Not only should universities encourage their students to acquire original "languages," but also to acquaint themselves with how various peoples, Westerners and non-Westerners, have perceived the texture of human experience and the nature of reality. They should not simply study non-Western languages, cultural and religious traditions, their histories and texts, through Western perspectives, utilizing primarily Western critical methods. It is readily apparent that non-Western peoples have very different conventions of perceiving the texture of human experience. Often some faculty members of religious studies on the graduate level stress only the "outer" meaning of religions at the expense of their "inner" meanings, which they tend to equate naively with the peculiar objective of "theological" studies. Or, some others frequently move to the opposite extreme and assert their own understanding of the inner meanings of (Jewish or Christian) religions as unbiased, neutral, and objective views, and the only meaning of the religion in question. In the main, graduate universities' programs of religious studies, even though they should refrain from "advocacy" of any particular religious tradition, should help students both to achieve mature and viable private and public ethical norms and to acquire sufficient skills in social, economic, cultural, and political "decision-making" and "engineering" which are consonant with their respective religious resourcefulness and convictions.

As we turn to the task of the free-standing seminaries and to a great extent to the "church-oriented" university-divinity schools of Jewish and Christian traditions, we realize that much misunderstanding exists in the minds of many people about the scholarly integrity of religious/theological studies focusing on "one" religion, and thus it may be prudent to try to untangle this complex issue. From the time of the Enlightenment, there has developed a general consensus that education, following the insights of Vico, Marx, and others, must be rational and critical, whereas seminary education—even though it does not repudiate the consensus view of education altogether—operates as well with the paradoxical religious insight that "one part" sometimes can and should represent the "wholeness" (not all-ness) of whatever reality is in question without distorting it.[18]

To illustrate this paradoxical principle, the so-called *"do"* ("Way") arts in Japan, e.g., the Way of Tea or *Cha-* or *Sa-do*, the Way of Swordsmanship of *Ken-do*, the Way of Flower Arrangement or *Ka-dō*, and the Way of Self-defense or *Ju-do*, are based on a Buddhist (Tendai) principle that observing with utter seriousness and devotion just "one" rule among numerous Buddhist disciplines (known as *Eton-kai* or Harmonious Round System of Rules) enables one to reach the depth of the "whole" reality (not equated with "all"). Or again, a famous Buddhist nature-poet, Saigyo, had an unshakable conviction that the "wholeness" of the reality of a cherry tree remained intact even when thousands of flower petals of "one" tree were scattered away before his own eyes due to blowing wind. Historically, many religious traditions have developed educational institutions of religious studies focusing on their respective

---

[18] See Alles and Kitagawa, "The Dialectic of the Parts and Whole. . ." *Retrospect and Prospect.*

"one" religion, stressing the importance of the "autobiographical" apprehension of the "inner" meaning of religion, which is not accessible to the "biographical" understanding of the "outer" meaning.

During its early period, Christianity, like many other religions, was closely related to "autobiographical" and "biographical" modes of apprehension common to all human beings. The Apostle Paul articulated such a double orientation ("monotheism" as the inner meaning and "monolatry" as the outer meaning). So long as Christianity was a minority religion, one of many rival traditions in the Mediterranean world, almost by necessity it retained its double religious orientation fairly well. Accordingly, the followers of Christ knew that the same items had two kinds of different but equally legitimate meanings, seen from the "autobiographical-inner" and "biographical-outer" perspectives: gospel vs. truth, salvation vs. enlightenment, affirmation vs. understanding, incarnation vs. nativity, *metanoia* vs. learning, church vs. Christian religion, will of God vs. God, the proclaimer (Jesus Christ) as savior and lord vs. historic Jesus of Nazareth who proclaimed the Kingdom of God.

In the history of Christianity, the first serious attempt to collapse the two different ("autobiographical-inner" and "biographical-outer") orientations in order to create a unified, coherent doctrinal system—a perennial temptation to intelligent religious people—arose when some erudite Gentiles, who unlike the poorly educated Galilean fishermen had been well-versed in Greek philosophy, came into the Christian fold. In order to make the Christian message more accessible to the wider public, these "apologists" followed the footsteps of Hellenistic Jews, who had earlier attempted to translate their "autobiographical" Jewish faith into a biographical mode of Greek thought and *koine*. These Hellenistic Jews were attracted to the Greek notion of the *logoi spermatikoi* or the "scattered seeds" of truth found in every cultural tradition. Some of the Christian Fathers, like Clement of Alexandria and Origen, appropriated the notion of the *logos* ("word," "reason," "rational faculty"), made famous by Philo Judeaus, and asserted that the divine *Logos,* the teacher (*logos paidagogos*), which had guided all pre- and non-Christian traditions, became the *logos incarnate* in Jesus Christ,[19] thus incorporating the Hellenistic Jews' biographical formula into their autobiographically-oriented "unified scheme." With this intellectual somersault, the small and powerless Christian community became convinced of the universal validity of its message. It gave a happy illusion to many Christian leaders that their

---

[19] Ernest Benz, "The Theological Meaning of the History of Religions," *The Journal of Religion*, Vol. XLI, No. 1 (January 1961), p. 5.

"autobiographical" understanding of the "inner" meaning of their religion can now boast the self-evident, objective truth claim open to everybody inside and outside the Christian fold.

Throughout the history of religions of the world, whenever one religion becomes a dominant tradition for any length of time at a certain place, e.g., Islam in Arabia, Hinduism in India, or Buddhism in Southeast Asia, adherents of that religion begin to assume that their autobiographical affirmation of the inner meaning of their faith must be objectively true. Christianity from the fourth century A.D. in Europe, where it became the dominant religion at the expense of Judaism which it suppressed and Islam which it rejected, until our own time has followed this familiar pattern. In their attempt to develop a coherent universal doctrinal formula, collapsing the autobiographical and biographical perceptions of Christianity, various European Christian thinkers, especially the Scholastics, tried to integrate Greek philosophical thought, especially Aristotelianism (which ironically they had learned through the mediation of Muslim and Jewish thinkers) into their Christian theological superstructure. The latter was considered the "queen of science" in the then rising medieval universities. Ironically, from that time until the present, the Christian "theological" enterprise has come to imply "Hellenization" of the Christian *kerygma*. Even today, according to Edward Farley's understanding of many Western Christians' "autobiographical" view:

> Theology is...a discipline, a course of studies, a career and teaching specialty, a necessity for ministry, a *Hellenistic-Christian mode of thinking* that no self-respecting Buddhist, Hindu, or Jew would dream of imitating. It is churchly, Christological, biblical, rationative, situational, chauvinistic, legitimating, critical, objectivist, personal, academic, concrete, and, of course, practical.[20]

Some non-Western Christians and other religionists tend to suspect that it was European Christians who domesticated and distorted Christian kerygma and Greek philosophy "theologically," so as to present Christianity as a more useful and believable (at least to Western Christians) tradition that can provide "cosmic legitimation" to the Western form of the religious-cultural-social-political synthesis.

It is clear that although free-standing seminaries share many concerns with *religious studies* programs in the college and the university, their differences are also many and marked. The most conspicuous fea-

---

[20] Edward Farley, "Theology and Practice Outside the Clerical Paradigm," Don S. Browning, ed., *Practical Theology* (San Francisco: Harper & Row, 1983), p. 22 (My italics).

ture of the seminaries is that they are academic as well as religious and professional schools, hence their emphasis on devotional life and spiritual formation of students in addition to academic (theological) requirements. Free-standing seminaries, unlike the *religious studies* programs, are dedicated to the study of one religion (Judaism or Christianity in many cases) as the embodiment of the "wholeness" of religious reality or (in Christian seminaries) as the supreme tradition not only to the current adherents of that religion but also potentially to all human beings. Moreover, to Christian seminaries, their religion has incomparable systems of doctrines and ethics but, more importantly, is incarnated into a unique religious institution called the "church." The main task of the Christian seminary is understood to be that of imparting and interpreting theologically the Christian faith, doctrine, and message, inherited by and through the church, to seminary students. For the most part, free-standing seminaries and most of the "church-oriented" university-divinity schools came into being for the training of clerical and other types of religious leadership for the church, even though it is the denominational churches (and not seminaries) which certify and ordain ministers.

Free-standing seminaries of various church traditions, especially those which are considered "mainline," share the agonies of their sponsoring churches. Today many church groups are confronted by increasing demands for extended agendas, e.g., worship, Christian education, community outreach programs, declining membership, budgetary constraints, and shortage of qualified personnel. The impact of these practical problems of the churches impinge upon the life and curriculum of seminaries. Under the circumstances, the seminaries in question find it very difficult to expand more scholarly research and training *vis à vis* the threat of scientific thinking, secularization, competition with other professions and careers, religious and moral illiteracy of the populace, political earthquakes in Eastern Europe, and threat of new and/or exotic religious-cultic groups. While the academic standards of free-standing seminaries have made tremendous advancement in recent years, even so, free-standing seminaries in the Christian tradition have a long way to go academically. Thanks to the persistent efforts of such organizations as the Association of Theological Schools (ATS) in the United States and Canada, there is a growing number of faculty members who have graduate degrees.

At the risk of oversimplification, listed below are some of the current problems that confront free-standing seminaries. For one thing, many faculty members, especially those who teach in sophisticated seminaries (which have been characterized earlier as *de facto* "theological colleges"), are very skillful in utilizing many critical, up-to-date scholarly methods. In the end, however, they regard these "specialized" analytical and hermeneutical methods, as well as what I call "biographical" approaches to "outer" meaning of religion, as subservient to "general" theological schemes based primarily on their "autobiographical" affirmation of Christian soteriology. However, we should caution ourselves against the temptation easily to collapse the "autobiographical-inner" and the "biographical-outer" orientations in dealing with philosophical, historical, psychological, or theological explorations of religious reality. Instead of attempting to concoct dubious, premature "unified orientations," it is imperative that we try to hold in balance, as did the Apostle Paul, the "autobiographical-inner" stance (Paul's singular affirmation of "monotheism" and of Jesus Christ as saviour) and the "biographical-outer" realization (his "monolatristic" recognition of other deities advocated by other religious traditions). Implicit in this discussion is the pressing issue of religious pluralism.

Traditionally, most Christian seminaries have considered non-Christians primarily as potential objects of Christian evangelism. The fact remains that the non-Biblical notion of *"extra ecclesiam nulla salus"* (the most extreme form of "autobiographical" affirmation of the ecclesiastical Christianity's soteriology) dies hard. Even some liberal seminary professors attempt to understand non-Christian religions and the syntheses of which they are parts primarily through the window of Christianity and Christian-inspired Western synthesis. It is high time for Christian seminaries to recognize that other religions take seriously the notion of their own embodiment of the "wholeness" of religious reality, just as does Christianity, and that the inner meanings of other traditions cannot be adjudicated directly through the inner meaning of your own.

These are but a few samples of some of the deep-seated problems that have historically complicated Christian theological scholarship which free-standing seminaries have inherited from church tradition. My hope is that the seminaries, expected though they are to attend to the task of clerical training and other chores to serve as academic arms of the sponsoring churches, should also be recognized as the critique, sounding board, think-tank, and intellectual spearhead for the churches. As such they should maintain a certain amount of real academic freedom as "educational institutions," which they are and must be.

VIII. *The Tasks of the University-Divinity School*

There are various kinds of universities (state, private, and church-related) and there are also at least two "ideal types," "church-oriented" and "university-oriented." For the moment, state universities seem to welcome "religious studies" programs but not the "divinity school." Thus practically speaking, our current attention should be addressed primarily to "private" and "church-related" universities. Contrary to expectation, there are no organic relationships between "university-oriented" programs and *private* universities or the "church-oriented" program and *church related* universities. "Church-oriented" university-divinity schools, even when they may not be organically related to specific "denominational church groups," share with free-standing seminaries of various denominations the conviction that it is legitimate to study "one religion" (usually Christianity) as the embodiment of the "wholeness" of religious reality. In this connection, there are a variety of "church-related" colleges or universities, e.g., historical, practical, and religious-theological. Of particular concern here is the combination of the church-related institutions based on religious-theological rationale (e.g., schools of the Roman Catholic, United Methodist, and others), and the "church-oriented" university-divinity schools. Institutions which represent this kind of combination seem to be particularly close in ethos to that of the free-standing seminaries.[21] In this regard, the "university-oriented" university-divinity school which aims at religiously-inspired intellectual enterprise is quite different.

The "church-related" university-divinity school and free-standing seminaries not only share the conviction of studying "one religion" but also stress the importance of *advocacy* as the necessary ingredient of that one religion which they pursue. Both types of institutions regard the training of clerical and other religious leaders as an important priority on their agendas. The university-divinity schools, even when they are "church-oriented," may not have automatic rapport with specific denominational church organizations. Both the "church-oriented" university-divinity schools and the free-standing seminaries seem to be convinced that the insiders' autobiographical affirmation of the inner truth of their religious tradition (e.g., Christianity) should constitute the central theological enterprise. It follows then that both institutions assume that what I have characterized as the "biographical" approach to the "outer meaning" of religion *can be* integrated, subordinated, and utilized theologi-

---

[21] For the "church-oriented" program of the university-divinity school, see Waits' illuminating article, "Church and School..."

cally with their autobiographical affirmation of the inner meaning of religion. Indeed, many scholars of those institutions have been attempting to unify the autobiographical and biographical approaches in their studies of scriptures, doctrines, ecclesiastical history, pastoral counseling, and social ethics. Opinions vary widely as to the success of their efforts. However, neither institution recognizes the legitimacy of an independent "biographical" approach to the "outer meaning" of religion, as such. In this regard, there may be some difference between the "church-oriented" university-divinity schools and free-standing seminaries. The former institutions are not against the "biographical-outer" orientation in principle. In fact, they may be quite congenial to having such orientations in other segments of the university, even though they offer very little along this line themselves. These programs, though "church-oriented" in nature as a matter of university policy, should be open to any academically-qualified students of their universities regardless of their religious motivation.

Unlike many free-standing seminaries which operate with the "generalist vision" of theological studies, the "church-oriented" university-divinity schools—and to a great extent the growing number of "cluster" seminaries—encourage "specialist vision" of theological studies (training men and women to be experts in chosen areas such as biblical studies, ecclesiastical history, ethics, counselling) without, however, repudiating the "generalist vision," as well.[22] On the other hand, free-standing seminaries, with the exception of heavily endowed institutions, usually do not have enough resources to accommodate independent "biographical-outer" oriented approaches which are more critically important for the "specialist vision" of theological studies. This may account for the attraction of the "cluster" arrangement (amply illustrated in this volume by the description of the Graduate Theological Union, Berkeley) which "as cluster" pursues the "specialist vision," realizing that it is not possible for individual seminaries to do so.

Ideally the "church-oriented" university-divinity schools ought to produce men and women who are equally at home in their "generalist" religious orientation and "specialist" vocations, the Christian counterparts of those eminent Jewish scholars mentioned by Edward Farley. In his words:

---

[22] Waits tells us that "in Candler's recent curriculum review, Professor Holifield urged that preparation for the ministry concern itself more with what he called 'specific knowledge' [which implies the 'specialist' mode without discarding the 'generalist' mode of the basic theological curriculum]." p. 4.

> An example of a graduate education which combines comprehensive and even theological understanding with the rigor of scholarship is the ideal evidently at work behind most Jewish scholarship. Rare is the Jewish scholar who is simply a narrow specialist, who lives in the specialist's world in such a way as to be unable to interpret Judaism with comprehensive historical insight and theological appraisal...The notion that specialized pursuit of scholarship would exclude the possibility of being a theological interpreter of Judaism would be utterly foreign to [eminent Jewish scholars].[23]

As one who shares Farley's admiration of eminent Jewish scholars, I too subscribe to the ideals of the "church-oriented" university-divinity schools which pursue "university-inspired theological studies," producing that kind of well-balanced specialist-generalist, theological/religious scholar and religious leader.[24]

IX. *The "University-Oriented" University-Divinity School*

Today most American university-divinity schools espouse the "church-oriented" orientation. I have always felt that the Divinity School at Harvard at one time had flirted more with the "university-oriented" mode, but that it made a dramatic switch to the "church-oriented" mode under the presidency of Nathan Pusey, even though the Divinity School—like its counterpart at Yale—is clearly not church owned, nor affiliated with any one denomination. I still think my feeling is not altogether wrong, but I must admit I am less certain about my feeling now, because, according to Harvey Cox, Harvard Divinity School has always been oriented toward "communities of faith." To be more specific, Cox began his address at the 1989-90 Convocation of his school with a theme close to what I consider the "church-oriented" perspective. In his own words:

> 'By virtue of the authority delegated to me, I confer on you the degree of Master of Theological Studies, Master of Divinity, Master of Theology, or Doctor of Theology, and declare that you are well prepared to foster the health and vitality of the community of faith.' These are the words intoned by the president of the University on Commencement Day, as he bestows degrees on the graduates of this school. I repeat them here...to remind us...that our purpose at HDS [Harvard Divinity School] is to foster the health and vitality of communities of faith.[25]

---

[23] Edward Farley, *Theologia: The Fragmentation and Unity of Theological Education* (Philadelphia: Fortress Press, 1983), pp. 202-203.
[24] This theme is well-developed in Waits, "Church and School..."
[25] Quoted in Harvard Divinity School Bulletin, Vol. XIX, No. 4 (Winter 1990), p. 10.

Whether Cox's statement contradicts my impression or not, it is evident that what I consider to be the "university-oriented" university-divinity school does not exist in unadulterated form at the present. Nevertheless, my comments on the subject may be important at least for future reference.

Briefly stated, the "university-oriented" mode aims at the kind of theological-religious study based on the reality of religious plurality of the world of our time. Thus, its objective is different from the "church-oriented" mode pursued by many university-divinity schools today which are committed to the study and advocacy of one religion with both specialist-and-generalist aspirations of studies within the context of one tradition (usually Christian). In so stating, it is not my intention to judge which orientation is better, "university-oriented" or "church-oriented." They are both important and legitimate but quite different. It is not easy to mix these two modes and orientations. My own reflections on the importance of the "university-oriented" university-divinity school is based on several factors:

1) I wish to avoid idle speculation about the future, but those of us who have witnessed the great changes of the world situation in our lifetime, from the end of Western colonialism in the non-Western world shortly after the Second World War to recent political upheavals in China, Eastern Europe, and South Africa, are not surprised by the notion that the world order as we have known it may be crumbling under our own feet. In this ever-changing world, the United States, which faces serious *internal* social and cultural changes due to growing "rainbowization" and secularization, can ill afford to ignore *externally* the "south-north" relationships as well as "east-west" relationships. I once stated in that connection:

> In a real sense the basic problem of our time is not the emergence of many new quarrelsome nations [e.g., the Philippines, India, Pakistan, Sri Lanka, Burma, South and North Korea, Indonesia, Vietnam, Cambodia, Laos, Malaysia, etc.] in the post-1945 era, but rather what both caused and resulted from their political independence, namely, the momentous redefinition of man's conception of dignity, value, and freedom of humankind.[26]

It is important for us to realize that this global change in human perception requires more than a simple re-arranging of old furniture in the cozy club of western philosophies, religions, and culture. Indeed, it demands

---

[26] J.M. Kitagawa, *The History of Religions: Understanding Human Experience* (Atlanta: Scholars Press, 1987), p. 163.

the hammering out of new linguistic and conceptual symbols transcending the present conflicting assertions and affirmations of various peoples and traditions. This implies, among other things, that Western logic and rhetoric based on a provincial convention of dividing human experience into a series of semi-autonomous pigeonholes (such as religion, ethics, philosophy, aesthetics) will no longer be sufficient.

2) In this rapidly shrinking world of the late twentieth and approaching twenty-first centuries, universities in every continent have to be oriented simultaneously to: (a) their own religious-cultural-social-political syntheses, and (b) the global community, so that intelligent men and women of various linguistic, ethnic, national, religious, and cultural backgrounds will learn how to live meaningfully in their own environments and yet live peacefully together with other peoples elsewhere in a global community. We in the United States should not be misled by the superficial external similarities between the America domestic synthesis and the global synthesis. At home, our task is to integrate a variety of cultural strands that come to our shores, domesticating them if need be, in order to hammer out a dynamic, ever-growing unique American brand of religious-cultural-social-political synthesis. Globally, our *métier* is to envision the new coherence of the world community based on, as Thomas Mann's Joseph realized in Egypt, a humble recognition that the world has many centers of "world of meaning" based on a variety of religious-cultural-social-political syntheses, including our own. To appreciate the existence of "many centers" in the world, we have to cherish the life of the university where these different kinds of "world of meaning" can be explored, examined, and pursued.[27] American "private" universities, which unlike state-universities and church-related universities are free from state or church interferences, have unique obligations to become important path-finders and paradigms for the kind of independent institutions of higher learning the world over.

3) Confronted by such stupendous cultural, social and political changes, both national and global, the "university-oriented" university-divinity school programs should realize special responsibilities to develop their coherent structures of theological/religious studies which supplement the programs of *religious studies* in the college and the university, as well as *theological studies* of free-standing seminaries. The "university-oriented" divinity school programs should cooperate with all the aforementioned programs; indeed, graduates of all the kinds of

---

[27] Ibid.

schools mentioned above should be welcomed to take advantage of the "university-oriented" programs. Perhaps in the future the "university-oriented" theological-religious programs of private universities may prove to serve as a sort of *"habilitation"* scheme already familiar in German universities.

4) The "university-oriented" programs have much in common with non-theological *religious studies* (*verstehen* mode) of the college and the university, especially because *religious studies* programs also take seriously the fact of religious plurality both on the global and national contexts. In sharp contrast to these programs, curricula of Jewish or Christian theological studies are committed to the study primarily of one religion, and even approach the phenomenon of religious plurality through the window of the one religion in question. Invariably, however, *religious studies* programs tend to stress the "biographical-outer" orientation in the study of religions at the expense of the "autobiographical-inner" approaches. In this regard, it is important for the "university-oriented" university-divinity schools to be mindful of pursuing both "autobiographical-inner" and "biographical-outer" approaches for the sake of acquiring a balanced notion of *religion* (singular).

In any religious inquiry, it is crucial, as Edward Farley reminds us, to present the determinate religious faith which is often soft-pedaled in *religious studies*:

> the student will be confronted with the critical appraisals which attend side by side with formal (theoretical, practical and sociological) manifestations of religions.
>
> ...this is exactly what should happen when Buddhism [for example] is taught in such a way as to do it justice. To teach Buddhism is not simply to communicate information about Buddhist history or present practices but to stage and evoke participation in its texts and their claims that the insightfulness of Buddhist meditation is insightfully grasped by the student.[28]

In this connection, there seem to be two issues that are involved in the usual *religious studies* programs. First, in order to be fair to competing religious traditions, and also in stressing the "biographical-outer" approaches to various religions, many *religious studies* programs tend to ignore what Farley enunciated as the important, but often neglected, approach to religious faith, so that "religion" is often treated like politics or economics. In some *religious studies* programs, Judaism and Christianity suffer more than other religions from the one-sided external

---

[28] Farley, *Theologia*, p. 198.

approach. Second, there are also cases of some narrow specialists, trained only in one religion, who expound that religion's insiders' views as the only valid theories of religion. At any rate, the double orientation of the "university-oriented" university-divinity school programs have something to offer (or supplement) the one-sided emphasis of *religious studies* programs.

5) The "university-oriented" university-divinity school has a totally different task from one-religion-based *theological studies* of free-standing seminaries and even of the "church-oriented" university-divinity schools and cluster schools. Vis à vis the latter, the "university-oriented" programs have to demonstrate (a) the validity of "biographical-outer" approaches to Christianity or Judaism, whichever the case may be, as an important methodological option, and (b) the necessary alternative approach to Judaism or Christianity as parts of the whole religious experience of humankind as seen from the perspective of the "whole." In both of these endeavors, we are required to have a tentative generalized understanding of "religion," based on careful objectification and empathetic multi-dimensional understanding of different religions of the world. This should happen not only through Westcentric or Christiancentric logic, symbol and rhetoric, but also through other [non-Western] peoples' conventions of perceiving human experience and reality.

6) Above all, the university-divinity school, especially when it is "university-oriented," has a heavy responsibility as an integral partner in the cooperative inquiry of the university at large. On the one hand, it must question and scrutinize the inherited orthodoxies of various religious traditions. On the other hand, it must criticize and restrain the absolutizing tendency of cultural ethnocentrism. It is not only the American university but universities in other continents which exhibit social, cultural, economic, and political tendencies toward idolatry. More often than not, the American university inherited from modern Western civilization two questionable dogmas, namely, the dogma affirming the unbiased, objective, universal validity of the Western perception of human experience and reality, based on the provincial Western convention of dividing human experience into a series of separable compartments of life, and the dogma asserting the irrelevance of religion for the serious pursuit of society and culture. As to the first dogma, the university-divinity school is duty-bound to dispel the Western illusion that the Western mode of thinking and inquiry, important though it is to European and American university circles, is not the most reliable tool

for the global intellectual enterprise of the understanding of human experience in the next century. Regarding the second dogma, no one should underestimate its tenacity, especially in the university community which has always resented the historical pattern of many church groups' frequent insistence that "religious authority" serve as a standard to adjudicate competing cognitive issues. Today, we have to be aware that the dogma of the irrelevance of religion is not confined to university circles alone. As Daniel Bell observed recently:

> From Voltaire to Marx every Enlightenment thinker thought that religion would disappear in the 20th century because religion was fetishism, animistic superstition ... [W]ell, it's not true, because religion is a response, and sometimes a very coherent response, to the existential predicaments faced by all men [and women] in all times. Empires have crumbled; economic systems have crumbled. The great historical religions have survived.[29]

Confronted by today's ambiguous situation, those in the "university-oriented" university-divinity schools are advised to realize both their *responsibilities* and *limitations*. On the one hand, they have the *responsibility* to persuade the university community on cognitive grounds of the significance of religion which is so pervasive in various dimensions of human experience. They must try to develop a coherent, cogent intellectual framework, not only based on the Western mode of inquiry but also taking into consideration the non-Western peoples' perception of the texture of history and anatomy of human experience. In this sense, the "university-oriented" university-divinity school is committed essentially to the "religiously-inspired" vocation of intellectual life, which is as important a vocation as those in the natural sciences, philosophy, art, humanity, and social sciences. In following the vocation of intellectual inquiry concerning the religious reality underlying human experience, probably the highest standard of the "university-oriented" university-divinity school may be illustrated by what Johann Gottlieeb Fichte once called *Die Bestimmung des Menschen*.

We are motivated, however, by the very vocation of intellectual inquiry to recognize its many *limitations*. We know only too well how the intellectual vocation has been shaped historically by Western religious-cultural-social-political experience in the particular institutional structure of *studium*, forerunner of the modern university. Although the Western form of university has become accepted widely in the non-Western parts

---

[29] Quoted by Richard Bernstein in his article, "Capitalism Undermining Capitalism," *New York Times*, July 7, 1989, p. B2.

of the world, the intellectual vocation—even in the West which originally produced the tradition of *studium*—has begun to ooze out of the confines of the university pattern. This is illustrated by serious research work in various laboratories beyond the university campus, training programs for experts and leaders by business, artistic, religious, and other communities. Thus, the "university-oriented" university-divinity schools as well as "church-oriented" university-divinity schools, should have a realistic sense of their *limitations* and pursue as genuine partners—neither "queen," nor appendix—co-operative inquiries in the university as much as in theological-religious endeavors, realizing honestly and humbly that *Die Bestimmung des Menschen* itself may not be the final end of the human journey in this mysterious universe.

The Marginalization of Theology in the University

JOSEPH C. HOUGH JR.

I. Introduction

In the earliest European universities, the place of Christian theological studies was simply assumed. It was the queen of the sciences, the organizing principle for all knowledge. Most of those who migrated to the medieval universities to become the earliest masters and professors were clerics. What they had mastered, for the most part, was theology, and what they professed, if not theology itself, certainly was understood to be in accord with theological knowledge.[1] Theological knowledge was of "supernatural" things, the things of God made known by revelation. Reason, too, was a source of knowledge, and the best of reason and revelation formed a harmonious whole. Yet, in the final analysis, reason was fallible, and revelation was not, so that the freedom of reason was circumscribed by the knowledge of revelation. No theory of knowledge could be complete unless that which was known by natural reason was crowned by theological knowledge. In fact, the university itself was understood theologically as were all the other institutions in society.

---

[1] I am aware of the fact that Salerno and Bologna were focused on medicine and law, but even in these universities, teaching that contradicted orthodox Christian theology in any way would not long have been tolerated. For a full description of the complex development of the early universities in Europe, see Hastings Rashdall, *The Universities of Europe in the Middle Ages*, 3 volumes, F. M. Powicke and A. B. Emden, editors (Oxford: Oxford University, 1936).

All of that has, of course, changed. For a variety of reasons, the place of theology in the university has become peripheral or even problematic. In the following essay, I shall develop a brief historical account of the way in which this situation has come about and then suggest some directions for the development of a contemporary rationale for the place of theological studies in the university.

II. Theology in the Medieval University

The earliest comprehensive idea of the university was theological. This was true with respect to its institutional role in society, the conception of a proper subject matter for studies, and the vocation of the professor. Of course, the idea of a university was rooted in much earlier Christian reflection and practice concerned with the relationship of learning and piety. As George H. Williams has demonstrated, a number of major themes surfaced in early Christian thinking concerning the nature of scholarship in general as well as the vocation of the Christian scholar, all of which influenced the emerging university ideal.[2] I shall not review these themes in detail, but a brief description of their main features is necessary for an understanding of the breadth of thinking underlying the medieval understanding of the university.

Very early, Christians affirmed the important role of scholarship. Usually this was understood in relation to the three offices of the ministry of Christ. The scholar was understood to be exercising the prophetic office, while the rulers and the church leaders were exercising respectively the kingly and priestly offices. Equally important for the development of a theology of the university was that Christian reflection which attempted to understand the relationship of specifically Christian teaching to the teaching and wisdom of antiquity. What some Christians argued was that God in her providential ordering of the world had made provision for the transfer of human learning from one generation of scholars to the next in such a way that the continuity of wisdom and truth was affirmed even though Christian teaching was finally to be authoritative. From Adam to Abraham; from Athens to Jerusalem to Rome; the torch was passed by a succession of learned persons committed to the truth. Later, scholars in the university would stand in that order as the designated bearers and guardians of basic human wisdom.

But there was a problem. Human reason had been impaired in the Fall of Adam and Eve, so that the possibility of the transfer of divinely

---

[2] George H. Williams, *Wilderness and Paradise in Christian Thought* (New York: Harper and Brothers, 1962) 140-231.

ordered knowledge was imperiled. Yet, a community of devoted Christian scholars could still hope that with discipline and faithful effort and with God's help, they could still provide for the safeguarding of knowledge and for its orderly transmission relatively free from error. Still the distortions of sin and the distractions of the world created confusion and discord. More and more, Christians saw the work of the scholar as a kind of spiritual warfare, and increasingly they withdrew into highly disciplined communities to fight against the temptations of the world as they carried on their scholarly work. In this way, the monasteries were certainly the precursors of university communities in medieval times.[3]

Over the years, such reflections about scholarship influenced the development of at least three important aspects of the medieval theology of the university. In the first place, there was a theological conception of the university as an institution set in the context of a comprehensive theology of the social order. As early as the thirteenth century, the notion of the university as one of the "pillars" of Christian civilization was clearly formulated. Alexander of Roes argued that the conception of a Christian society required "preservation of centers of relative autonomy in order to secure Christian society against aberrations in the name of piety or patriotism." He insisted that each must be kept distinct from the other because God had willed it so. Otherwise, disaster would befall the Christian social order.[4]

Secondly, within the structure of Christian society, the distinctiveness of the Christian university did not imply its complete autonomy, for it was clear that while the university should have relative institutional autonomy, its subject matter was to be pursued in the service of piety. The roots of this idea of university instruction lay in the emphasis on the importance of learning that appeared in the early church fathers. It was exemplified in Jerome's call for a "learned celibacy."[5] It was especially prominent in medieval monastic theology at the time of the founding of the university. The monastics held that the study of the classics was important for the development of spirituality. To be sure, the study of the ancients was always carried on under the authority of the scriptures, and classical teaching was always to be brought into conformity with Christian revelation,[6] but the result of this kind of pedagogy was "to set

---

[3] Ibid., 158f.
[4] Ibid., 172; see also Rashdall, op. cit., especially volume I, 2f.
[5] Williams, op. cit., 158-59.
[6] Jean LeClerq, *The Love of Learning and the Desire for God*, translated by Catharine Misrahi (London: SPCK, 1978) 139ff.

free the conscience of both teachers and pupils with regard to the pagan authors." As a result there emerged what Jean LeClerq called an "integral humanism" that was finally directed toward increasing in the student "the influence of Him who alone is 'perfect man,' Christ the Son of God."[7] The love of God and the love of learning were combined, and this Christian humanism remained a potent force in the university long after the institutional form of the medieval Christian university had disappeared.

Third, in all of this it is obvious that the vocation of the teacher in the university was hardly distinguishable from the vocation of ministry in general. The professors, like the university, had a distinctive responsibility for learning, but they were all clerics, and it was clear that as teachers or masters in the university their primary loyalty was to the church. Theology was the highest pinnacle of university study, and even those who studied for the other learned professions were schooled in theology as well.

Neither the church nor the university always rested easily with this ideal.[8] But it was there, nonetheless, and the struggles and distortions that occurred were very visible only because the idea of the university carried such force. Not everyone in the university, the state or the church was Christian, nor even understood the theological construct undergirding the *corpus christianum*—or even cared about it at all for that matter. Yet the overwhelming power of the church, the customs of the society and general public opinion favored the Christian understanding, and there were ample religious and legal sanctions to enforce conformity of practice in most cases.

The Reformation did little at first to challenge this essential idea of the university. According to George H. Williams, no distinctly Protestant notion of the university was ever developed,[9] and the important elements of the medieval theology of the social order remained intact, particularly in Calvin. Using a Christological formula, he developed at Geneva the most complete integration of society and church that has appeared in Christian history.[10] He undertook "...to insure that society would in actual practice and in every detail be an expression of the

---

[7] Ibid., 149, 179.
[8] Cf. John W. Baldwin and Richard Goldthwaite, editors, *Universities in Politics* (Baltimore: Johns Hopkins, 1972) and R.N. Swanson, *Universities, Academics and the Great Schism* (Cambridge: Cambridge University, 1979).
[9] Williams, op. cit., 220.
[10] John Baillie, *What is Christian Civilization* (New York: Harper and Row, 1945) 22.

kingly rule of Christ,"[11] and that included the university, whose teachers were *docteurs,* one of the four offices of ministry described in the Ecclesiastical Ordinances of 1561.[12] Yet, in Calvin's case the *corpus christianum* was confined to Geneva. Elsewhere, where Calvinists were a minority movement, they set out to christianize the universities.

Meanwhile, both the Lutherans and the Anglicans, due to their intense conflict with the papacy, were disposed to bring the university more under the authority of a ruler who would enforce their own orthodoxy.[13] It is true that there was an early alliance between some Protestants, especially Melancthon, and Renaissance humanists in German universities. However, that alliance was forged primarily to do battle with the papacy, and it ultimately collapsed before the surging pressure in Lutheran universities for a confessional university protected by the state. From the middle of the sixteenth century until the close of the seventeenth century, the Christian confessional university was dominant. In the Reformation countries, the idea of the university as one of the coordinate and relatively autonomous pillars of society had disappeared. In its place was the territorial Christian university whose teaching was clearly under the dogmatic authority of the dominant church of the region.[14]

In both the medieval period and the Reformation, however, there was this much in common. The university was understood to be a theological institution, both in terms of its place in society and the internal ordering of its subject matter. Learning, of whatever form, was primarily, if not entirely, in the service of Christian piety.

III. Theology in the Modern University

Because my interest is in a typological sketch of the place of theology in the university, I have neglected to present the full complexity of the historical development of universities in Medieval or Reformation times in Western Europe. For example, Bologna and Salerno were earlier than Paris, and neither of them really fit my description of the medieval university very well.[15] Moreover, Christian humanism was constantly threatened by a scholastic dogmatism, so much so that the university

---

[11] Quoted in Baillie, op. cit., 23.
[12] Williams, op. cit., 190-191.
[13] Ibid., 185.
[14] Friedrich Paulsen, *The German Universities and University Study* (London: Longmans,1906) 14ff.
[15] Cf. footnote no. 1.

was often more interested in censorship than in learning.[16] In contrast to that tendency, under the impact of the Renaissance, humanism began to break loose from its Christian moorings. For example, by the middle of the fifteenth century in Germany, Griefswald was already dominated by the Renaissance humanists. To this conquest were added Freiburg, Basel and others in just a few years, and at the end of the second decade of the sixteenth century, this secular humanism had effected a remarkable change in all the major German speaking universities.

As I indicated earlier, Protestants at first cooperated with the humanists in a struggle to displace Catholic domination of the universities. Moreover, it is important to remember that many of the Renaissance humanists, including Erasmus and Grotius, were Christian. Learning was still in the service of piety. What was unacceptable to the humanists was the restriction of classical learning by the religious dogmatism of an authoritarian church. Since Calvin and Melancthon both had strong humanistic interests, cooperation was not difficult during the early stages of the Reformation. But the cooperation was transitory and enmity soon appeared as confessional interests increasingly dominated the thinking of the Protestant reformers about the university. Erasmus declared that "knowledge perished wherever Lutheranism became dominant," and by the end of the sixteenth century, Protestantism had swept the humanists out of Protestant dominated universities. The scholastics began a revival in Catholic dominated areas during the sixteenth and seventeenth centuries, though they did not gain ascendency in any of the German universities until the nineteenth century.[17]

What was occurring, though hardly obvious at first glance, was the breakdown of the old pattern of the Christian university. It should be noted, however, that during the period when humanists dominated the field, it was only the institutional aspect of the Christian university that came under attack. Not until the very end of the seventeenth century with the establishment of the University of Halle in Germany was the place of theology in the university seriously challenged. Under the leadership of Thomasius Wolff, philosophy replaced theology at the center of the university. He championed the pursuit of truth based on reason alone. Morality and law, Wolff argued, were no longer to be grounded theologically, but would be based on rational knowledge of the human person and society. Moreover, rational knowledge was to be advanced by research. Knowledge was no longer seen to be the wisdom of the past

---

[16] Cf. Swanson, op. cit.
[17] Paulsen, op. cit., 14-34.

that was simply to be transmitted to students, nor was it the function of the university to preserve and secure ancient truths against challenge. The assumption on which the new university instruction was to be based was that truth was to be discovered.[18] The university professor was to be free of any regulations by state or church which would limit research leading to discovery, and he also would, of necessity, be free to encourage students to follow a similar path.

At Halle, then, the emphasis was on research with special attention to philosophy, mathematics and physics. Some fifty years later, Göttingen moved in a similar direction but with a primary added dimension. The neo-humanists at Göttingen were fascinated with the literature of the Enlightenment as well as with the classics. But none of this was to be in the service of piety. It was to serve a rational and human purpose, namely: the development of appreciation for and an identification with culture.[19]

At both Göttingen and at Halle, German pietism was also an important influence on the university. The pietists opposed the old classical notion of spiritual formation and orthodox theology. This they shared with the humanists and the rationalists. Moreover, with their emphasis on the development of the individual soul and the value of the individual, they were easily assimilated into the neo-humanist ideal of spiritual cultivation, the elevation of the individual spirit, "...the transformation of the entire character, the making of a new cultural person."[20] Incidentally, a similar, though by no means identical, movement took place in England during the eighteenth century.[21]

What I have illustrated briefly here about changes in the university was but a case in point of the changes occurring everywhere in society. Under the impact of multiple forces, the whole medieval social structure crumbled. The Reformation, the Enlightenment, the Industrial Revolution, and the rise of the nation states together created a radically new situation by the end of the eighteenth century. The concept of a "Christian" society was eroded in a variety of ways. One could discuss any number of significant changes, but one that is important for my pur-

---

[18] Ibid., 42-48. This idea of the university as the discoverer of knowledge reached England during the nineteenth century, by the time of Newman's classic essay *The Idea of a University*. Cf. Sheldon Rothblatt, *Tradition and Change in English Liberal Education* (London: Faber and Faber, 1976) 157-166.

[19] Paulsen, op. cit., 42-48; see also Fritz Ringer, *The Decline of the German Mandarins: The German Academic Community 1890-1933* (Cambridge, Mass.: Harvard University, 1969) Chapter 1.

[20] Ringer, op. cit., 18-20.

[21] Rothblatt, op. cit.

poses here is the change in general religious beliefs. During the Middle ages, there were, as I have indicated earlier, certainly persons who professed to be orthodox believers who were not. Hypocrisy is not new. What was new after the Enlightenment was the presence of thousands of persons who professed no religious beliefs at all; many others whose beliefs were amorphous and ill-defined; and some whose beliefs were hostile to religious belief as such. Still, as was the case in the new universities, value systems rooted in Christian teachings were widely accepted, and often used as weapons against religious authority. What had emerged was what John Baillie has called the "open" Christian civilization, a civilization in which values rooted in Christian theological understanding had become autonomous and were justified without any necessary reference to their Christian foundations.[22] Such values as freedom, the worth and dignity of the individual, toleration and civil rights cannot be fully understood without reference to their historical grounding in the Christian ideals of the image of God in each human and the worth of the individual soul's salvation as exemplified in the death of Christ. The idea of equality is similarly rooted and also was an outgrowth of the notion that all persons were equally sinners before God.[23] The open Christian society, then, is at once "Christian incognito" (to use a Tillichian phrase) and in its "depth dimension" still Christian. It is, in Maritain's words, "not consecrationally but secularly Christian."[24] But why call such a society Christian? T.S. Eliot's answer was, "A society has not ceased to be Christian until it has become positively something else."[25]

What happened generally in the society, of course, happened also in the university. The emergence of the modern liberal idea of the university was very early affirmed by Christian theologians as a secular embodiment of a Christian ideal. Nowhere was this more evident than in Germany where philosophy, literature and culture "grew up in the soil of Protestantism."[26] The idealism that emerged under the leadership of

---

[22] Baillie, op. cit.(whole book). The term, "open Christian civilization," appears on p. 41.

[23] Cf. Joseph C. Hough, Jr. "The Reapportionment Controversy: A Critical Examination From the Perspective of Christian Ethics," Unpublished Dissertation, Yale University, 1965. But see also Gregory Vlastos' excellent article in which he explodes any easy assumption of a causal connection or even the compatibility of some types of Christianity with democracy (Gregory Vlastos, "Religion and Democracy," in Amos N. Wilder, editor, *Liberal Learning and Religion* [New York: Harper and Brothers, 1951] 267-295x).

[24] Jacques Maritain, *True Humanism*, translated by Margot R. Adamson (London: Geoffrey Bles: Centenary, 1938) 200.

[25] T.S. Eliot, *The Idea of a Christian Society* (London: Faber and Faber, 1939) 13.

[26] Paulsen, op. cit., 37.

Kant, and later Hegel, Fichte and Shelling, really never rejected Protestant Christianity. The idealists were its "modernizers."[27] It is, therefore, not surprising at all that early in the nineteenth century Schleiermacher, the leading Christian theologian of the time, wrote with strong conviction about the new university at Berlin. He agreed with von Humboldt, Fichte, Kant, Hegel and others that the organizing principle of the new university was to be freedom —freedom to teach and freedom to learn. Following the pattern laid out by Wolff at Halle, Schleiermacher argued that scholarship based on research was the primary function of the university and that the goal of university-based research was the discovery of a comprehensive and unified principle of knowledge by which the whole of knowledge and its parts could be interpreted and integrated. The key to this search was not only freedom to teach and learn but also free communication of ideas between the various special fields of knowledge. "It is," said Schleiermacher, "the duty of all scholars to reunite in comparative studies that which by virtue of language appears in separation."[28] All knowledge is grounded in scientific scholarship, by which he meant not any narrow empiricism but relentless and critical pursuit of new knowledge through research. The essential duty of the university, he concluded, was "…to generate and to train the scholarly spirit," the final outcome of which would be "…a totally new form of the intellectual life."[29] Specialized advanced research belonged to another institution —the academy. But in the university, the concern was to be with the interconnectedness of disciplines and the principle of cognition itself. It seemed obvious, therefore, to Schleiermacher, that instruction in philosophy was basic to all other instruction,[30] and only those professors who were established in some field of pure scholarship in the philosophical faculty would be allowed to teach in the schools of the professions.[31]

The new university was to provide an important service to the state as well. It was to develop an intellectual elite which was broadly "cultured," one whose personalities were formed in accordance with a cultural ideal or a system of the highest and most universal ethical and aesthetic norms. This particular legacy of German neo-humanism and

---

[27] Ringer, op. cit., 83.
[28] Friedrich Schleiermacher, "Reflections Concerning the Nature and Function of Universities," (1808) Gerhard E. Spiegler, editor and translator, *The Christian Scholar*, volume 48, Summer 1965, 141.
[29] Ibid., 146.
[30] Ibid., 147, 154.
[31] Ibid., 155-156.

pietism was not explicit in Schleiermacher's essay, but it appears clearly in other writings on the new university published at the same time. Here one finds the final contours of the modern university in Germany. The effort to enculturate the whole person was directed toward the formation of a leader class with a clear worldview composed of the highest values of liberal culture. These leaders would use the state as a vehicle for creating an objective cultural state in which the spirit of the cultured person would be concretely and corporately manifest.[32]

It is obvious from what has been said, that even in Schleiermacher's conception of the university, theology was not the organizing center. He did assume, however, that the study of theology belonged in the university.[33] So did Immanuel Kant, although he assigned to the philosophy faculty the task of determining the validity of the basic truth claims of theologians.[34] But this did not seem obvious at all to other leading figures in the discussion about the new university at Berlin. For example, Fichte did not think that theology as such belonged in the new university because it was not a positive science, that is, it had no identifiable unified subject matter of its own. He argued that historical theology and philological studies in theology could easily be assigned to other historical sciences. Because dogmatics could not yield scientific knowledge, it had no place in a scientific university. There was, therefore, no reason to include a theological faculty in the university at all.[35]

Schleiermacher argued that theology was in fact a positive science. It was a positive science because it represented a "body of scientific elements which [had] a connectedness of their own." This connectedness resided first in the essential relation of all the elements of theological studies to a determinate faith, a mode of God-consciousness. Since the issue was focused exclusively on Christian theological studies, all of the elements refer, of course, to Christian faith. But Schleiermacher goes on to say that the sciences cannot merely be speculative. They must be prac-

---

[32] Ringer, op. cit., 1-127. For a later version than that of Schleiermacher, see Karl Jaspers, *Die Idee der Universität* (Berlin: Springer, 1923).

[33] Friedrich Schleiermacher, *Brief Outline of the Study of Theology*, translated by William Farrar (Edinburgh, 1850, ATLA edition, 1963 [published by Schleiermacher in 1811]).

[34] See Immanuel Kant, *The Conflict of the Faculties*, translated by Mary J. Gregor (New York: Abaris Books, 1979 [published by Kant in 1798]).

[35] See Johann Gottlieb Fichte, "Deduzierter Plan Einer Zu Berlin Zu Errichtenden Hohern Lehranstalt", in Ernst Anrich, editor, *Die Idee der Deutschen Universität: Die fünf Grundschriften aus der Zeit ihrer Neubegrundung durch klassischen Idealismus und romantischen Realismus*, (Darmstadt: Wissenschaftliche Buchgesellschaft, 1964 [published by Fichte in 1807]) 125f. Fichte's argument is discussed briefly in Wolfhart Pannenberg, *Theology and the Philosophy of Science*, translated by Francis McDonagh (Philadelphia: Westminster, 1976) 373n.

tical. Therefore, theology is a science to the degree that it provides guidance for the church in the broadest sense possible. There is yet one more caveat. Theological studies are not for everyone. The unity of theological studies finally lies in the fact that each of the elements is necessary for the preparation of those who will lead the church.[36] In other words, theological science is in complete harmony with the purpose of the university—namely to produce an educated leadership class for one of the major professions essential to the life of the state. Thus Schleiermacher indirectly answers Fichte by changing the terms of the discussion.[37]

The "scientific" character of theological studies as a whole resides in their reference to the possibility of advancing a particular kind of knowledge, namely, knowledge concerning the character of God-consciousness represented in Christian faith. Thus not only do theological studies belong in the new scientific university, dogmatic theology itself belongs in historical theology, because knowledge of the contemporary state of Christian thinking about God (i.e. dogmatics) is necessary for a comprehensive understanding of the historical manifestation of Christian faith right through to the present. But the scientific character of theological studies as a whole is also secured by the test of practicality. It is knowledge of faith that is directed toward the practical manifestation of that God-consciousness in the institutional life of the church.

The debate at Berlin involved two separate but related issues. On the one hand there was the question as to whether theological studies necessary for the preparation of leaders of the church would be included in the university at all. In other words, the future of the program in theological studies including all matters of science and those matters affecting the life and governance of the church was at stake. Should these studies be carried on in the new university? On the other hand, there was the question about the appropriateness of including dogmatic theology as such in university theological studies. Could any dogmatic studies be scientific? Schleiermacher had to answer both at once. If studies of determinate faiths did not include dogmatics, Fichte could win the argument. Theological studies could be dispersed among other related sciences. But this would mean that in the new university no specific attention would be paid to the matters affecting the guidance and governance of the church. Thus even if there were room for historical, philosophical and philological studies focused on Christianity, theological studies as a

---

[36] Schleiermacher, *Brief Outline*, op. cit., 1963, 91ff.
[37] Pannenberg thinks that Schleiermacher wrote much of his work before Fichte published his essay in 1807. Pannenberg, op. cit., 373n.

coherent subject matter would have no practical base in the university at all.

In the immediate setting of the controversy, Schleiermacher was successful.[38] But two problems were created in his argument that are at the center of the discussion of theology in the university today. First, though his argument in the *Brief Outline* focused specifically on the needs of leadership for the church, he was close to Kant. Kant had argued that it was in the interest of the state to insist on the presence in the university of the faculties of medicine, law and theology so that there could be some control over the quality and even the content of training for the leaders of key social institutions.[39] Politically, this might also have been a necessary argument for Schleiermacher to make, but it did tend to subordinate the more substantive argument for the scientific nature of theological studies as a unified approach to knowledge of a certain kind.[40] A second problem was Schleiermacher's argument in his essay on the university that professors responsible for theological studies must have standing in another of the scientific faculties in the university in order to be considered for teaching theological subjects. This concession by implication conceded much that had been won. Though the *place* of theological *studies* in the university had been secured, the *status* of theological *faculty* was derivative, and by implication, this cast doubt on the status of theology as a scientific subject matter appropriate for university study.

I have focused on developments in the German universities, but it should be noted that similar developments occurred in England as well, though at a much slower pace. The new learning of Renaissance humanism generated considerable interest in England as early as the sixteenth century. Erasmus was influential, and for a time, both Corpus Christi at Oxford and Saint John's at Cambridge seemed to be moving away from the scholasticism inherited from Paris. Yet, on the whole, the inherited pattern remained dominant even into the eighteenth century. There were certainly critics of the established universities who attacked both Cambridge and Oxford for their rigidity and narrowness and their failure to humanize or form the character of the whole person, but their criticism had little impact on the major universities. Thus in England, the

---

[38] There was strong oppostition to the teaching of theology in the university in Germany throughout the nineteenth century. It continues to be a major subject of debate today. For a history of the debate about the "science" of theology, see Pannenberg, op. cit.

[39] Kant, op. cit., especially the Introduction by Mary Gregor. Kant's major interest was not, of course, in justifying the presence of either theology, law or medicine. It was primarily a political document calculated to secure the freedom of the philosophical faculty from any kind of religious or political censorship.

[40] See Edward Farley, *Theologia* (Philadelphia: Fortress, 1983) Chapter 4.

search for "liberal" education mostly occurred outside the university until well into the eighteenth century.[41] By the time of Newman's classic *Idea of a University*, this situation had changed in very complex ways. No longer was education seen to be in the service of piety. It was for the cultivation of the mind. In Newman's case, remnants of the older ideal persisted. For example, he was still deeply committed to the study of theology as a necessary component in university education. All knowledge must be perfected, he argued, in the Thomistic virtues of the spirit.[42] Yet, the university's purpose was clearly not simply to produce orthodox clergy or laity. It was to form an educated elite who would give leadership to the whole society as "cultured gentlemen." The university would introduce them to and immerse them in their cultural heritage. This was to be accomplished by the study of the classics with a view to cultivating the intellect in such a way that students would develop a liberal "habit of mind." This habit of mind, which would last through life, possessed the attributes of "freedom, equitableness, calmness, moderation, and wisdom."[43] A cultivated intellect, in Newman's view, was the most adequate preparation for the professions and, what is more, it yielded a better person and hence contributed to the betterment of society.[44] Newman was close to the German ideal at this point. But one does not yet see the emphasis on research and investigation nor the emphasis on science. That would come later in the nineteenth century as the debate over the inclusion of natural scientific studies in university curricula was finally won on economic and political grounds after the failure of British industry at the Paris exhibition of 1867.[45] In Newman's university, the culture of the "cultured gentleman" was Western classical and somewhat Christian though neither dogmatic nor orthodox. In this his idea of the university was similar to that of Schleiermacher. But with Newman the place of theology in the university was secure. It was assumed to be subject matter essential to the true understanding of culture.

IV. Theology and the University in the United States

The medieval pattern for the university found its way early to the new world. Paris, after all, was the mother of Cambridge. Cambridge, later a center of Puritan influence during the seventeenth century, was

---

[41] Rothblatt, op. cit., 75ff.
[42] John Henry Newman, *The Idea of a University* (Garden City, N. Y.: Doubleday, 1959 [Doubleday Image Book]) 111-113.
[43] Ibid., 129.
[44] Ibid., 179ff.
[45] Eric Ashby, *Technology and the Academics* (London: Macmillan, 1958) 57.

the alma mater of the men who founded Harvard, the first college in America. The founders of Harvard brought their idea of a university with them from England. Steeped in the tradition of Cambridge and the theology of Calvin, they tried to recreate in the new Cambridge what they knew on the banks of the Cam. In the early history of Harvard, its leaders, particularly Increase and Cotton Mather, sounded all of the major theological themes that undergirded the medieval theology of the university. Harvard's earliest presidents were all clergymen, and it was clear that learning was to be in the service of piety, mainly through the agency of learned ministers for the churches. Though their Cambridge experience had led them to be suspicious of establishment theology, so much so that theology was not even included in the curriculum, the rules of the college specified that the student was to "consider the main end of his life and studies to know God and Jesus Christ which is eternal life."[46] Furthermore, one main impetus for the founding of Harvard was to provide a learned ministry, and most of the students during the early years were studying for the Christian ministry.[47]

The curriculum, for the most part, reflected the classical studies of Cambridge, except in place of the teaching of theology it was assumed that the study of scripture and regular prayer and worship were to be practiced by all outside the classroom. What was required for a learned ministry and orthodox laymen alike was the study of the ancient trivium and quadrivium, together with the languages required for the reading of classical texts and scripture. Thus, while the ethos of the college was geared to promote true piety, the course of study was designed to discipline the mind so that the graduate could put learning to the service of Christian commonwealth. Most professors were ministers who were seen to be the prophets who struggled to transfer the learning of the ages bequeathed to Abraham to Greece, Paris and Cambridge.[48] The Puritans, as John Brubacher suggested, had achieved "the continuance of the medieval tradition in a new world setting."[49]

This transplanted medieval pattern, which probably owed more to the Geneva model than to Paris, was not long to survive in America. Though the rhetoric persisted, the struggle over religious establishment

---

[46] Charles F. Thwing, *A History of Higher Education in America* (New York: D. Appleton,1906) 34.
[47] Ibid., 45.
[48] Ibid., 1-49; see also, Robert Handy, *A Christian America* (New York: Oxford University, 1984) 6, 11; Williams, op. cit., 143-157; and John Brubacher and Willis Rudy, *Higher Education in Transition* (New York: Harper and Row,1977) Chapter 1.
[49] Brubacher and Rudy, op. cit., 7.

in America undermined the possibility of any unified Christian conceptions of society like that of the medieval times. Rival groups established competing colleges, and confessionalism had its day. But the dearth of resources and students, together with developing religious pluralism, required a search for some sort of religious detente. Thus, by the middle of the eighteenth century, religious tests for admissions were non-existent and toleration was extended even to diversity of religious practices on many college campuses.[50]

The developing tolerance did not extend to curriculum development. Like Harvard, the other eastern colleges taught much the same subjects, at least until about 1765. After that, a series of modifications were introduced that broadened the curriculum offerings significantly. Still the classical pattern together with an emphasis on mental discipline persevered, and the residential college system inherited from Cambridge was duplicated everywhere. Religion dominated student life, and Christian orthodoxy was the norm. College eduction was liberal education for leaders in a Christianized society, even though not all of the Christians meant the same thing when they imagined what it was for a society to be Christian.[51]

Though this pattern of education remained dominant in the colleges through the colonial period, there was, at no time, general agreement that it was the best kind of education for the new world. It was elitist, and that did not go down well among the colonials. It was mental discipline, and that did not suit the practical bent of many of the new Americans. Critics began to agitate for change. In the first half of the eighteenth century, Benjamin Franklin argued for the founding of a college in Pennsylvania clearly secular in conception and directed toward the practical needs of a growing population in the new world. In the constitutional statement of the new college there was no mention of religion, the church, or the ministry.[52] Thomas Jefferson, most likely influenced by the Philadelphia model, proposed for William and Mary a similar model that was deeply indebted to French Enlightenment thinkers. His proposal was also thoroughly secular and oriented to higher standards of professional excellence. Shortly after Jefferson became governor, his proposals were introduced to William and Mary though they were never fully implemented.[53] Thus by the time of the famous Yale Report

---

[50] Ibid., 8-9.
[51] Ibid., 14, 22, 23 and 42ff.
[52] Thwing, op. cit., 112ff.
[53] Ibid., 112-116, 192, 202.

of 1828, pressure for reform was extensive. Even though that report affirmed the old pattern for the colleges, the harbingers of change had already inspired their prophetic followers, and the days of the old college pattern were numbered.[54]

As in Europe, important changes were underway in American society that undermined any semblance of a total Christian theological conception of society. Very early, it became obvious that even the regionally established churches could not survive the waves of immigration coming from a variety of locations. Most of the early settlers were inspired by their own religious visions, and those visions were very different. Baptists contested the pressure for uniformity in New England. The government of Virginia adopted the principles of Madison's Remonstrances, and the First Amendment of the new federal constitution contained provisions for freedom of religious expression and the anti-establishment clause. After the Great Awakening, all of the various religious groups gained in strength, and religious pluralism was a reality everywhere.[55]

In all of this diversity, however, the various fledgling denominations had one thing in common. They believed in education. As Douglas Sloan has pointed out, "when Jonathan Edwards expressed his conviction that an advancement in learning had preceded and gone hand in hand with the recovery of 'true religion' in the Reformation, he was simply repeating an attitude already commonplace among Protestants."[56] To be sure, the confidence in education did not always extend to that provided at Yale and Harvard, but even the "new side Presbyterians," who found Yale and Harvard too liberal, moved quickly to establish the College of New Jersey. Their faith in education as an important means of achieving their Christian social ideals had not diminished. By the end of the eighteenth century, the College of New Jersey had a president who thought

---

[54] Laurence, Veysey, *The Emergence of the American University* (Chicago: University of Chicago, 1965) Chapter 1.

[55] Handy, op. cit., 13ff. None of this is meant to indicate that religious domination of the colleges in America disappeared. Even the earliest state universities were controlled by religious groups that had achieved dominance in the region. Oddly enough both Yale and Harvard, having been chartered by the state, were subject to the control of more orthodox Puritans, long after they were relatively free internally of orthodox control. Yale was only freed from this type of state-mediated pressure in 1818 and Harvard teetered on the brink of becoming a state university from 1851-1865 (cf. George H. Williams, editor, *The Harvard Divinity School*, [Boston: Beacon, 1954] 15 and Roland Bainton, *Yale and the Ministry* [New York: Harper and Brothers,1957] 79). The freeing of these universities from state control also tended to release them from ecclesiastical control as well because most pressure for orthodoxy was coming, by this time, from state officials and not church officials.

[56] Douglas Sloan, *The Great Awakening and American Education* (New York: Teachers' College, Columbia University, 1973) 12.

that education was more important than conversion in shaping human character and the social order.57

Thus, by the middle of the nineteenth century there had developed in America a new Christian understanding of education. The logic of it was something like the following: Religion was the essential foundation of morals, a term American Protestants equated with the best and most desirable civilization. This civilization, a clearly Protestant one, was best promoted by education. Alexander Campbell, the great Disciples of Christ leader, spoke for most Protestants when he argued that Protestantism, universal education and free republican institutions were much the same thing.58

This developing Protestant theory of education was very vague. It had to be, given the deep tensions which existed between the various Protestant denominations. However, vagueness has never been an obstacle to Protestant moral fervor, so it was with considerable confidence that Protestants marched together during the early nineteenth century in pursuit of Christian civilization.59 Each of them may have had something different in mind when speaking of Christian civilization, but they were united in their pursuit of the dream.

Since education was viewed as central to the development and maintenance of the hope for a Christian civilization, it is not at all surprising that university presidents spoke of their institutions as centers for the promotion of Christian civilization. However, it is important to remember that their conceptions of their universities did not include any notion of the centrality of theology in the university. As Laurence Veysey has pointed out, very few of the presidents of colleges and universities at the end of the nineteenth century spoke much about theology as such. It certainly never occurred to them that universities or colleges constituted one of the pillars of a theologically constructed vision of society.60 They viewed the universities as the pinnacle of an educational system promoting a civilized society. To be sure, that civilization incorporated Christian values and ideals, but their notion of a Christian society was an autonomous one, characterized by decent morals, democratic values and stability. When they championed the Christian religion, it was more

---

57 Douglas Sloan, *The Scottish Enlightenment and the American College Ideal* (New York: Teachers' College, Columbia University, 1971) 157.

58 David Harrel, Jr., *The Quest for a Christian America: The Disciples of Christ and American Society to 1866* (Nashville: Abingdon, 1966) 219 cited in Handy, op. cit., 37.

59 Handy, op. cit.,37.

60 Veysey, op. cit., 28.

likely because they thought that religion helped to promote these general social goods.

This thinking probably reflected a subtle shift in the use of the term Christian civilization, one which took place, according to Handy, just after 1860. In the earlier version of Christian civilization, it was Christianity which was the "best part of civilization." Before the end of the century the emphasis had shifted to civilization itself because it was understood to have absorbed the spirit of Christianity. Thus the churches were now positively assessed in relation to their contributions to civilization. Hope was now centered in civilization itself—religion was a help in the process, but the progress of civilization was increasingly autonomous.[61]

In principle, however, the basic commitment to learning in the service of piety had not been surrendered, though the piety now had a distinctly moralistic tone. Moreover, as late as 1865 ninety percent of college presidents were still clergymen.[62] Rhetoric reminiscent of the main themes of medieval theology thus abounded on ceremonial occasions, and in formal pronouncements about the purpose of the university, a sort of moralistic piety was still a prominent theme. But even this was not long to endure.

During the latter half of the nineteenth century, war, reconstruction, massive immigration, urbanization and industrialization had combined to change the face of America. In the process, it rendered the old concept of a Christian civilization obsolete. That conception grew out of the consensus on values that emerged in white Anglo-Saxon Protestant rural and small town America. Like the Puritan society that preceded it, it gave way to a new kind of social and religious pluralism.

As these changes took place, the discussion of the purpose of the university also took a decidedly different turn. The idea of the modern university in Germany clashed with the liberal idea from England, and both of them were subject to increasingly critical scrutiny by advocates of democratization and the ideal of utility in America. The controversies surrounding these ideals generated the most creative debate over the theory of the university in American history. In all of this, there were continuing vague references to the service of Christian civilization in presidential speeches from time to time. But the discussion went on without any reference to religion or theology at all. In America, the place of theology in the university was not a subject of interest to the major

---

[61] Handy, op. cit., 95, 96.
[62] Veysey, op. cit., 7.

participants in the battle over the future shape of the university. To be sure, theologians continued to speak about the possibility of Christianizing the social order. As late as 1916, Walter Rauschenbusch was arguing that the Christianization of most American institutions was complete, but none of the key leaders of the universities took note of that fact.[63]

V. The Marginalization of Theology in the University in the United States

The marginalization of theology in the debate over the idea of the university in America was accompanied historically by a gradual change in the understanding of what constituted theological studies. It will be recalled that the founders of Harvard did not include any teaching of theology as such in their proposed curriculum. Though it was the passion for a learned ministry that was the most important factor in the founding of the earliest colonial colleges, the curriculum itself was a general course of study in the classical mode deemed appropriate for all students. Students who aspired to be ministers in the churches often did complete their studies at the colleges, but that preparation did not include any instruction in the matters specifically related to the functions of the minister in the churches. As a result, an increasing number of ministerial candidates took advantage of what Bainton has called, the "Schools of the Prophets," that is, they took up residence in a parsonage and apprenticed themselves to a senior practicing clergyman. They read under his tutelage, observed him as he performed his pastoral duties and preached an occasional sermon to be scrutinized and criticized. Therefore, the quality of the parsonage school was often too much a function of the time and interest of the tutor. Where students resided in the college, supervision was provided by a professor or even the college president on occasion. Since most of the presidents were clergy, they were certainly as competent as anyone in the college to oversee the young ministers in training. They were often sympathetic and helpful, but in most cases insufficient attention was given by pastors or presidents to practical training for the ministerial functions in a local congregation. As a result, concern in the churches about the adequacy of ministerial education began to mount.[64] In the state universities, the question about the place of theology had a different dimension. Though early state

---

[63] Walter Rauschenbusch, *Christianizing the Social Order* (New York: MacMillan,1912).
[64] Bainton, op. cit., 49; Conrad Wright, "The Early Period," in Williams, *The Harvard Divinity School*, op.cit., 22.

universities were often controlled by specific denominational groups, Jefferson's proposals for William and Mary in the late eighteenth century deliberately excluded the teaching of theology in the university. When the university of Virginia opened in 1818, it had no theological faculty, nor was there any provision for religious activities on campus. All religious studies were relegated to "Schools on the Confines," that is, outside the curriculum and off the campus of the university.[65] That pattern continued for a time in state supported institutions, essentially for many of the same reasons.

Henry Tappen's proposal for the University of Michigan is a good example. In Tappan's proposal for a "true" university there was no suggestion for a faculty of theology. Given his professed admiration for the German universities, Tappan was aware that this would seem odd. He proceeded to give an explanation for this puzzling omission:

> It will be remarked that we have omitted a Faculty of Theology in the constitution of this University. As each denomination of Christians has its peculiar Theological views and interests, it would be impossible to unite them harmoniously in one faculty. It is most expedient, therefore, to leave this branch to the Theological Institutions already established by the several denominations. But still a connection of an unobjectionable character might be formed between Theological Institutes, especially those existing in this city, and the University.[66]

He then suggested the possibility of cross registration of students and inter-institutional accreditation of work toward degrees as means for creating a cooperative relationship between the state university and private sectarian theological schools. Tappan's exclusion of theological study from the university, then, was surely not based on any question about its academic respectability. Nor was his objection to the study of theology in the university due to any kind of bias against religion as such. He was an ordained minister committed to the maintenance of a strong Christian ethos in the university. He was even committed to the support of compulsory religious practices for the students though he would countenance no denominational tests for the faculty or students.[67]

His opposition to the study of theology in the university was based on his observations and his direct experience of the contentiousness and

---

[65] Robert M. Healy, *Jefferson on Religion and Public Education* (New Haven: Yale University, 1962) 217f.

[66] Henry Tappan, *University Education* (New York, 1851) quoted in Richard Hofstadter and Wilson Smith, *American Higher Education: A Documentary History* (Chicago: University of Chicago, 1961) 506.

[67] Ibid., 507.

competitiveness between the various denominations, each of which wished to gain control of the university and thus to control the teaching of theology in the university. Tappan could see no end to that problem. He had concluded that in a community of religious pluralism under the constitutional provisions for separation of church and state, it was simply impossible to have theological instruction in public institutions.

That this was essentially Tappan's reasoning becomes even more clear in a lecture he delivered in 1858 after his losing fight against legislation allowing the chartering of denominational colleges in Michigan. "In an institution professedly belonging to a particular religious denomination, or belonging to the State where a State religion exists," he wrote, "a Theological Faculty can be established as freely as any other."[68] But not so in the state university. It belongs to no denomination, but only to the people of the state. "It is designed for a simple purpose—advancing knowledge and promoting education. It is a purely literary and scientific institution; it is in no sense ecclesiastical."[69] No longer was Tappan open even to the joint denominational control of any aspect of the university. The scars of the ugly fight with the competing denominations had made him a true believer in the total separation of church and the state university.

The University of Michigan was the most important of the state universities in the West. Its charter was the basic document used in the establishment of the University of Minnesota, and it was also influential in the deliberations leading to the founding of the University of Wisconsin.[70] Tappan was also a major influence on Andrew White, a professor of history at the University of Michigan, who was later to become the founding president of Cornell, the first major land grant university in the United States.[71] Tappan's thinking about the place of theology in the university, therefore, continued the Jeffersonian model and was influential in setting the pattern followed by most state universities established in the nineteenth century.

At the turn of the century, the sort of controversy over the place of theology in the university which came into focus during the founding of the University of Berlin began to bedevil American colleges and universities as well. The issue here was not the separation of church and state but the nature of scientific scholarship. Even as early as the seventeenth

---

[68] Henry Tappan, "The University: Its Constitution and Its Relations, Political and Religious," in Hofstadter and Smith, op. cit., 530.
[69] Ibid., 536.
[70] Brubacher and Rudy, op. cit., 156.
[71] See White's reflections on his days at Michigan in Hofstadter and Smith, op. cit., 545f.

century, there had been some uneasiness at Harvard about whether or not a theology closely related to the churches could really be open to objective research.[72] But it was not until a little after the mid point of the nineteenth century that nearly all American theological faculties were being affected specifically by German theology and scholarship.[73]

A large number of theological students had gone to Germany during the nineteenth century. From their professorial mentors they learned new ways of studying the Bible that proved simultaneously shaking and liberating. The German scientific theologians had developed a critical methodology for approaching the Bible. One group, the lower critics, began with textual study, applying the methodology of grammar and philology. Their aim was to recover the exact wording of the original text. The higher critics were interested in interpretation, and they deployed the tools of historical and literary studies to the texts in order to expose the meaning of the text.

Biblical critics of all sorts challenged the validity of belief in the literal interpretation of the scriptures. Literary critics applied the same tools of analysis that were applied to the study of literature in general, identifying sections of the scriptures as myth, poetry and legend. Historical critics challenged the received wisdom concerning the authorship of biblical materials, the development of doctrine, and the growth of the church. Their conclusions began to undermine the hold of orthodox teaching on their students and raised questions about the traditional doctrine of divine inspiration of the scriptures.[74]

As more and more theological students returned from Germany to teach in American colleges, universities, and theological seminaries, the teaching of religion in the colleges and universities changed radically. At Harvard, especially, fascination with "scientific" theology had given a historical cast to all theological studies by the end of the nineteenth century. Though specific reference to "scientific" theology faded along the way, the dominance of the historical method made it difficult to sustain strong interest in and support for systematic theology, the descendent of the old dogmatics. Even though President Eliot gave a ringing endorsement to theological studies in the university in 1879, it was clearly theo-

---

[72] Williams, *The Harvard Divinity School*, op.cit., 7.
[73] Sydney Ahlstrom, "The Middle Period," in Williams, *The Harvard Divinity School*, op.cit., 117ff.
[74] See Jurgen Herbst, *The German Historical School in American Scholarship: A Study in the Transfer of Culture* (Ithaca, N. Y.: Cornell University, 1965) 73f.

logical studies in the historical mode that he had in mind.⁷⁵ This was true not only at the leadership schools like Harvard but also in the small denominationally related colleges as well.⁷⁶

Many of the teachers of religion were older clergy who were not able or willing to adjust to the new understanding of the teaching of theology and religion, nor could they really hold their own intellectually in the vigorous atmosphere of the newly developing universities with their devotion to advanced graduate studies. A new breed of teachers emerged emphasizing research and objectivity in the study of religion, both in college departments of religion and divinity school faculties.⁷⁷

The growing hegemony of scientific theological studies exacerbated the doctrinal disputes that early in the nineteenth century had created turmoil in the colleges where theology was taught. This was particularly true at Harvard, where the dispute between the Unitarians and the orthodox Congregationalists came to a focus in the controversy surrounding the appointment of Henry Ware as Hollis Professor of Divinity in 1805. That event signaled the end of orthodox control of Harvard, and it was obvious that the confidence of the Calvinists in Harvard as a place suitable for ministerial education was shaken. As a result, they moved to establish Andover Theological Seminary in 1808, an event which set in motion what George Williams has called a "disastrous pattern in American higher education...the separation of theological studies and other studies for the professions from the university."⁷⁸ Harvard responded by establishing the first university divinity school in America in 1811. This was followed by Princeton in 1812 and Yale in 1822. Following Andover, other denominational groups moved to establish free standing theological seminaries as well.

This development cannot be understood merely as the fragmentation of theological education as a result of theological differences. It was at least partially a reflection of the concerns about the inadequacy of theo-

---

⁷⁵ Ibid., 146 and Levering Reynolds, Jr., "The Later Years," in Williams, *The Harvard Divinity School*, op. cit., 170ff.

⁷⁶ For example, Oberlin College's teaching of religion underwent a very dramatic change during the latter part of the nineteenth century, and the change was a direct result of German influence. David Palmer, student at Oberlin, has described the changes in an unpublished student paper written in 1989. I am grateful to him for sharing the paper with me.

⁷⁷ See, for example, Robert Handy, *A History of Union Theological Seminary in New York* (New York: Columbia University, 1987) 11ff. See also, Thornton Meriam, "Religion in Higher Education Through the Past Twenty-Five Years," in Amos Wilder, op. cit., 3-23.

⁷⁸ Conrad Wright, "The Early Period," in Williams, *The Harvard Divinity School*, op. cit., p. 23; and Williams, *The Harvard Divinity School*, op. cit., 5ff. See also, William Adams Brown, *The Case for Theology in the University* (Chicago: University of Chicago,1938) 33f.

logical education mentioned earlier. Moreover, as Bainton has argued, the formation of divinity schools and seminaries must also be seen as part of the dawn of professional schools in general.[79] Whether one sees the separation of the seminaries from the universities in the apocalyptic terms of Williams or in the more measured view of Bainton, however, the creation of theological seminaries outside the university raised the question as to whether the university was really the best place for the education of ministers. This was partly due to the dogmatism and contentiousness of church leaders, the characteristic attitudes of doctrinal purists which had offended Jefferson and exasperated Tappan. It also reflected, however, the legitimate concern of church leaders about the capacity of the university to give due attention specifically to those matters which, in Schleiermacher's terms, affected the life and governance of the churches. If from their perspective, the scholarship of the university was not only out of touch with the practical needs of the churches but the scholars were downright disdainful of the orthodox beliefs and practice, it was quite evident that there was a problem for the churches with locating the educational programs for young ministers in the universities.

The tensions waned after a time. Harvard and Andover even joined forces for a brief time, and soon the new theology had captured the denominational seminaries as well as the university divinity schools. By the close of the nineteenth century there was a detente. The best of the seminaries, Union in New York, moved closer to Columbia in order to educate ministers in an ethos of cooperative scholarly study of religion and theology.

Meanwhile the growing dominance of scientific theological studies was making it possible for American university leaders to consider the study of religion as an appropriate field for study in the modern research university apart from divinity studies as such. William Rainey Harper was a key figure in the launching of the study of the Bible in undergraduate colleges and university graduate programs. He began teaching at Yale in the Semitics Department and the Divinity School. As he became the most popular teacher in the Divinity School, he was able to initiate the first course in English Bible in the college. By 1890 Yale had an official chair of English Bible in the university faculty, and Harper was the first incumbent. Harper also spearheaded a national movement to promote the teaching of the English Bible, to train competent teachers, and to place academic unit value on the study of the Bible. He believed that

---

[79] Bainton, op. cit., 79ff.

the proper approach was to develop methods of inquiry which were in accord with the latest critical scientific scholarship.

In 1893, Harper sent one of his students, J. L. Willett, to the University of Michigan to teach English Bible. Soon thereafter Michigan became the first state university to establish a chair in the English study of the Bible. Other state institutions followed suit, including Jefferson's Virginia, and Georgia, Texas, Missouri and Illinois. Usually instruction in the Bible began where both Jefferson and Tappan had defined its place - at the periphery of the campus - often as a project of a pastor in the "university church." Universities gradually incorporated these courses into their curricula, first granting academic credit for courses and then granting faculty status to the instructors.[80] A few years later, under leadership of Charles Kent of Yale, the National Council on Religion moved to establish privately funded "schools of religion," near state universities in which religious subjects would be taught in a manner consonant with the highest standards for scientific scholarship. Though few of these schools survived the Second World War, what they portended was the development of university departments of religion operating independently of theological studies as such.[81]

In universities with divinity schools already present, separate departments of religion, both graduate and undergraduate, were established. For obvious reasons, this development created some difficulties. Just after the turn of the century, for example, new curriculum developments led Yale Divinity School to re-name itself the Yale School of Religion, a move which was reversed in 1920 for fear of confusion with the emerging Department of Religion.[82] That fear was not unfounded. In the major private universities there was little to distinguish the research methodology or content of teaching of departments of religion and the historical disciplines in the divinity schools, and systematic theology was often hardly distinguishable from philosophy of religion.[83] But there was nothing in the emerging departments of religion comparable to the "disciplines" of religious education, pastoral counseling, or homiletics. As a result, the formation of graduate departments of religion in the uni-

---

[80] James P. Wind, *The Bible and the University: The Messianic Vision of William Rainey Harper* (Atlanta: Scholars, 1987) 102-103—refers to material from Herbert Lockwood Willett, "The Corridor of Years,"Unpublished autobiography, *The archives of The Christian Century* (Chicago, Illinois) 92-94.

[81] See Thornton Meriam, "Religion in Higher Education Through the Past Twenty-five Years," in Amos Wilder, op. cit., 3-23.

[82] Bainton, op. cit., 209.

[83] See Conrad Cherry, "The Study of Religion and the Rise of the American University," below, 117ff.

versities underscored the dividing line between the so-called "academic" and "practical" disciplines in the divinity school. The former were included among the graduate faculty in religion. The latter were not. Thus while the place of the so-called academic disciplines in the university seemed to be more secure within the new graduate departments of religion, the presence of the practical disciplines in the university was secure only so long as the divinity school itself was seen to be a necessary part of the private universities.

By the end of the 1920s, however, the presence of the divinity school in the modern university seemed to some to be a serious problem. This time, the problem was not only sectarian strife, but the perceived lack of academic integrity of theological studies. In his 1930 lectures, Abraham Flexner was especially clear about his view that divinity schools had no place in a modern university. Because of their commitment to presuppositions not capable of scientific verification and their inevitable denominational biases, said Flexner, they were an anomaly in a university dedicated to disinterested, objective research.[84] Shortly thereafter, President Conant at Harvard was complaining about the continued financial deficits of the Divinity School and openly expressing his opinion that theology as such was a divisive rather than a unitive principle in the university.[85] In his attack on the current state of the university, Robert Hutchins declared that theology had compromised itself to such an extent that it could no longer provide the central organizing principle of the university.[86] In fact, theological studies in the divinity school, succumbing to the pressures of vocationalism, had become "a feeble imitation" of all the other professional schools.[87] Since Hutchins thought that the university should be clearly separate from all vocational and utilitarian education, he doubted whether such a divinity school really belonged in the university.[88] Hutchins' position is especially interesting since he was a successor of William Rainey Harper. Harper had practically organized the university around the divinity school. In 1905, moreover, he had suggested reforms in theological education to conform with a distinctively vocational or "functional" orientation.[89] Here was a

---

[84] Abraham Flexner, *Universities, American, English and German* (New York: Oxford University, 1968 edition [originally published 1930]) 29.
[85] Reynolds, op. cit., 212ff.
[86] Robert Maynard Hutchins, *The Higher Learning in America* (New Haven: Yale University,1936) 94ff.
[87] Ibid.,102.
[88] Ibid., 43ff.
[89] William Rainey Harper, "Shall the Theological Curriculum be Modified and How?" *The Trend in Higher Education in America* (Chicago: University of Chicago, 1905) 234-67.

definitive indication of the distance between Harvard of 1636 and Chicago of 1936. Theological education, once identical to university education, now found its place in the universities being questioned, even in one founded on the rock of Baptist piety! William Adams Brown of Union Theological Seminary in New York fought a vigorous rear-guard action, arguing for the central place of a reconceived theology in the university. His arguments appear almost quaint today. He assumed a unity of theology in general and made an appeal to a version of Christian America, an idea which had lost its historical footing. This led him to a condescending theological triumphalism which was questionable even then.[90] Brown, nonetheless, won a concession from Hutchins that there was a place in the university for theology that was not dogmatic, but Hutchins never retracted his judgment that theology was no longer capable of serving as a unifying force in the university. In the American university it had a dwelling place, but it was at the margins. The teaching of theology for the most part, was confined to the divinity schools. In contrast, by the late 1920s, support for the teaching of religion, even in state universities was very strong. In 1927, Herbert Searles of the University of Iowa argued that the study of religion must be included in any university which pretended to provide a complete education. Any university, he said, which aspires to interpret and understand the highest and best of culture in the past and present, must make a place for the study of religion in its curriculum.[91] His view was fairly typical among the leaders of state universities.[92]

In 1954 at Harvard, George H. Williams again pleaded the case for the centrality of theology in the university. The withdrawal of theology from the university, Williams argued, would seriously weaken the constitution of the university and place in jeopardy its connection with its past. He argued that the time was ripe for the revival of interest in the "larger dimension of life," a subject matter that could be addressed adequately in the university only by theology.[93] Furthermore, he believed that the "integrity of the university, the conservation of its universality, its refusal to accommodate itself to mere expediency, "might finally depend in our generation upon courageous and prophetic church leaders

---

[90] Brown, op. cit., 51, 77, 83f.
[91] Herbert L. Searles, *The Study of Religion in State Universities* (University of Iowa Studies, Studies in Character, Volume I/3, 15 October 1927) 10.
[92] See Merrimon Cuniggim, *The College Seeks Religion* (New Haven: Yale University, 1947) 77f.
[93] Williams, *The Harvard Divinity School*, op. cit., 5-6.

who could insist on freedom for the university in the pursuit of truth."[94] But there is no evidence that Williams' views were credible outside the divinity school. Theology was no longer queen. The discussion of theology and the university was henceforth to focus on the question whether the deposed royalty any longer had a home in the realm.

Conclusion

Do theological studies have a home in the modern secular university? The answer to that question, of course, can move in several directions. Pointing to the growing professionalism of American life, one could make the case specifically for the divinity school in the university with an argument somewhat similar to the one Kant advanced in the nineteenth century. However, instead of Kant's focus on the ruler's interest in the well-being of the state, one could argue that the university has a responsibility for the common good of society. Assuming that this is true, the university has a legitimate interest in, and an obligation to insure that it makes a significant contribution to the development of excellent leadership in all of the various professions. Since the churches are still very important and influential institutions in American society, the university has, therefore, an obligation to provide for the professional education of ministers for the churches in order to ensure the most learned and competent leadership for these social institutions. Whether that obligation is best fulfilled by the maintenance of schools for ministerial education as such or by some other means is an important matter for careful reflection and consideration.

My argument here is not intended to address the question of whether or not the university divinity schools are the best place for ministerial education. It is rather intended to address the justification for having a university divinity school at all. It is, of course, not self-evident that only university divinity schools are capable of ensuring the highest standards of competence and learning in the ministry. In fact, there is a case to be made that in light of the clearly secular, if not anti-religious, bias of the ethos of the modern university and the prevailing epistemological commitments of most university disciplines to an "objectivist" epistemology, ministers could be better prepared in free-standing seminaries. The view of the university as a hostile environment for faith had strong support among the working group of distinguished Christian scholars who, in the late 1940s, inspired Sir Walter Moberly to write THE CRISIS IN

---

[94] Ibid., 246-47.

THE UNIVERSITY. Moberly concluded that the modern university was, even if unintentionally, anti-Christian in both its assumptions and its organization.[95] In the 1970s, even such a devoted university scholar as Gerhard Ebeling hinted that the location of ministry studies in the university might not be as desirable as a separate location in proximity to the university.[96] It is also clearly the case that the fact that a divinity school is located in a university is no indication of its intellectual proximity to the university. If the university divinity school is to claim advantages for ministerial studies done in the context of the larger horizon of university studies, there must be some evidence that the divinity students are somehow connected to the university by more than central heating. In my view, the most convincing argument for the divinity school's importance to the profession of ministry does not rest on the claim that ministerial education in the university is inherently superior to that of free standing seminaries. It is rather the fact that the faculty of the university schools continue to be the chief educators of the leadership of all theological education, particularly those who teach in the divinity schools and seminaries This has been the most important contribution of university divinity schools to the elevation of professional standards for ministry in recent years. It will probably continue to be a major contribution in the future. Therefore, if the university has an obligation to provide for leadership education in the major institutions of society, it should continue to support the presence of superior divinity schools as part of its contribution to the common good.

A second argument for the importance of theological studies in the university focuses on the importance of the contribution that radical theological thinking might make to critical thinking in the university. This argument, a much more modest version of the ones advanced by Brown and Williams, has been advanced by writers such as Richard Niebuhr and, lately, Edward Farley. In Niebuhr's case, it is the constant reference to God the absolute, the "one beyond the many" that constantly brings into question any claims to the possession of knowledge that is final and absolute by parties in the university, the state, or the church. But theology not only has the function of relativizing all knowledge. Niebuhr insists that it serves the university in a positive way as well. For one thing, the relativizing effect of radical theological thinking invites freedom for new voices and facilitates mutual correction and creative conflict. It can also be the basis for the university's resistance to

---

[95] London, SCM, 1949.
[96] *The Study of Theology*, translated by Duane Priebe (Philadelphia: Westminster, 1978).

domination by the church or the state. In addition, the radically *monotheistic* posture of theological discourse points beyond the disunity and fragmentation of life toward a shared loyalty to the good of the whole. In this sense, theological thinking at its best serves as a reminder to the parts of the university of their obligation for the good of the whole of knowledge as well as the university's obligation for the common good of the human community.[97]

Farley calls this two-sided contribution to the life of the university a "third critical principle," one that is as important to knowledge in its own way as the critical principles of the Enlightenment. The Enlightenment, he says, grasped the relativity of knowledge and the necessity for the university to be free from dogmatism. It also grasped the multidimensionality of things, the necessity for completing and correcting paradigms of knowing. It did not, however, understand fully the dialectical character of human striving, that all of our efforts at correction themselves are subject to corruption. Thinking grounded in the Christian mythos provides an understanding of the depth, reality, and persistence of human corruption in a way not comprehended by the other critical principles of the Enlightenment. Thus, radical theological thinking invites a kind of modesty about truth claims that is important for the promotion of intellectual discourse across the entire university. But this is not the end of the matter, for the promise of redemption is also at the heart of the Christian mythos. Recognition of the corruptibility of knowledge is always set in the context of new possibilities of knowing. This undergirds a positive commitment to the human quest for truth while avoiding the temptation to see that quest as capable of perfecting knowledge. This, in turn, might create a tendency in university discourse to anticipate new paradigms of knowledge. In other words, theological thinking might provide a mirror of redemptive possibilities in the pursuit of knowledge that is scarcely present elsewhere in the fragmented life of the modern university.[98] Thus, Niebuhr and Farley have argued that theological thinking contributes not only to the common good of the whole society by educating leadership for the profession, but it can also make an important contribution to the common discourse of the university. This in itself would advance the "internal" common good of the university.[99]

---

[97] H. Richard Niebuhr, "Theology in the University" in *Radical Monotheism and Western Culture* (New York: Harper and Row, 1960) 93-99.

[98] Edward Farley, *The Fragility of Knowledge* (Philadelphia: Fortress, 1988) 17-28.

[99] For a full discussion of the responsibility of the university for the common good, including the distinction between the external and internal common good of the university,

There is a third possible line of reasoning for the importance of theological studies in the university. One might argue as did Schleiermacher (and more recently Pannenberg and Farley) that theological studies belong in the university because the study of theology is a necessary part of the study of religion. As I have indicated earlier, Schleiermacher believed that "dogmatic theology" belonged in the university because any study of the history of religion that ignored both past and contemporary belief systems was simply not complete. A religion, after all, is an historical "determinate faith." Therefore, the "scientific" study of religion must include dogmatic theology because one cannot comprehend historical faith apart from an examination of the study of historical and contemporary belief systems. In the context of the modern American university, one might argue that in addition to the history of religion, the sociology of religion and so on, theological studies are a necessary part of religious studies because the nature of religion cannot be fully understood apart from some clear understanding of the religious belief systems that arise in response to religious experience and constitute the subject matter from which religious communities form their shared identity. In a pluralistic religious world, of course, this sort of study must include theological thinking in its broadest sense, namely the study of belief systems of a variety of the world's great religions. In sum, it is the integrity of university based religious studies itself which requires the inclusion of theological studies in the university. Of course, any argument of this sort rests on the assumption that religious studies itself constitutes an appropriate and coherent field of inquiry in the modern university. And the ghost of Fichte is ever present to remind us that it is conceivable that the history of religion properly belongs to history, the sociology of religion to sociology, the philosophy of religion to philosophy and so on. Thus it could be conceded that study of religion is important in the university without conceding the need for a separate department of religious studies. But that is not a matter I shall argue here.

Whether these or any other arguments will have much impact on the leadership of major universities will depend to a large extent on the clarity of vision and determination with which theological faculties turn

---

see my essay, "The University and the Common Good," in David R. Griffin and Joseph C. Hough, Jr., editors, *Theology and the University* (Albany, N.Y.: SUNY, 1991).

their attention from narrow disciplinary pursuits to the broader question of their role as citizens in the university and the society. There are signs now that there is at least a new level of intensity in these broader conversations.[100]

---

[100] I refer to the growing number of publications appearing that are focusing on the nature of theological education as such. For a partial listing of the major works see, Clark Gilpin, "Basic Issues in Theological Education: A Selected Bibliography, 1980-1988," *Theological Education*, Volume 25/2, Spring 1989, 115f.

UBI THEOLOGIA, IBI ECCLESIA?
Schleiermacher, Troeltsch, and the Prospect for an Academic Theology

B. A. GERRISH

> How precisely everything fits and locks together in the realm of knowledge! You can say that the more a subject is dealt with in isolation, the more incomprehensible and confused it appears. — FRIEDRICH SCHLEIERMACHER

> Schleiermacher believed vigorously in the oneness of the world of the mind and delighted in it.... Anyone who does not see him in this light will never quite understand him. —HEINRICH SCHOLZ

> The problem is the lack of any unity of the sciences and the loss of the will or the means even to discuss the issue. —ALLAN BLOOM

The term "academic theology" is often used scornfully, to mean a theology that has lost touch with the life of the church and the duties of working ministers and is therefore good for nothing, like salt that has lost its savor. But I use it here, without prejudice, simply to mean theology done in a university, not in a seminary or theological college. The university, no less than the church, is an institution with its own set of aims and values; an "academic theology" considers itself answerable to these aims and values, whether or not the results are useful to the churches or help to make good clergy.[1] Perhaps the German term

---

[1] In one educator's words, the university's only excuse for existence is "to provide a haven where the search for truth may go on unhampered by utility or pressure for 'results.'" Robert Maynard Hutchins, *The Higher Learning in America*, Storr Lectures (New Haven: Yale

wissenschaftliche Theologie ("scientific theology") would do as well. For whether theology has a legitimate place in the universities depends, in large part, on the scientific respectability of its method: that is, on how well theologians can state and justify the rules by which they profess to attain knowledge. But in view of the general problem to which this volume is addressed, the nature of the university-based divinity schools, I have preferred the institutional to the methodological term, and I want to avoid any odious suggestion that a scientific theology (in the sense given) could be pursued only in a university, not in a seminary or a monastery. It is arguable in any case that in English the word "scientific" has been preempted by the *natural* sciences, and that even the *social* sciences employ it only by license. For this reason, too, "academic theology" is usually my preferred term.

How one thinks of the university-based divinity school is bound to reflect one's estimate of the distinctively theological task. The linguistic, literary, and historical activities of the theologian's immediate neighbors in the divinity school are not usually felt to be problematic in themselves, although their location in the divinity school, rather than in the humanities, may be judged compromising precisely because of the theological company they keep. Colleagues outside the divinity school, and sometimes even colleagues inside, are inclined to view the theologian as like some agent of a foreign power: because the theologian's ultimate loyalty lies elsewhere, she or he cannot be trusted to keep the law of the land or to contribute to the common good.[2] Whether what is done under the rubric of "academic theology" is salutary to the churches, then, is not here the issue. Is it salutary to the universities?

An enormous literature in several languages has addressed the question in the last two hundred years; if we posed it in terms of the scientific status of theology, we would have to add that it already engaged some acute minds in the Middle Ages. Unfortunately, however, the discussion these days is often queered by ambiguity, so that instead of answering it one may end in confusion over what the question really is. In particular, the word "theology" is commonly used as though everyone knew what it meant, whereas in fact theologies come in several varieties, and the

---

University Press, 1936), p. 43. On the two hindrances, "vocationalism" and "empiricism" (the mere piling up of information), see further ibid., pp. 111, 117-18.

[2] The image is suggested by Sir Walter Moberly on behalf of the critics of designing Christians: "However high-minded your intentions, you are like government servants who use their position to further the interests of a foreign power .... [Y]ou are not serving the university but are seeking to use it as an instrument for purposes which are not its own" (*The Crisis in the University* [London: SCM Press, 1949], p. 28).

question might better be phrased: *What* theology, if any, has a legitimate place in the academy?

My purpose in this essay is accordingly to check the academic credentials of just one way of doing theology: Friedrich Schleiermacher's (1768-1834). Naturally, I choose the model that, in my opinion, still has the strongest claims to potential fruitfulness in the American universities, although it was developed not in America but in Germany. My own theological interest at present is, in fact, in the historical development and continued viability of this mode of theologizing. Here I simply ask about its institutional home, and I am convinced that Schleiermacher's thoughts on this question have been widely misrepresented, not least by Ernst Troeltsch (1865-1923). I recognize, of course, that there are varieties of university, too, as well as varieties of theology. But, for now, I intend to approach the problem of theology and the university from the standpoint of one concept of theology. To begin with, I want to explore the reasons why there is a problem at all.

I.

It goes without saying, I assume, that the place of theology in the modern university can be defended only where its abdication as queen of the sciences is presupposed. Granted that Christian theology can no longer provide, as it did in the Middle Ages, the unifying principles of the entire system of human knowledge, can it nonetheless claim a legitimate, if humbler place in the university? It may be that theology has its own small niche, along with other arts and sciences, in an academy that has become in principle more egalitarian. But it may also be that the academy should remain vigilant even after the ancient crown of theology has been quietly encased in the museum of history.

Take, for instance, John Henry Newman's (1801-1890) plea for theology in his classic study *The Idea of a University* (1852), the literary product of his association with the new Catholic University of Ireland.[3] The uni-

---

[3] The book has been through several editions. My page references are to John Henry Cardinal Newman, *The Idea of a University Defined and Illustrated, I: In Nine Discourses Delivered to the Catholics of Dublin, II: In Occasional Lectures and Essays Addressed to the Members of the Catholic University*, new impression (Westminster, Md.: Christian Classics Inc., 1973), which follows Newman's second revision, published in 1873, and accordingly includes the lectures and essays he added at that time to the 1852 discourses. I shall also refer to the important original fifth discourse, "General Knowledge Viewed as One Philosophy," which Newman excised when he made the first main revision in 1859. My page references for the fifth discourse (1852) are to Newman, *The Idea of a University*, etc., new ed., ed. Charles Frederick Harrold (New York: Longmans, Green, 1947), appendix, pp. 389-406.

versity, he says, is "a place of *teaching* universal *knowledge*."[4] It is not a place where truth is simply discovered, which would not require students. Nor is it a place where an assortment of truths are mechanically acquired. The requisite knowledge is philosophical: not a mere pile of information, it calls for actively organizing what is learned, a systematizing of it to assign things their value in relation to one another.[5] Hence, the communication of knowledge belongs to the formation of the *person*: it imparts a virtue, a habit of mind, to be esteemed for its own sake and not as an instrument for acquiring or doing anything else, although the cultivated intellect does, as a matter of fact, help equip us for many kinds of activity.[6]

Now the system of universal or organized knowledge would of course be broken if any domain of inquiry were omitted. The circle, Newman insists, is an undivided whole from which each science is only an abstraction, a portion of truth.[7] And that is why there must be theology in the university. Theology is a branch of knowledge with as much right as astronomy to have a place in the university; it is the science of God, the truths we know about God put into system.[8] University teaching without theology would accordingly be unphilosophical, lacking in wholeness. This could indeed be said of the absence of any portion of knowledge. But Newman cannot resist claiming a little more for theology. Its exclusion would not only break the circle in the sense of leaving it incomplete; it would disrupt the unity of learning for the further reason that the science of God touches on so many other sciences. He concludes that religious truth is not only a portion, but a condition, of general knowledge, and that theology is therefore the highest and widest branch of knowledge—though it does not interfere with the freedom of any secular science in its own department.[9] And the special need for theology suggests to him the need for the beneficent presence of the church.

---

[4] *Idea*, p. ix. In his essay "What is a University?" (first published in 1854) Newman defines the university as "a place for the communication and circulation *of thought* [my emphasis], by means of personal intercourse." See "Rise and Progress of Universities," chap. 2, in Newman, *Historical Sketches*, vol. 3, new ed. (London: Longmans, Green, 1889), p. 6.

[5] *Idea*, pp. 111, 125, 130, 134, 137. In the original fifth discourse Newman said: "The assemblage of Sciences, which together make up Universal Knowledge, is not an accidental or a varying heap of acquisitions, but a system, and may be said to be *in equilibrio*, as long as all its portions are secured to it" ("General Knowledge," p. 389). This conveys as well as any of his utterances what Newman meant by the idea or form that gives the university unity (cf. ibid., pp. 394, 396).

[6] *Idea*, pp. ix, 101, 114, 121, 125-26, 165-67, 177-78.

[7] Ibid., pp. 50, 60, 72.

[8] Ibid., pp. 19-20, 42, 61.

[9] Ibid., pp. 66-67, 70; "General Knowledge," p. 399.

Newman's theme, to be sure, at any rate in the first eight discourses, is not the Catholic university but simply the university. In this sense, his discourses are only, as he says, preliminary.[10] But the ultimate goal—a truly Catholic university—is already reflected proleptically in his idea of a university in general, and the argument threatens to fall apart. For, on the one hand, the university is certainly not a convent or a seminary: its purpose is to fit persons for *this* world, not for the next. And what goes with this purpose is not so much the Catholic faith as a religion or philosophy of reason, or of civilization, which is ambivalent from the Catholic point of view. Partly present alongside the Catholic faith, partly in conflict with it, the religion of reason contains elements of truth, which are nonetheless false because they are not the whole truth.[11] On the other hand, however, the university *as such* ought to teach revealed or Catholic theology since it is, after all, truth.[12] And it would be absurd not to recognize that the church has an interest in such an activity. "The Church has no call to watch over and protect Science: but towards Theology she has a distinct duty.... Where Theology is, there she must be...."[13]

Ubi theologia, ibi ecclesia! That is the problem in a nutshell, though Newman hardly recognized it as such. The surrender of her crown has not quite left theology to struggle alone in a competitive, democratic environment. The church is still there to assist from above, and the idea of a university passes over gently into the idea of a Catholic university.[14] It is easy to see why the citizens of a secular and pluralistic university would still be anxious about the possibility of a divided loyalty. History has taught them that the church, when weary of argument, will reach for a stick. And they may begin to suspect that from a common or garden university, as distinct from a Catholic or other sectarian one, theology had best be excluded; at most they could make room for an objective description of theology, not for doing it, and there seems to be no reason why such description would require a theological faculty. Besides, can it seriously be maintained that theology is a science? How can it be if it is

---

[10] *Idea*, p. 214.
[11] Ibid., p. 232; pp. 182, 200, 214.
[12] The conclusion to the original fifth discourse states bluntly: "A University, so called, which refuses to profess the Catholic Creed, is, from the nature of the case, hostile both to the Church and to Philosophy" ("General Knowledge," p. 406). For this reason, Newman opposed not only the absence of religion in education but also the introduction of a "general religion": that is, a deliberately non-sectarian Christianity or a natural religion that would embrace Judaism and Islam as well (ibid., pp. 400-1).
[13] *Idea*, pp. 214, 215, 227.
[14] Ibid., p. ix.

subject to the church's well-meant, but wholly inappropriate supervision?[15]

Not every champion of theology sees the church in Newman's authoritarian terms. But their dilemma, I suspect, *mutatis mutandis*, remains essentially the same: either a bloodless religion of reason that fits comfortably into the academy, or else a frankly Christian theology that awakens the suspicion of a divided loyalty. Newman grasped the second horn of the dilemma; others have found themselves impaled on the first. An instructive example can be found in the exchange between Robert Maynard Hutchins (1899-1977) and William Adams Brown (1865-1943). In reply to the thesis put forward by Hutchins, that the ordering of knowledge in the university calls not for Christian theology but for Greek metaphysics,[16] Brown took up the cause of theology. He meant a theology that uses Christian faith as at once a clue to understanding the universe and a religious basis for the democratic tradition.[17] But his argument carried him so far away from everything distinctively Christian that Hutchins could retort, in effect: *Your* theology is *my* metaphysics. "Everything that Mr. Brown puts in the category of theology," he said, "I should call natural theology."[18]

Similar, it seems to me, was the dilemma Sir Walter Moberly (1881-1974) fell into in his winsome book *The Crisis of the University* (1949). He started from a muscular Christian viewpoint, expressed in bold talk of "Christianization," but was driven to the lame conclusion that Christians will have to settle for the principle of the half-loaf. Half a loaf is better than none: the Christian can at least work for rational reforms in the university that are not incompatible with Christianity.[19] But this implies, surely, that they are at home in the university just insofar as they set aside their ecclesiastical commitments and work with the same rational and humanistic assumptions as the non-Christians—even, indeed, the non-theists. Moberly did believe that the theological faculty, as the custodian of Revelation (with a capital R), still had its special mission: not only to educate clergy but to confront the entire student body with the Christian challenge. But theology, so conceived, is inevitably isolated and embattled, and Moberly expressly rejected any attempt to assimilate it to

---

[15] In *The Idea of a University*, at least, Newman does not seriously entertain the possibility that the minor premiss of his argument—that theology is a science—could be questioned. See pp. 19-20, 67.

[16] Hutchins, *Higher Learning*, chap. 4.

[17] Brown, *The Case for Theology in the University* (Chicago: University of Chicago Press, 1938), pp. 13, 112.

[18] Preface to Brown, *Case for Theology*, p. vii.

[19] *Crisis*, p. 310.

other academic studies.[20] His image of the Christians in the university as "government servants who use their position to further the interests of a foreign power" seems only too apt.

The question, then, has now become this: Is the connection of an explicitly Christian theology with the claims of the church such that it must necessarily march out of step with everyone else in the academy, or else be honorably retired? Hutchins, for one, gave an unfavorable verdict with all his usual forthrightness: "Theology is banned by law from some universities. It might as well be from the rest. Theology is based on revealed truth and on articles of faith. We are a faithless generation and take no stock in revelation. Theology implies orthodoxy and an orthodox church. We have neither."[21] And we are back with the rule (or the warning): *Ubi theologia, ibi ecclesia.*[22] Whether or not we agree with Hutchins will depend, or should depend, on what theology we have in mind.

II.

At first glance, Schleiermacher appears to afford very little help. Though not quite in Newman's manner, he too subordinates theology to the church, and, quite *unlike* Newman, he seems uncertain of theology's right to a place among the sciences. While plans were being drawn up for the new University of Berlin, he put together his *Occasional Thoughts on Universities in the German Sense* (1808), in which he directly addressed the question of the theological faculty and its place in the academic community. Taken together with his sketch of the theological curriculum in his *Brief Outline of the Study of Theology* (1811, 1830²), his remarks seem to permit theology at best a lower rank among the university disciplines and to justify its existence purely on the grounds of its service to the church. It is easy to see why later German theologians found his position to be objectionable in itself and an open door to still more objectionable theologies that came after him—without sufficient reason, as I shall try to show.

---

[20] Ibid., pp. 278-92, 306-8.
[21] *Higher Learning*, p. 97. Note that it is specifically a dogmatic theology that Hutchins disapproves of: "When . . . I said that theology could not assist us, I was thinking only of dogmatic theology, which rests upon faith, or supernatural knowledge" (preface to Brown, *Case for Theology*, p. vi).
[22] I do not mean to imply that this formula conveys the *only* problem with theology; it is a *root* problem in the sense that others grow out of it. Two additional objections, that theology talks about non-empirical objects and that it isolates Christianity from other religions, will be touched on along the way. Still others (theology rationalizes religion, privatizes religion, and so on) are ignored here but would call for the same approach, which asks: *What theology?*

For Schleiermacher, "science" (*Wissenschaft*) was not, as it has become for us, one of several divisions of human knowledge. As he explained it in his thoughts on universities, science is the collective enterprise in which every researcher, in every field of inquiry, is engaged, and the fragments of knowledge that each contributes can be fully appreciated only in their relation to the whole.[23] External pressures, such as the immediate needs of the state, or competition between one state and another, may impose limits on the ideal of a single community of learning. But true scholars and scientists everywhere, whatever the demands of specialization, understand themselves to be mutually dependent in one inclusive enterprise, and they are bound to concern themselves intensely with the general principles that define knowledge in every department of inquiry. The state, no doubt, is inclined to dismiss such a concern as fruitless speculation and to demand instead new discoveries and the spread of factual information in fields presumed to be useful. The scientific spirit, however, is by its very nature systematic: it cannot grow to full consciousness where there is no conception of one whole domain of knowledge, at least in outline.[24]

By a *university* Schleiermacher understood precisely the institutional home for the awareness of science as a single activity powered by a common interest in the unity and form of knowledge. A *school*, by contrast, exists for education—to impart the elements of knowledge in certain basic fields—and can only strike the initial spark of the scientific spirit in a few, naturally gifted youths. And the *academy*, or learned society, the third main type of institution for the pursuit of learning, exists for the advancement of knowledge in a particular discipline by masters, who already have the scientific spirit. The burden of maintaining the idea of a common scientific enterprise therefore falls squarely on the university, which stands between the school and the academy; and it would be disastrous, Schleiermacher thought, if the university became either an advanced school or a cluster of academies and specialized institutes. The true scientific spirit requires that every field of knowledge must be cultivated, and each only as a part of the whole.[25] It was this recognition, he believed, that had given birth to the distinctively German university, and

---

[23] Schleiermacher, *Gelegentliche Gedanken über Universitäten in deutschem Sinn, nebst einem Anhang über eine neu zu errichtende* (1808), in Ernst Anrich, ed., *Die Idee der deutschen Universität: Die fünf Grundschriften aus der Zeit ihrer Neubegründung durch klassischen Idealismus und romantischen Realismus* (Darmstadt: Hermann Gentner, 1956), pp. 223-24. This is the passage from which my first epigraph is taken at the beginning of this essay.

[24] Ibid., pp. 226-32, 238, 246.

[25] Ibid., pp. 233-45. It is interesting to note how closely agreed Schleiermacher and Newman were at this point—for all their obvious differences in other respects.

in effect it made the faculty of philosophy ("arts and sciences," as we would say) the new queen of the sciences (*in der Tat Herrin*). For in the faculty of philosophy the sciences are bound together as one and made the object of an all-inclusive critical scrutiny.[26] Philosophical instruction is the basis for all other pursuits in the university; indeed, the actual university is contained in the faculty of philosophy alone—or would be if the university were purely the creation of the scientific community.[27]

Where, then, does theology fit in? The problem is that it finds its home *outside* the faculty of philosophy, in one of three "special schools" (*Spezialschulen*), or "positive faculties," that owe their existence to certain social needs sponsored by the state. The faculties of law, medicine, and theology—"professional schools," as we now call them—do not spring naturally out of the scientific impulse; each arises from the necessity to ground an indispensable practice or profession securely in an explicit theory and in the transmission of accumulated knowledge (*Tradition von Kenntnissen*). Thus the theological faculty

> took shape in the church to preserve the wisdom of the fathers; to prevent the future loss of what was already done in former times to separate truth from error; to give a historical basis, a secure and definite direction, and a common spirit to the further development of doctrine (*der weiteren Fortbildung der Lehre*) and of the church. And as the state became more closely tied to the church, it had to sanction these provisions too and take them under its care.[28]

Now what professional education in theology, law, or medicine requires, according to Schleiermacher, is not so much a single academic discipline as a mixture of several disciplines that have their natural home in the faculty of philosophy. This is what he means by a "positive science": an assemblage of sciences, or fragments of sciences, brought together to equip practitioners in one of the professions. "Theology," as he uses the word, is just such a positive science, so that the theological faculty does not find its unity directly in the nature of knowledge but brings it in from the outside, so to say, to meet the complex needs of church leadership. Theology as a whole, then, manifests the scientific spirit imperfectly because its parts are put together accidentally—for a strictly practical end. Take away the practical end, and the parts will naturally revert to whatever departments of the philosophical faculty they were taken from; there alone, in the faculty of philosophy, is the sense for

---

[26] Ibid., pp. 258, 260.
[27] Ibid., pp. 240, 250, 257. Clearly, Schleiermacher uses the adjective "philosophical" sometimes to refer to a faculty, sometimes to a department within the faculty.
[28] Ibid., p. 258. Translations from the German in this essay are mine.

the inner connection of all knowledge maintained and the natural drive and organization of the scientific enterprise fully expressed.[29] In this sense, the discipline of theology and so the theological faculty itself lead a kind of parasitical existence in the academic community.

It is undeniable that this line of argument implies a marginalization not only of the theological faculty but of the schools of law and medicine as well; the center of the university lies elsewhere. Schleiermacher even admits the risk that the "professional schools" (to use our term) may come to resemble mere trade schools and fall into unscientific superficiality. But if the creative advancement of science finds its proper home in the faculty of philosophy, the remedy, he thinks, is for those who teach in the professional schools to establish their credentials in the field of pure science: unless they hold simultaneous appointments in the faculty of philosophy, they should be required at least to give occasional lectures in one of the disciplines the faculty of philosophy embraces, without worrying about the relevance of the lectures to the work of their own school. Only in this way can the vital connection of law, medicine, and theology with pure science, and so the place of professional education in the university, be made secure. In short, the scientific standing of a professional school and its teaching staff is externally accredited, and any teacher of law or theology who lacks the inner drive to achieve success in some department of pure science deserves to be laughed out of the university.[30] The vocation of the theologian certainly appears to bear the burden of a divided loyalty. In the eyes of some interpreters, notably Troeltsch, Schleiermacher must be held responsible for the fact that after him an actual antagonism between ecclesiastical and scientific interests threatened to split the theological faculty itself.

III.

It is often said that in nineteenth-century Germany the Protestant theological faculties became polarized into two factions; sometimes the explanation is added that it was Schleiermacher who at least opened the door to the conflict between them. Repeated efforts to establish a strictly scientific theology had to distance themselves from his view of theology as a practical and churchly discipline. Even so sympathetic an interpreter as Heinrich Scholz (1884-1956), who hailed the return to Schleiermacher

---

[29] Ibid., p. 259; *Kurze Darstellung des theologischen Studiums zum Behuf einleitender Vorlesungen* (hereafter *KD*), 3d, critical ed., ed. Heinrich Scholz (1910; reprint ed., Darmstadt: Wissenschaftliche Buchgesellschaft, 1961), §§ 1, 5, 6.

[30] *Gelegentliche Gedanken*, pp. 261-62.

after the passing of Albrecht Ritschl (1822-1889) and reissued the *Brief Outline* in 1910, looked back to what he admitted to be at least an apparent flaw in the book's theological program. By deriving theology from church leadership, Schleiermacher seemed to have moved into the center a merely external, practical motif: alien to science and a danger to pure inquiry, it threatened to ruin theology by reducing it to a higher technology.[31] Scholz exonerated Schleiermacher by arguing that another strand in the *Brief Outline* makes the understanding of Christianity, rather than the need for church leadership, the actual goal and organizing principle of theological studies.[32] But it is unquestionably the practical, churchly strand that has dominated the secondary literature. Troeltsch's opinion is particularly interesting because he professed himself to be Schleiermacher's disciple.[33]

Writing at about the same time as Scholz, in the *Journal for Scientific Theology* (1908), Troeltsch noted that much Protestant theology in the second half of the nineteenth century had become largely indifferent to the problems of the church. Since the theological faculties were state institutions, they were relatively independent of the churches. There was no necessity for the biblical scholars or the church historians, at least, to relate their work to the needs of the church; they shared the presuppositions and methods of cognate disciplines located elsewhere in the university and remained unconcerned with the latest ecclesiastical causes. This, of course, Troeltsch points out, placed the burden of churchly concerns all the more heavily on the systematic and practical theologians, and dogmatics came to be perceived as merely a matter of personal conviction. A frightful gap had opened up between dogmatic theology and scientific, historical theology.[34]

The theoretical basis for this frightful gap, Troeltsch believed, could be traced back to none other than Schleiermacher, who conceded the

---

[31] *KD*, pp. ix, xxviii.

[32] Ibid., pp. xxx-xxxi. I think myself that an even more important point is the one Scholz makes in the passage from which I have taken my second epigraph (pp. xxxvi-xxxvii). Cf. Newman's remark that "a truly great intellect . . . is one which takes a connected view of old and new, past and present, far and near, and which has an insight into the influence of all these one on another . . ." (*Idea*, p. 134).

[33] See my essay "The Possibility of a Historical Theology: An Appraisal of Troeltsch's Dogmatics" (1976), in Gerrish, *The Old Protestantism and the New: Essays on the Reformation Heritage* (Chicago: University of Chicago Press, 1982), pp. 208-229; further, Walter E. Wyman, Jr., *The Concept of Glaubenslehre: Ernst Troeltsch and the Theological Heritage of Schleiermacher*, American Academy of Religion Series, vol. 44 (Chico, California: Scholars Press, 1983).

[34] "Rückblick auf ein halbes Jahrhundert der theologischen Wissenschaft" (1908), in Troeltsch, *Gesammelte Schriften* (hereafter *GS*), 4 vols. (1912-25; reprint ed., Aalen: Scientia Verlag, 1961-66), 2:194-99; cf. p. 221.

impossibility of strict, scientific knowledge of the transcendent and assigned dogmatics to practical theology.[35] Dogmatics is then a discipline that makes use of the methods and findings of science but is not itself a science.[36] And if theology exists simply to influence practical life, the way is cleared for theologians who take science much less seriously than Schleiermacher did. Troeltsch's favorite example was Ritschl, who lifted out of the normal, profane course of history just as much as his Lutheranism required—notably, the personality of Jesus, which he proclaimed a miracle of revelation—and calmly continued to affirm the anthropocentric view of the world as made for humanity, not troubling himself one bit about the theory of evolution.[37]

Like Scholz, Troeltsch was willing to absolve Schleiermacher from some of the blame for this unhappy turn, though he did not doubt that it was the *Brief Outline* that prepared the way with its basic theological type.[38] For Schleiermacher did at least see the necessity to link dogmatics with *philosophical* theology. In Troeltsch's mind, that set the agenda for the present: what we need is a philosophy of religion, or *Religionswissenschaft*, that will justify religious symbols as a genuine, if inadequate form of knowledge and will demonstrate the supreme validity (*Höchstgeltung*) of Christianity among the religions of the world. Apart from such philosophical support, the very existence of our Christian theological faculties cannot be defended, unless we are prepared to say that we have them for purely accidental and cultural reasons—because we happen to be Christians. A philosophy of religion is the common presupposition for the work of both the historical and the dogmatic theologians, and Schleiermacher's program remains the unfinished program of all scientific theology.[39]

In his later years, as is well known, Troeltsch himself undermined his own grand design for Christian theology as his confidence in the

---

[35] "Die Dogmatik wurde . . . von Schleiermacher geradezu der praktischen (er selbst sagt freilich 'historischen') Theologie zugewiesen . . ." (ibid., p. 201). The significance of Troeltsch's departure from Schleiermacher's actual language will become apparent below (sec. 4). It is in fact the character of dogmatics as *historical* theology that, in Schleiermacher's view, makes it the science it is: what it knows is the Christian way of believing as a historical phenomenon. Troeltsch's terminological shift, innocent though he makes it sound, conceals a confusion between piety, which is *not* knowledge (i.e., of God), and dogmatic science, which *is* knowledge (i.e., of piety). See the references given in n. 71 below.

[36] Ibid., p. 207.

[37] Ibid., pp. 204-5, 211, 218. On *theologische Scheinhistorie*, see also pp. 221-22.

[38] Schleiermacher was the man "der mit der Trennung der wissenschaftlich-historischen und der praktisch-vermittelnden Disziplinen die ganze Situation geschaffen und erkannt hat" (ibid., p. 225; cf. pp. 205-6, 208, 210).

[39] Ibid., pp. 219, 223-26.

supreme validity of Christianity faded.⁴⁰ But I do not believe it follows that Schleiermacher's concept of theology has no future. It is hard, perhaps impossible, to claim that Troeltsch's program ever was, in the respect indicated, an authentic development of Schleiermacher's.⁴¹ Despite a few puzzling ambiguities, it seems clear to me that in the end Schleiermacher thought a proof of the superiority of Christianity to be as impossible for the philosophy of religion as it is unnecessary for dogmatics.⁴² But be that as it may, what, we must ask, was the consequence of Troeltsch's program for dogmatics itself? The answer is that dogmatics remained in his eyes—though without disapprobation—purely an expression of personal conviction, undertaken for the ends of preaching and teaching in a church; it was not a science in the true sense but a part of practical theology.⁴³ If, then, Schleiermacher's conception of the practical goal of theology was a problem, Troeltsch hardly solved it. He made it worse.

Perhaps one moral to be gleaned from the story of German theology from Schleiermacher to Troeltsch is that dutiful professions of allegiance to scientific theology or the science of religion (*Religionswissenschaft*) have not automatically proved to be a safe prophylactic against personal religious commitments. The same moral could be drawn from Adolf von Harnack's (1851-1930) famous resistance to the introduction of chairs for the "general history of religion" into the German theological faculties. He marshalled several arguments for his position, but the decisive one was that Christianity is not one religion, Jesus Christ not one master, among others.⁴⁴ A lingering Christian absolutism, it seems, may cling to the thought even of a historical scholar who can virtuously assert that "in our historical work we cannot and must not consider the doctrines of the

---

⁴⁰ See, in particular, "The Place of Christianity among the World Religions," one of the lectures he was to have delivered in England in 1923: Troeltsch, *Christian Thought: Its History and Application*, ed. F[riedrich] von Hügel (1923; reprint ed., New York: Meridian Books, 1957), pp. 33-63, esp. pp. 51-57. The lectures appeared in German the following year with the title *Der Historismus und seine Überwindung: Fünf Vorträge*, ed. Friedrich von Hügel (1924; reprint ed., Aalen: Scientia Verlag, 1966); see pp. 74-79.

⁴¹ In *other* respects, it certainly *was*. See the literature cited in n. 33 above.

⁴² The point is a controversial one, but see, in particular, Schleiermacher, *Der christliche Glaube nach den Grundsätzen der evangelischen Kirche im Zusammenhange dargestellt* (hereafter Gl.), 7th ed., based on the 2d ed. of 1830-31, ed. Martin Redeker, 2 vols. (Berlin: Walter de Gruyter, 1960), § 11.5; cf. § 7.3, § 33.3.

⁴³ Troeltsch, "Die Dogmatik der 'religionsgeschichtlichen Schule'" (1913), GS, 2:500-24, esp. pp. 514-15. The article first appeared in English in the *American Journal of Theology* 17 (1913): 1-21.

⁴⁴ Harnack, "Die Aufgabe der theologischen Fakultäten und die allgemeine Religionsgeschichte, nebst einem Nachwort" (1901), *Reden und Aufsätze*, 2d ed., 2 vols. (Giessen: Alfred Töpelmann [J. Ricker], 1906), 2:159-87. esp. pp. 172-73.

churches."⁴⁵ For the present, however, I wish to keep the focus on Schleiermacher, who held unequivocally that not only the systematic theologian but the church historian, too, *should* think about the needs of the church.

One final testimony, closer to our own day, may be cited concerning the alleged problematic consequences of his stand; it demonstrates that Troeltsch's line of interpretation is still very much alive. In his informative study *Theology and the Theory of Science* (1973), Wolfhart Pannenberg writes:

> The result of Schleiermacher's attempt to base theology on the requirements of church leadership was that a confessional and ecclesiastical standpoint (*eine konfessionelle Kirchlichkeit*) functioned as unquestioned foundation of theology and could therefore be immunized against criticism. That, of course, was not Schleiermacher's intention, but it clearly shows up a limitation in the way he defined theology.⁴⁶

It is difficult to see how such an ecclesiastical complacency could ever appeal to any pertinent "limitation" in Schleiermacher's definition of theology. His understanding of the ecclesiastical *goal* of theological studies never implied that the interests of the church might control the actual *content* of the theologian's work. On the contrary, he took care to prevent any such implication. What he said of the study of church history can surely be generalized to every branch of theological study, as he understood it: the interests of the church and the interests of scholarship (*das wissenschaftliche Interesse*) cannot contradict each other for the very good reason that absolute impartiality is in the church's best interests.

> Hence even the liveliest interest of the evangelical theologian in his church must not prejudice either his research or his presentation of it. And it is just as little to be feared that the results of this research will weaken his interest in the church; at worst, they can only give him the impulse to work with others for the removal of recognized defects.⁴⁷

No one can seriously doubt that this was Schleiermacher's procedure in his own labors. It is not the theologian's task merely to preserve, or to produce on demand, whatever the church currently thinks it needs, but to help bring the language of the church into closer conformity with the

---

⁴⁵ Ibid., p. 176.
⁴⁶ Pannenberg, *Wissenschaftstheorie und Theologie* (Frankfurt am Main: Suhrkamp Verlag, 1973), p. 255. Like Heinrich Scholz, Pannenberg recognizes (a little grudgingly) the other strand in the *Brief Outline*, according to which the *material* unity of theology is derived from its overall concern with the nature or essence of Christianity; it is the science of Christianity or of the Christian religion (pp. 253-54, 430).
⁴⁷ *KD*, § 193.

authentic essence of Christian faith.⁴⁸ Such a conception of the task was possible for him only because he derived the scientific character of the several parts of theology not from their practical end, but from their place in a carefully articulated theory of science.⁴⁹ He would not in fact disagree when Pannenberg says that "the science of Christianity is surely not *constituted* by the church's and society's interest in it."⁵⁰

IV.

The practical, professional, and ecclesiastical organization of theology, so much in evidence in the *Thoughts on Universities* and the *Brief Outline*, gives us one side of Schleiermacher's thinking on the nature of the discipline, not the whole. It by no means tells us all he has to say about an "academic theology" in the sense in which I am using the term: roughly, for what he himself calls "dogmatic theology" or *Glaubenslehre* (literally: "doctrine of faith").⁵¹ "Theology" (without further qualification) is his word for the entire theological curriculum. Dogmatics is one of the pieces that make up the whole.⁵² The pieces are put together from sciences that have their natural home in the faculty of philosophy. It follows that the scientific status of dogmatics cannot be settled simply from its place in the theological curriculum, or its institutional location in the theological faculty; it depends more properly on its *theoretical* location in the system of sciences.⁵³

There are admittedly some tensions in Schleiermacher's pertinent utterances on dogmatics. In one place, for instance, he asserts that dog-

---

⁴⁸ *Gl.*, §§ 21-22; *KD*, §§ 60, 84.

⁴⁹ Schleiermacher's *Wissenschaftslehre* is less readily accessible than the thoughts on universities and brief outline; it has to be put together chiefly from lectures that he himself never published. An admirable sketch, particularly helpful in showing the location of theology in Schleiermacher's organization of the sciences, is given by Hans-Joachim Birkner, *Schleiermachers Christliche Sittenlehre im Zusammenhang seines philosophisch-theologischen Systems*, Theologische Bibliothek Töpelmann, vol. 8 (Berlin: Alfred Töpelmann, 1964), esp. pp. 30-87. For further discussion, with a wealth of references to the secondary literature, see Gunter Scholtz, *Die Philosophie Schleiermachers*, Erträge der Forschung, vol. 217 (Darmstadt: Wissenschaftliche Buchgesellschaft, 1984), esp. pp. 64-78, 127-40.

⁵⁰ *Wissenschaftstheorie*, p. 254.

⁵¹ "Darstellung des Glaubens ist Glaubenslehre" (*Gl.*, § 1.1, handwritten note).

⁵² *KD*, §§ 97, 195-231.

⁵³ This is not the place to present Schleiermacher's theory of science in general. It is intricate not only because of its ambitious scope but also because of what must seem to us to be an eccentric terminology. I have tried to state the main points very briefly in "Friedrich Schleiermacher," in Ninian Smart et al., eds., *Nineteenth-Century Religious Thought in the West*, 3 vols. (Cambridge: Cambridge University Press, 1985), 1:123-56, esp. pp. 127-30. In the present essay, I must be content simply to document Schleiermacher's classification of dogmatics as an empirical-historical science, although it is neither a *mindless* empiricism nor a mere historical *report* (see notes 58 and 80 below.)

matics (*das dogmatische Verfahren*) only exists for the sake of the Christian proclamation.[54] But I see no reason to doubt that if there were no practical need for ministers to proclaim the Christian message, dogmatics must be one of the fragments of theological study that could in principle, with whatever modifications, revert to the philosophical faculty—that is, to what we would call "the humanities." In Schleiermacher's theory of the sciences dogmatics is an *empirical* science: its data are facts of human experience, since it attempts to give an account of a particular way of believing or being religious.[55] More exactly, dogmatics is classified as *historical* theology: it is a part of the scientific treatment of a historical phenomenon—the part, namely, that deals with the present state of the Christian community's beliefs. The past state of those beliefs is assigned to church history, which is also, in Schleiermacher's scheme, a part of historical theology.[56] Hence it would hardly have been possible for him to drive such a wedge between dogmatic theology and history of Christianity as Troeltsch imagined—as though one were and the other were not a science.[57] Both are parts of historical theology, and when Schleiermacher says that historical theology "coheres (*zusammenhängt*) with science proper through philosophical theology," he cannot mean that church history and dogmatics are *not* sciences; he means that this is how they *are* sciences. They would lack scientific status if they confronted the mass of data without the organizing concepts that philosoph-

---

[54] *Gl.*, § 19.1. See also n. 65 below.

[55] The entire positive science of theology is concerned with Christianity understood as a *Glaubensweise*, or a particular way of being conscious of God (*KD*, § 1). Accordingly, dogmatics has no other purpose than to give a description or elucidation of the Christian consciousness; its subject matter is actual facts of experience. See *Schleiermachers Sendschreiben über seine Glaubenslehre an Lücke* (1829), new ed., ed. Hermann Mulert, Studien zur Geschichte des neueren Protestantismus, 2. Quellenheft (Giessen: Alfred Töpelmann [J. Ricker], 1908), pp. 20-21 (where Schleiermacher expressly uses the word *empirisch*), 33-34. Cf. *Gl.*, §28.2.

[56] *KD*, §§ 81, 97, 195, 252. In *KD*, § 195, doctrine is expressly taken to be simply one part of the church's social condition. Schleiermacher's language is (to us) confusing because we normally contrast empirical and historical sciences and apply the word "historical" only to past events or the study of past events. For him, by contrast, historical facts are just as much empirical data as are the objects of immediate sense perception (*Gl.*, § 28.2), and a discipline is historical not because its data are past events but because it deals with the flux of human existence—including its present, which can be understood only as the product of the past and the germ of the future (*KD*, § 26). A complication in Schleiermacher's position surfaces clearly in *Gl.*, § 28.2, where he points to a double distinction: dogmatics differs not only from deductive-conceptual sciences (because it starts from a fact, not from an axiom), but also from those historical sciences that embrace a "definite field of *outward* perception" (because the fundamental fact of Christian piety, which dogmatics postulates, is an *"inner* fact").

[57] See, eg., Troeltsch, *GS*, 2:514-15.

ical theology supplies; for that would be *mindless* traditioning (*geistlose Überlieferung*).⁵⁸

Schleiermacher expressly states that by reason of its content historical theology, which includes dogmatics, is a part of the modern study of history (*neuere Geschichtskunde*).⁵⁹ Presumably, then, the dogmatic theologian would be required in Schleiermacher's order of things to give occasional lectures in the department of history; and if the theological faculty went out of business tomorrow, dogmaticians could seek employment in the faculty of philosophy, though it is not entirely clear how, or how far, they would have to adapt their discipline in making the move. Perhaps dogmatics in some form would become one of the special divisions of historical science that "are annexed to the philosophical faculty just so long as they are not dealt with pragmatically in the interests of some practical goal."⁶⁰

Now, of course, Schleiermacher's terms (*Geschichtskunde, empirisch*, and so on) seldom, if ever, coincide exactly with our English equivalents, and the proliferation of divisions, departments, and professional schools in our present-day American universities complicates the picture still further. But the cardinal point, even if it is little more than a bare hint, remains: he thought it possible so to conceive of theology (dogmatics) that it could in principle have a place in the humanities. It may be replied that what belongs in the humanities is history of religions or *Religionswissenschaft*, not theology, and that history of religions can establish its legitimacy only insofar as it remains untarnished by any taint of theology. But what Schleiermacher in fact did was exactly to move *theology* a good step closer to what came to be called "the scientific study of religion." It is his conception of the theological *faculty* that has obscured this fundamental move.

Schleiermacher did not represent dogmatics as the science of supernaturally revealed truths or the science of God, but held it to be a strictly human science that deals with one variety of one fundamental aspect of human experience. For precisely this reason, he could launch his dogmatic project only by placing the Christian way of believing in the context of other religious faiths and bringing religion in general into

---

⁵⁸ *KD*, §§ 28-29, 65. A *merely* empirical treatment, or *mindless* empiricism, is insufficient (§§ 21, 59, 256). History is not chronicle (§§ 153, 252).

⁵⁹ Ibid., § 69.

⁶⁰ *Gelegentliche Gedanken*, p. 259. The examples Schleiermacher gives of scientific areas in which professors of law and theology should want to distinguish themselves are *reine Philosophie, Sittenlehre, philosophische Geschichtsbetrachtung*, and *Philologie* (ibid., pp. 261-62).

relation with other types of human experience.⁶¹ And while he followed tradition in giving dogmatic propositions also in the form of statements about God's activities and attributes, as well as in the form of statements about human experience, he could envision a future theology that would confine itself wholly to the description of the religious affections, as befits a consistently empirical discipline.⁶²

Naturally, this vision of the theology of the future has been greeted with horror by many other theologians, and their objections need much more careful attention than I can possibly hope to give them here. Even so judicious a theologian as Pannenberg asserts that Schleiermacher contributed unintentionally to the discrediting of talk about God: he treated religion only as a form of subjective experience, not as the self-manifestation of divine reality.⁶³ I do not myself think the criticism is just: Schleiermacher held religion generally to be a revelation of the divine in the depths of every human consciousness, and the Christian religion to be the effect of the historical revelation in Jesus of Nazareth.⁶⁴ He thought that he had shown *how* to talk about God. But, for the moment, I am more interested in the fact that his anthropological dogmatics of the future does, in a sense, approach the methodological "bracketing" of reality claims that is recommended by historians of religions. The truth of dogmatic assertions is the correctness with which they describe the Christian way of believing; they do not strictly *assert* the Christian way of believing or claim that what Christians believe is true, even if the dogmatician, as a Christian, *thinks* it is true.⁶⁵

---

⁶¹ The twofold placement (*Ortsbestimmung*) of the Christian way of believing was the main purpose of the opening sections of the *Glaubenslehre* (*Gl.*, §§ 2-11; *KD*, §§ 21-22; *Sendschreiben*, pp. 54-55).

⁶² *Gl.*, § 30; *Sendschreiben*, pp. 47-48.

⁶³ *Wissenschaftstheorie*, pp. 266, 374.

⁶⁴ *Gl.*, § 4.4, § 10.

⁶⁵ On bracketing reality claims, see, e.g., Joachim Wach, *Introduction to the History of Religions*, ed. Joseph M. Kitagawa et al. (New York: Macmillan, 1988), pp. 22-27. Cf. Ninian Smart on methodological agnosticism or neutralism (*The Science of Religion and the Sociology of Knowledge: Some Methodological Questions* [Princeton, New Jersey: Princeton University Press, 1973], pp. 57, 66, 158-59) and Peter L. Berger on other worlds and human projections (*The Sacred Canopy: Elements of a Sociological Theory of Religion* [Garden City, New York: Doubleday, 1967], pp. 88-89, 179-88). The varieties of truth claim that one finds made, or reported, in a work of theology need to be disentangled more carefully than they can be here. But I think Wach is too hasty when he writes: "[T]he assertion that a particular religion is true...will always be the first and last assertion of every dogmatics" (*Introduction*, p. 46). Schleiermacher, at least, thought that adherents of another religion could assent to his definition of Christianity without adopting Christianity as true for them (*Gl.*, § 11.5); perhaps he could have hoped for similar understanding for the rest of the *Glaubenslehre*. Unfortunately, however, he immediately goes on to say that dogmatics is "only for Christians" (cf. also *Gl.*, § 2).

No doubt, what distinguishes Schleiermacher's dogmatics from *Religionswissenschaft*, as usually understood, is chiefly that he did not think a correct account of the Christian way of believing *could* be given by anyone who did *not* believe. He offered, not an outsider's reading of a historical tradition, but an insider's, and this entailed for him the attempt to put the best construction on it, to cast it in the most suitable form, and so to open up possibilities for its future. "Development of doctrine" is a key phrase in his understanding of theology. The dogmatic theologian does not reproduce a static system of beliefs, nor even chart the course of a living tradition, but is rather a conscious agent of a tradition's continuing vitality, adaptation, and change.[66] For while the essence of the dogmatic task is simply *describing* the religious affections correctly (which is what makes it an empirical task),[67] it can only be carried out by *developing* the inherited doctrinal forms—subjecting them to a critical appropriation that immerses itself as far as possible both in the particular tradition and in the current state of knowledge generally.[68]

Clearly, no such constructive task is normally undertaken by the practitioners of *Religionswissenschaft*. But the difference between *Religionswissenschaft* and *Glaubenslehre* is by no means that the latter has a less scientific, purely churchly and practical, intent. Even what Schleiermacher calls the "ecclesiastical value" of dogmatic propositions is strictly an empirical, and to this extent scientific, criterion: their fidelity to the Christian religious affections. The "scientific value" of the propositions only makes the reference to the religious affections more exact and systematic.[69] The necessity to do dogmatics from within the tradition—a necessity he expressly affirms[70] —did not require of him a surrender of his scientific principles (a point to which I shall return later). In his own intention at least, dogmatics was to be a science, part of the scientific treatment of the historical career of Christianity.[71] The prospect for

---

[66] *Gelegentliche Gedanken*, p. 258; *Gl.*, § 19.3-4, § 25.2, § 27.2. Cf. Schleiermacher's letter to F. H. Jacobi (30 March 1818): text in Martin Cordes, "Der Brief Schleiermachers an Jacobi: Ein Beitrag zu seiner Entstehung und Überlieferung," *Zeitschrift für Theologie und Kirche* 68 (1971):195-212; see p. 209.

[67] *Gl.*, § 15-16.

[68] *Gl.*, § 16 (Zusatz), § 19 (Zusatz); *KD*, §§ 177, 180-81; *Sendschreiben*, pp. 64-66. Philosophical language is borrowed only to aid in giving the form of dogmatic propositions; their content is given by the religious affections themselves (*Gl.*, § 16 [Zusatz], § 19 [Zusatz]; *Sendschreiben*, pp. 59-61, 66).

[69] *Gl.*, § 17; cf. *Gl.*, § 28.1.

[70] It is already affirmed in the Anselmian motto on the title page of the *Glaubenslehre*. See also *Gl.*, § 13 (Zusatz), § 19.1; *KD*, § 196. Philosophical theology, on the other hand, adopts a neutral standpoint "above" Christianity (*KD*, § 33).

[71] *Gl.*, § 19, § 31.1; *KD*, § 252.

an academic theology looks very different from Schleiermacher's perspective than it did later from Troeltsch's. If the theology of the future were reconceived as a humanistic discipline, the church's faith would be there not to control the inquiry but to provide the subject matter of a science that asks for no special favors.

V.

The picture of theology in Schleiermacher's *Thoughts on Universities* and *Brief Outline* inevitably strikes us as remote. It is not simply that theology, as he saw it, was in the service of the church (which, by and large, is how we still see it), but that in his world one church had a privileged social status; its clergy were in effect civil servants or, as Kant liked to say, tools and instruments of the government.[72] The theological faculty was there because the state had taken the education of the clergy under its wing. Pannenberg doubts if Schleiermacher ever realized just how dependent he left theology on the interests of the state as well as on the interests of the church.[73] In any case, whether or not he realized it, the theological faculty, as Schleiermacher conceived of it, was bound to be threatened if the social standing of the church took a turn for the worse. And that is clearly what has happened, at least in the eyes of our present-day intelligentsia.

Even though his actual *thoughts* on the subject are partly dated, it need not follow that Schleiermacher's *concern* for the relation of theology to church and society is of no interest any more. It can be translated, up to a point, into the language of our own discussions on religion and public life, or the university and the common good. Perhaps in our situation the mission of the university-based divinity school will be less exclusively oriented toward church and ministry, more directly toward the social order, than Schleiermacher could have thought. Within the university, the divinity school may help nurture candid, self-critical appraisals of the social role of the academy itself. For while the free quest for truth is a good in itself, it is still pertinent to ask how it is related to other goods, especially since "truth for truth's sake" tends to coincide with the self-interest of university professors. But that is not my theme here. I am more interested in seeing that the *other* side of

---

[72] Immanuel Kant (1724-1804), *Der Streit der Fakultäten/The Conflict of the Faculties* (1798), trans. and ed. Mary J. Gregor, Janus Library (New York: Abaris Books, 1979), p. 24. The clergy administer a "statutory religion": a religion contained in writings authorized by the government, which accordingly have the force of law (pp. 32-34).

[73] *Wissenschaftstheorie*, p. 250.

Schleiermacher's thoughts on theology as an academic discipline will not be overlooked.

My thesis has been that anyone who turns to him for possible insight on the place of theology in the university will very likely learn more from what he says about the theoretical unity of science than from what he says about the pragmatic unity of theological studies. I do not of course suppose that in our world his dogmatics could pass as unproblematic, or that it could be adopted without further ado once the terminological eccentricities are removed; only that its possibilities as an academic theology have still not been exhausted, but rather obscured. Most of the objections levelled against theology as a university discipline either miss him completely or at least need to be reconsidered, and we have hardly begun to explore the possibilities of theology ("dogmatics," in his parlance) as a humanistic rather than a professional discipline. Naturally, such a change, if ever made, would shape the discipline even while providing it with a home. An academic theology would be motivated by "the scientific spirit": it would have to show its place on the scientific map, to share its methodological principles with other disciplines, and to relate its own findings as far as possible with theirs.[74] It should even have something to contribute to the common enterprise besides its actual findings, because the fact is that in the historicizing of knowledge theology was a pioneering discipline; other disciplines, which mistook theological reform for a discrediting of theology, have had to catch up.[75]

I realize, of course, that in the university it is easier to make a case for philosophical, or natural, theology than for an explicitly Christian, constructive theology. I am certainly in favor of a philosophical theology, though I doubt if it could ever do all that Troeltsch once expected of it.[76] If, with David Tracy, we distinguish the three communities to which theology is addressed as the academy, the church, and society, then I agree with him that the kind of theology that is *primarily* related to the academy will be philosophical or fundamental. But my question here has

---

[74] See, in addition to the citations already given, the famous passage on the "eternal covenant" in *Sendschreiben*, p. 40.

[75] See the interesting reflections of Stephen Toulmin on "The Historicization of Natural Science: Its Implications for Theology," in Hans Küng and David Tracy, eds., *Paradigm Change in Theology: A Symposium for the Future*, trans. Margaret Kohl (New York: Crossroad, 1989), pp. 233-41.

[76] If the question of the truth or validity of religious claims is in effect bracketed in dogmatic theology, the need for a philosophical theology to take it up becomes all the more urgent. But Troeltsch himself finally abandoned the attempt to prove the *highest* validity of Christianity (see n. 40 above).

been whether there is *also* a place in the academy for what he calls a "systematic theology," the discipline to which he assigns the task Schleiermacher gave to *Glaubenslehre*—the task of reinterpreting the tradition for the present.[77] The old names for this discipline, "dogmatic theology" or simply "dogmatics"—names Schleiermacher himself never gave up—are no longer very helpful, because "dogmatic" has acquired the pejorative sense of obstinate and overbearing insistence on a dogma. The association may not be entirely accidental. Theodor Reik has argued that the formation of a dogma in the church, such as the dogma of the Trinity, resembles psychologically the emergence of an obsessional idea in neurotic patients. "To such people," he says, "the dogma appears eternal and released from all temporal limitations."[78] Be that as it may, the label "dogmatics" is probably irretrievable in the academy and perhaps should be abandoned even in the church. For, as Troeltsch put it, dogmatics is no longer dogmatics when it knows no dogmas any more.[79] What is left, however, according to Schleiermacher, is not a mere personal confession of faith for the inspiration of future clergy, as Troeltsch supposed, but a *scientific* description of a particular way of believing *as seen from the inside*. And there, perhaps, in the last phrase, are the grounds for a lingering suspicion on the part of the academy. Is the church—mediately, at least, in the form of an ecclesiastical commitment—still present, only better hidden?

Well, Schleiermacher was probably right in holding that dogmatics, in his sense, could be done only from the inside—by someone who shared the faith to be scrutinized. That followed from his definition of the dogmatic task. A *report* on what Christians say they believe could be undertaken by any outsider with sufficient information. But it is unlikely that an outsider could, or would even wish to, engage in bringing about a *development* of the doctrines in which the faith is expressed. The question is, then, whether such development—such an "act of traditioning," as we say—is out of line with what goes on in other university disciplines. Schleiermacher apparently did not think so. Although he freely used the Anselmian language of faith seeking understanding, he was not claiming to possess information supernaturally communicated to the elect, but rather affirming a hermeneutic principle: inner facts cannot be

---

[77] Tracy, *The Analogical Imagination: Christian Theology and the Culture of Pluralism* (New York: Crossroad, 1981), pp. 56-57, 64, 68.

[78] Reik, *Dogma and Compulsion: Psychoanalytic Studies of Religion and Myths* (New York: International Universities Press, 1951), pp. 48, 69.

[79] Troeltsch, "Dogmatik," in Michael Schiele and Leopold Zscharnack, eds., *Die Religion in Geschichte und Gegenwart*, 5 vols. (Tübingen: J.C.B. Mohr [Paul Siebeck], 1909-13), 2:109.

simply observed but call for introspection, participation, and even commitment.⁸⁰ Presumably, the transmission of knowledge in the schools of law and medicine is not subject to the same limitation. But is there perhaps at least an analogy to the theologian's commitment in the humanities?⁸¹

Even in the natural sciences, in which so high a premium is placed on fresh observation and novel discoveries, commitment to a tradition of inquiry and discovery is by no means out of place. But since I was myself a student of Greek and Latin before I turned to theology, it is more natural for me to try a comparison between theology and the classics (not, I hope, between one losing cause and another). In school, those of us who took the "classical side" (as we put it) were not merely taught the rudiments of the Greek and Latin languages. Even a journeyman philologist could have dragged us through Homer's Greek. But we learned to appreciate Homer from an exuberant master who found our labored efforts at word-by-word translation so painful that he would interrupt us—usually with the theological expletive, "Oh, *God!*"—and would then race through page after page translating for us, chuckling happily as he went. He wanted us not just to construe the *Iliad* correctly, but to love Homer and to let him shape our spirits.

But more than that, we were constantly plied with something like tracts on behalf of the gospel of Hellenism. In an address delivered at the annual meeting of the Classical Association in 1954, the then secretary frankly classified some of the association's publications as "protreptic" (a nicer word, he thought, than "propaganda").⁸² Printed as handy booklets, small enough to slip into your pocket, these evangelistic tracts—mostly lectures or addresses in origin—could be distributed by schoolmasters to their eager pupils. Even more ambitious were whole volumes that raised the banner of a classical education. Sir Richard Livingstone (1880-1960) was perhaps the outstanding master of the genre. By means

---

⁸⁰ *Gl.*, § 13 (*Zusatz*). In *KD*, § 196, Schleiermacher makes the interesting observation that without personal conviction one could give a historical report but not a persuasive presentation of the *Zusammenhang* of doctrine—the way it hangs together (cf. *KD*, § 195). Dogmatic theology is *die Wissenschaft von dem Zusammenhange* and calls for an "apologetic" taking of sides (*Gl.*, § 19.1).

⁸¹ An analogy is *all* I am here looking for. The precise form in which Schleiermacher gives the Anselmian model of theologizing is, in my opinion, dubious. "[Q]ui expertus non fuerit, non intelliget" risks making theology esoteric. It is one thing to insist that the theologian needs to be *expertus* to give an adequate presentation of the Christian way of believing, quite another to infer that nobody else will understand what is said unless he or she is also *expertus* or *experta*.

⁸² L.J.D. Richardson, "The Classical Association: The First Fifty Years," *Proceedings of the Classical Association* 51 (1954): 23-41 see p. 32.

of a selective and highly idealized portrait of ancient Athens, he assured us that Greek ideals could help us with the chief weakness of our age: the lack of a definite view of life. He did not conceal from us the partial antagonism between Hellenism and Christianity but left us to make the choice for ourselves—or to follow the early church into a happy syncretism.[83]

I do not believe that we ever felt our minds were being violated; and we did not all become true believers, as some of our essays on the benefits of a classical education made only too clear. (I recall one impudent schoolboy arguing that a classical education teaches us many things we would not even wish to know without the benefit of a classical education.) We were not offended. We smiled a bit. But there was, I think, a danger: we were convinced of our intellectual superiority to pupils in what C. P. Snow (1905-1980) would call the *other* culture[84] and did not realize the deprivation our education actually entailed. Like the little band of Spartans at Thermopylae, we were delaying the advance of the barbarian hordes. The philosopher G. E. Moore (1873-1958), who sixty years earlier sat in the same classroom I did, told of the many hours he spent on his weekly quota of prose and verse composition in Greek and Latin, and wondered in retrospect: "Possibly it would have been better for me if some of those hours had been spent upon some of the Natural Sciences, of which I learned absolutely nothing at school...."[85]

When those of us who were loyal to the classics moved on to university, we were excited by E. R. Dodds's (1893-1979) brilliant study *The Greeks and the Irrational* (1951), not only because it offered a somewhat iconoclastic reinterpretation of the ancient Athenians (though that was appealing enough to the undergraduate mind), but also because he was plainly talking about the Dionysian passions that lurk behind the Apollonian smile of every reasonable, civilized man or woman. His work brought together the ancient texts and the newest anthropological and psychological theories, and we saw at once that his interpretation of Euripides as both the spokesman of the Greek enlightenment and its adversary was a comment on human nature. "Primitive," as Dodds

---

[83] R.W. Livingstone, *Greek Ideals and Modern Life* (London: Oxford University Press [Geoffrey Cumberlege], 1935), pp. 2-6, 37, 174-75; idem, *The Greek Genius and Its Meaning to Us*, 2d ed. (ibid., 1915), pp. 123-24.

[84] C[harles] P[ercy] Snow, *The Two Cultures and the Scientific Revolution*, Rede Lecture (Cambridge: Cambridge University Press, 1959).

[85] Moore, "An Autobiography," in Paul Arthur Schilpp, ed., *The Philosophy of G. E. Moore*, Library of Living Philosophers, 2nd ed. (New York: Tudor Publishing Company, 1952), p. 6.

remarked, is a fair enough description of most people's mental behavior most of the time. The Greeks were no exception: they illustrate the rule.[86]

My point, then, if I dare generalize from these shamelessly personal recollections, is that in varying degrees the best humanistic scholarship arises out of a powerful sense of the abiding value and universal significance of some tradition of learning. It is never a cold autopsy on a dead body. As Newman says, a little effusively, the university is "the place where the professor becomes eloquent, and is a missionary and a preacher, displaying his science in its most complete and most winning form, pouring it forth with the zeal of enthusiasm, and lighting up his own love of it in the breasts of his hearers."[87] It does not follow, of course, that *any* kind of advocacy, propaganda, or proselytism is justified, much less apocalyptic warnings of the wrath to come. But we can hardly demand of our theologians a more ascetic standard of detachment than we expect of their colleagues in other departments of the university. The Athanasian Creed claims too much for its obscure propositions when it promises eternal destruction to anyone who doubts them. In a secular university, at any rate, the theologian does not say, "This is the Catholic Faith, which except a man believe faithfully, he cannot be saved." She says rather: "Here is something of value that our world cannot afford to lose, something still alive that I cannot bring myself to treat as though it were dead." And then she proceeds to put the best construction on it.

Reinterpretation for the sake of transmitting something perceived to be of enduring worth lies at the heart of our humanistic enterprise. But so do the right and duty to test everything for oneself and the freedom to reject what is commended by one's teachers, however earnest and winsome they may be. Hence, although the academy does not need to exclude the creative development of a religious tradition by an insider (who else could develop it creatively?), it does have a responsibility not to give *absolute* precedence to one religion over another. Ideally, it should want to find room for theologians and philosophers who are working on, and within, other religious traditions than Christianity. This, too, is the logic of Schleiermacher's position—once the subordination of theological studies to the needs of church leadership is put in perspective. Within what he calls the "faculty of philosophy" only a *relative* precedence, at

---

[86] E[ric] R[obertson] Dodds, *The Greeks and the Irrational* (1968), 6th printing, Sather Classical Lectures, vol. 25 (Berkeley and Los Angeles: University of California Press, 1968), pp. viii, 188.

[87] "What is a University?" p. 16.

most, could be given to Christianity as the dominant religious tradition in our own culture.

Perhaps the future for the divinity schools, too, lies in the same, genuinely ecumenical direction. But it has not been my purpose in this essay to justify university-based divinity schools, only to explore the main reason why they are often found to be problematic. My conviction is that the existence of divinity schools is a further question on which we have yet to learn all we could from Schleiermacher. Once again, the most important texts are not the *Thoughts on Universities* or the *Brief Outline*; there is more to learn from his epoch-making reflections on religion and the religions in his famous *Speeches* to the cultured despisers.[88] For, as far as I can see, a divinity school (or something like it under another name) is required in a secular and pluralistic university only if religion is an "independent variable" (as the sociologists put it), worthy of exploration from every possible perspective, including the perspective of church leadership.

This, clearly, is another large question. But it is not unrelated to the question I have tried to explore: What kind of a theology belongs in the academy? I do not pretend that Schleiermacher's is the only, or even the most widely accepted, view of theology at the present time. But I do think it is at least defensible as an academic theology. Anyone who believes that theology is possible and meaningful in the church alone, that it begins with God in his Revelation in Jesus Christ, and that it is scientific just insofar as it corresponds to the Word of God through the obedience of faith, will need to come up with a quite different account of theology's credentials as a university discipline, or may prefer to pursue it somewhere else.

---

[88] *Friedrich Schleiermacher's Reden über die Religion*, critical ed., ed. G. Ch. Bernhard Pünjer (Brunswick: C.A. Schwetschke and Son [M. Bruhn], 1879). Not least among Schleiermacher's pertinent insights in the *Reden* is that if you want to know what it means to be religious, you have to settle *somewhere* (p. 257). This is a quite different justification for particularity than Harnack's claim that anyone who knows *this* religion (Christianity) knows them all ("Die Aufgabe," p. 168).

Three Revolutions in Theology and Theological Education

GLENN T. MILLER

Contemporary scholars have thoroughly researched the concept of revolution.[1] The word originated in the writings of ancient and medieval astronomers who used it to refer to the periodic return of the planets to their expected positions. During the seventeenth century, "revolution" became a useful political metaphor to describe the events in England where the King, then Commons, then the King again, and finally Commons yet again seized political power.[2] The term was later applied to the great eighteenth-century political upheavals in France and America.

The use of the metaphor of the return of the planets for violent change is paradoxical. Every revolution returns to some predetermined position. Thus the English absolved their removal of Charles I as a restoration of the ancient Anglo-Saxon liberties guaranteed in the common law; the Americans justified their independence by appealing to

---

[1] See J. Bernard Cohen, *Revolution in Science* (Cambridge: Massachusetts and London, England, 1985), pp. 51-76.

[2] Thus, for example, Thomas Hobbes: "I have seen in this revolution a circular motion of the sovereign power through two usurpers from the late King to his son. For...it moved King Charles I to the Long Parliament; from thence to the Rump; from the Rump to Oliver Cromwell and then back again from Richard Cromwell to the Rump; thence to the Long Parliament; and then to King Charles II, where long it may remain." (*Behemoth*, Book IV) cited in:
Felix Gilbert,"Revolution," in *The Dictionary of the History of Ideas: Studies of Selected Pivotal Ideas*, ed. by Philip Wiener (New York: Charles Scribner's Sons, 1973), vol. 4, col.2, 153.

England's ancient constitution; and the French claimed a rebirth of humankind's original state of liberty, equality, and fraternity.

Karl Marx, perhaps the nineteenth-century's greatest connoisseur of revolution, had a lively appreciation for the dialectic of past and future in social upheaval. His own metaphysics of history revolved around the ancient myth of a golden age that was destroyed by the evil of property. History was progressive. As the upper classes' control of wealth and privilege increased, human freedom, dignity, and equality decreased. In time, the rich established structures of law, religion, government, and inheritance that concealed their deprecations from their fellows. The denouncement, however, was at hand. Industrial capitalism, the final stage of economic aggrandizement, threatened to enslave everybody alike. The grandiose nature of modern capitalism, its unprecedented domination of human life, left people only one option: violent revolution. After that purifying fire, the state must wither away, and humankind would resume control of its destiny.

The metaphor of revolution was too rich and evocative to be confined to politics. People needed a metaphor for the rapid rate of social, political, technical, and economic change. The image of revolution, now twice removed from Copernicus' planets, was a favored simile. Philosophy, computers, and soap powders have had their "revolutions." The word has been used so often as to seem hackneyed, trite, or cliche. After all, if every novelty is a "revolution," then the word has no meaning beyond the rather mundane observation that things are different today than they were yesterday. Nonetheless, short of a brilliant new coinage or the fortunate redefinition of a latin polysyllable, we have no other idiom that describes radical change as clearly or graphically as revolution.

I.

Historians of science have found the image of revolution to be particularly fruitful. Such pace setting scholars as T. S. Kuhn[3] have explained the dramatic shifts in humankind's apprehension of the natural order by comparing them to political revolutions. Newton, Darwin, and Einstein overturned existing understandings of the world by a stroke of brilliance that enabled others to see long familiar phenomenon in a

---

[3] Thomas S. Kuhn, *The Structure of Scientific Revolutions* (Chicago, London, 1962). See also T. S. Kuhn, *The Essential Tension: Selected Studies in Scientific Tradition and Change* (Chicago, London: The University of Chicago Press, 1977).

new way.⁴ Once the scientific community accepted the reinterpretation, investigators used a new paradigm that, like earlier theories, sufficed until the next discovery was made.

Kuhn's work raised as many questions as it answered. Perhaps the most serious of these was definition: what is a scientific revolution? J. Bernard Cohen provided a insightful solution to that problem in his *The Newtonian Revolution* (1980) and more recent *Revolution in Science* (1985). According to Cohen, a true scientific revolution must pass through the following stages:

1. The advent of a new idea or theory (the creative act, original research, etc.);

2. The communication of the theory and, especially, its publication in the appropriate forums;

3. Acceptance of the new concept by other scientists as shown by their use of the theory as part of their own work. These stages provided Cohen with the material that he needed to suggest criteria that historians may employ to determine when a scientific revolution has occurred. These include the recognition of other scientists that a fundamental change has taken place, the acceptance of the new idea or theory as the basis for further research, and the consensus of later historians that an authentic scientific reorientation occurred.

The most important mark, however, was social. A genuine scientific revolution changes the institutions where science is pursued and taught. Cohen writes:

> The scientific revolution, which produced a new kind of knowledge and a new method of obtaining it, also produced new institutions for the advancement, recording, and dissemination of that knowledge. These were societies or academies of like-minded scientists who met to do experiments in concert, to see performances and tests of experiments done elsewhere.⁵

New ideas mandate the establishment or reestablishment of a "formal network of information."⁶ In the past such new networks have included

---

⁴ Kuhn's metaphor depends, as does almost all revolutionary thinking, on the idea that the basic substrata was already present when innovation occurred. Each of his examples returns, in effect, to a new interpretation of the data. Einstein's use of the electric motor (or generator) for his theory of relativity illustrates Kuhn's point. Physicists had known and pondered the example for decades, but only Einstein saw the structural relationship between the various parts of the device.

⁵ Cohen, *Revolution*, 81.
⁶ Cohen, *Revolution*, 82.

scientific societies, research laboratories, formal academic departments, and specialized journals. True scientific revolution thus is not only a change in perception, but it is a renovation of the social matrix in which perception takes place.

Can we transpose Cohen's understanding of a scientific revolution to a theological key? There are some reasons for caution. The history of theology and of science are different. For instance, the history of theology[7] (probably because of the influence of ecclesiastical communities and traditions in determining religious affirmations) has rarely been as punctual as the development of science. Further, present-day theologians are cautious in their claims to have advanced their discipline. Yet, there are some values in the use of the metaphor of a theological revolution that are difficult to express in other ways. The history of theological expression was not only the slow and steady accumulation of precedents or the gradual development of foundational concepts. Seasons of rapid change have occurred that have changed the way that theologians approach problems, and these periods have changed the institutions in which theology is studied.

The linkage between theological change and the transformation of theological institutions is not accidental. As in Cohen's analysis of science, the metaphor of a theological revolution assumes that any truly foundational change must produce a new network of information sharing and instruction. If no social changes occur, it is highly improbable that any real transformation has occurred.[8]

Many developments in theology met Cohen's criteria for a scientific revolution, and my choice of examples—Abelard's new scholasticism, Luther's discovery of Scripture, and Bushnell's redefinition of religion—is admittedly arbitrary. I do not claim that these are the only events that could be described as theological revolutions or that these are necessarily the best examples that could be found.

My goals are more modest. I want to show that each of these examples fits Cohen's picture of fundamental intellectual change. In each case, a new idea was presented, was widely published and discussed, and

---

[7] The word theology is used in this essay to refer to the intellectual study and examination of Christianity, especially as that academic discipline developed in western Europe and the United States.

[8] The question of theological revolutions needs to be separated from the question of the value of a particular theologians work. At this point in the twentieth century, for example, it seems evident that Karl Barth was arguably the most able theologian of our time. Yet, Barth's theology did not meet the criteria of a true revolution. The European (and American) systems of Protestant theological education did not change nor did the nature of theological communication.

within a generation or two had contributed to the transformation of the environment in which serious theological study was conducted. New institutions were needed for new ideas. The case of Bushnell is somewhat different from the others. Bushnell was not a theologian of the first rank, and many of his most creative ideas were derivative. But, Bushnell's work had revolutionary effects in the provincial atmosphere of North America and demanded (and got) basic changes in the nation's understanding of theological education. I have included him because the concept of revolution, if the metaphor is to be useful, must have a place for the Lenin who builds socialism in one country as well as for the Marx who inspires action everywhere.

II.

Peter Abelard (Abailard: 1079-1142) is a good candidate for the role of revolutionary. By all accounts, he lived in tension with his own times. One of the first professional (non-clerical) teachers, he lived a life suspended between the coming secularity of the various faculties of arts and the monastic past of European education. His famed affair with Heloise was as misinterpreted as his scholarly identity. Heloise's uncle, convinced (incorrectly) that the dashing young professor wanted to make his ward a priest's whore, had him castrated.

The same ambiguity was part of his professional career. Abelard's scholarly life began in a series of unrelenting intellectual battles with his former teachers, William of Champeuax and Anselm of Laon and ended in the historic donnybrook with Bernard that resulted in Abelard's excommunication by Rome. Abelard died in exile in a cluniac house, hated by many of his contemporaries, but remembered by Peter the Venerable, his abbot, as "the Socrates of the Gauls, the great Plato of the West, our Aristotle."[9] Abelard was an exceptional teacher, an able theologian who pioneered new ground in the doctrines of the trinity and of the atonement, and a pioneer in the use of dialectic or logic.

The historical evidence for Abelard's effect on theology is incomplete. Abelard lost his battle with Bernard (despite substantial support from former students and from friends in Rome), and the means of transmission of his thought to other thinkers is often obscure. The winners, after all, preserved the records of the battle and, alas, few of Abelard's successors were brave (or foolhardy) enough to note fully their dependence on a condemned heretic.

---

[9] Leif Grane, *Peter Abelard: Philosophy and Christianity in the Middle Ages* (London: Allen & Unwin, 1970), 157.

Nineteenth-century liberal interpreters of Abelard stressed the freshness and creativity of his contribution. Among others, Victor Cousins, Charles de Remussat, Albert Reville, and S. M. Deutsch found inspiration in Abelard for the nineteenth-century's rejection of traditional authority.[10] In part, their interpretation was a continuation of the misunderstanding of Abelard's theology found in such contemporaries as Bernard who wrote: "he (Abelard) defines faith as opinion...as if it were allowable for each one to think and speak as he likes concerning matters of faith."[11] Many editions of Abelard's writings seemed to support the most secular interpretations of his works. For example, many redactors of his *Scholastic Theology* read a crucial passage as "it is not believed because God said it, but because it is proved to be so."[12] A more careful examination of the manuscripts suggests, however, that the famous quote was the result of the omission of a number of lines by later copyists. If the liberal picture of Abelard as an emancipator of reason was exaggerated, the liberals' scholarly instincts were sure. Abelard's work turned theology upside down and forced it to redefine its tasks, its methods, and, ultimately, the institutions in which sacred doctrine was studied.

Abelard's revolution was centered in the most confusing of theological puzzles: how can theologians know whether their statements (or those given by tradition) are true or false. Before Abelard, the answer was deceptively simple: authority and reason. As any reader of the Church Fathers or early medieval thinkers knows, the traditional theological argument was a string of scriptural citations, supported more or less by a connecting argument. Even Origen, the most speculative and scholastic of the Fathers, assumed that his work was primarily exegetical. Augustine, the font of much western theology, derived his theological method from latin rhetoric and literary criticism. His best theology was written using the conventions of the essay (largely as defined by Cicero). But the heart of his theology, as of Origen's, was the appeal to the Bible. The theologians of the early Middle Ages multiplied the number of accepted authorities who might be cited, especially by including Augustine's known works, but the method varied little from patristic precedent.

Patristic and early medieval theologians were vague about the place of reason. Anselm of Canterbury (1033-1109)—a convinced August-

---

[10] Richard A. Weingard, *The Logic of Divine Love: A Critical Analysis of the Soteriology of Peter Abelard* (Oxford: Clarendon Press, 1970), 1.

[11] *de erroribus Abaelardi* cited in Weingard, The Logic, 4.

[12] Weingard, *The Logic*, 6.

inian—continued his master's Christian Platonism with its certainty that faith preceded reason, but his thought carefully preserved the Bible (and Church Dogma) from rational examination. One could think about what Scripture said but not about Scripture's right to say it. The present-day reader of *Cur Deus Homo*, the *Monologion*, and the *Proslogion* is amazed, not at their philosophical realism, but at Anselm's confidence that dogma and reason dealt with the same "things" and possessed an inherent affinity for each other.

Abelard's contribution was his demonstration (at least to his fellow teachers' satisfaction) that the "House of Authority"[13] had to be rebuilt. Abelard's attack on traditional dialectics often has been interpreted primarily as an attempt to offer a third way between the extremes of realism and nominalism; but, as useful as that reading may be, it ignores Abelard's basic point. For him, logic or dialectics was a method. The logician's purpose is to protect and nurture the logical procedures that make and keep intellectual life honest. In more recent theological language, dialectics are the guarantee of the public character of theological language.[14]

In this context, Abelard's attack on the traditional use of authority was incisive. In *Sic et Non* (Yes and No), Abelard carefully arranged the various theological texts, commonly accepted in his own day, so that their apparent contradictions were obvious to any reader. Abelard, a widely read scholar, was familiar with the technique of the *Florilegia* (collection of authorities) used by earlier scholars and in particular with struggles of the canon lawyers to impose order on the confusing mass of materials from past church councils. Whether Grabmann's (1911) attempt to identify the collection of precedents of Bernhold of Constance (d. 1100) as the exemplar of *Sic et Non* was correct or not, *Sic et Non's* patterns of arrangement suggest the legal tradition's use of precedent.

In his "Introduction," Abelard explained that he "aimed only to incite others to think."[15] To aid others' appreciation of the meaning of an authoritative text, he suggested that the scholar needed to determine the correct reading of the document, to place the work in its proper biographical context, to avoid misrepresenting its arguments, and, above all,

---

[13] I am indebted to Edward Farley for this wonderful image.
[14] For an interpretation of public theology, see David Tracy, *Blessed Rage For Order: The New Pluralism in Theology* (New York: The Seabury Press, 1975); also his *The Analogical Imagination: Christian Theology and the Culture of Pluralism* (New York: The Seabury Press, 1981).
[15] Jeffrey Garrett Sikes, *Peter Abailard* (New York: Russell and Russell, 1965), 82.

to exegete carefully the meaning and form of the words quoted.[16] Once this scholarly groundwork had been done, the theologian used logic to discover (as nearly as possible) the best contemporary statement of a doctrine or position.

The argument in *Sic et non* had great implications for theology. After Abelard, theologians were unable to assume that authority and rational organization were sufficient to settle disputes. As theology developed, Abelard's analytical approach was adopted almost universally. Peter Lombard (c. 1100-1160), whose *Sententiarum liber quartor* [c. 1155-58] became the key theological textbook for the medieval university, went beyond Abelard in the size and comprehension of his collection of texts and of his system of classification. Apprentice theologians at Paris received their first degree in Sacred Scripture, and then progressed to the mastery of the technical (scholarly) theology of the *Sentences*. This order became normative for all Northern European universities. Theologians were judged by their ability to defend controversial propositions before a critical audience. The disputation, which Abelard pioneered to showcase his approach, became the equivalent of a modern comprehensive examination, and students' progress through the various degrees was determined by their success or failure in dialectical exercises.

In short, Abelard discovered theology as a "technical" discipline. Not only was Abelard among the first to use the latin word *theologia*[17] to describe a type of intellectual enterprise, but he gave the term a very precise meaning.[18] Unlike "Sacred Doctrine"—the earlier term for the sum of Christian teaching—*theologia* was more and less than the statement of what the church had believed traditionally. *Theologia* was the result of the application of a method to the church's teaching and the subsequent logical determination of the most adequate formulations of that doctrine.

Once this understanding of *theologia* was established, the days of the monastic and cathedral schools were numbered. Abelard's significance

---

[16] Abelard's application of this method to the charter of the monastery of St. Dennis (Dionysus) in Paris so argued the monks that they wanted to expel Abelard. It is interesting that this method was used years before Valla used similar analysis to disprove the Donation of Constantine.

[17] The term, of course, originally was used in Greek philosophy to describe the philosophical criticisms of the inherited ideas of the gods or to describe the philosophical arguments for monotheism. Origen and the other Greek Fathers appear to have used the word in this way in their writings.

[18] For another (and somewhat idealized) understanding of theologia, see Edward Farley, *Theologia: The Fragmentation and Unity of Theological Education* (Philadelphia: Fortress Press, 1983).

for the development of university theology did not lie, as Rashdall argued in the fact that "the fame of Abelard...first drew to the streets of Paris the hordes of students whose presence involved that multiplication of masters by whom the university was ultimately formed."[19] (Rashdall I, 278, 1938). But, Abelard's achievement was more basic: he redefined the study of Christian doctrine so completely that earlier institutions were no longer adequate for the task. His mode of theological enquiry demanded the concentration of talent, the establishment of formal standards of advancement, and the creation of clear criteria of intellectual adequacy. In short, it demanded more than the best cathedral school or monastery could provide.[20]

III.

The revolutionary character of the Reformation is self-evident. The Northern portions of Europe dissolved their political and religious ties to the papacy, created new ecclesiastical institutions, and shifted the internal balance of wealth in their "countries" from the church to the nobility and the middle classes. A thousand years of mass gave way to the sermon and the catechism. In those western countries where Protestantism was rejected, the new faith posed sufficient threats to the political and social order to provoke civil war (France), severe repression (Spain, Italy), or international war (Austria).

What made Luther's theology revolutionary? To Adolph Harnack, Luther's work was the watershed in the history of theology:

> This completed whole, however, which he outlined with a firm hand, not merely to this or that particular dogma, but *to dogmatic Christianity in its entirety*: Christianity is something else than a sum of traditional doctrines....Any one who lets Luther be Luther, and regards his main

---

[19] Hastings Rashdall, *The Universities of Europe in the Middle Ages* (Oxford: The Clarendon Press, 1936) I, 278.

[20] In arguing for the revolutionary significance of Abelard's method for theology, I am mindful of the advances made in other areas, including medicine and law, at the same time. The period from 1100-1300 was one of the most creative in the history of Western Europe. Schools of law and medicine could (and in some areas did) develop into universities without theology. What Abelard did was to devise a method for theology that demanded a broader university context and made theology central to the cultural life of the new five centuries. There was no inevitability to that development, and teachers of sacred doctrine might have remained in the monasteries or cathedral schools. The merging cities and their wealth provided the financial wealth necessary for the universities, but resources may be used for a variety of purposes, including wine and song, and only a powerful vision turns their employment from private to public ends, It is fruitful to compare the rise of Western technical theology with theology's more traditional role in the Christian East, where greater wealth existed at the time, but where no theological revolution occurred.

positions as the valuable possession of the evangelical church—who does not merely tolerate them, that is to say under stress of circumstances (*per augustias temporum*)—has the lofty title and the strict obligation to end the history of dogma with him.[21]

If Harnack's confidence in the end of dogma appears today to be more a pious hope than a reality, his appraisal of Luther's significance was accurate. Stephen Ozment's observation that Luther was the "the age's most brilliant theologian" was an understatement.[22] Luther's theology provided the issues that occupied theologians for more than a hundred and fifty years of intense investigation, speculation, and debate. Whenever Protestantism has difficulty in finding its place in new intellectual contexts, a new interpretation of Luther has spurred creative theological work. Pietists, rationalists, confessionalists, and neo-orthodox have all created their own Luther as well as worn his mantle.

Luther's opponents provided evidence of the extent of the Lutheran theological revolution. The Council of Trent that met from 1545 to 1563 marked a new departure from the medieval church.[23] In formulating their response to the new national Protestant churches, the Bishops produced more legislation than the previous eighteen general councils recognized by Rome.[24] Almost all the dogmatic decisions referred in one way or another, directly or indirectly, to Luther's theology, his method, or to Protestant institutions. Ironically, the Tredentine reassertion of tradition transformed the medieval church more than the bishops (or many

---

[21] Harnack, *The History of Dogma* (London: William and Norgate, 1899), VII (trans by W. M. M'Gilchrist), 268. In contrast, Jaroslav Pelikan, *The History of the Christian Tradition :
VI. The Reformation of Church and Dogma* (Chicago: The University of Chicago, 1984) has interpreted Luther's theology as part of a more or less unified development of thought from 1300 to 1700. Pelikan's perspective has two foci. Historiographically, his primary point (and one that is carefully researched and documented) is that Luther worked within the doctrinal traditions of the church of his own day. Luther was an able(perhaps the most able) ecclesiastical thinker of the sixteenth century,. The same continuity between Lutheran and later Protestant thinkers. Theologically, Pelikan maintains (building on the thought of John Henry Newman) that the Christian tradition has slowly unfolded from its New Testament foundations. See Jaroslav Pelikan, *The Vindication of Tradition* (New Haven: Yale University Press, 1984). While granting the sophistication and depth of these methodological commitments, the basic question—whether theological change is possible or desirable—should be asked of both presuppositions. Has Pelikan ruled revolutionary changes in theology and church life out of court?

[22] Stephen Ozment, *The Age of the Reformation: 1250-1550: The Intellectual and Religious History of Late Medieval and Reformation Europe* (New Haven: Yale, 1980), 231

[23] J. Dulumeneau, *Catholicism between Luther and Voltaire* (Philadelphia: The Westminster Press, 1977).

[24] F. S. Piggin, "The Council of Trent," *The Evangelical Dictionary of Theology*, ed. by Walter Elwell (Grand Rapids: Baker 1984), 1100.

of Protestant contemporaries) recognized. After Trent, the ancient Church of the West was the Roman Catholic Church.

Luther's theology was rich and varied. Although Luther was a master of the traditional forms of theological discourse, including the disputation, much of his creative writing was done in response to an immediate situation, such an attack by an opponent, his congregation's need for a sermon on a particular subject, or the desire of a friend for spiritual guidance. Luther's literary talents, like those of his great contemporary Erasmus, were considerable, and he often yielded to the temptation to defeat an opponent with a quip rather than an argument. Luther developed the nuances of his theology over decades of academic and ecclesiastical life, but one thing in his approach to theology did not vary from his earliest days as an instructor in Bible to his death: his relentless effort to identify Christianity with the Word of God found in Scripture. The Bible was the center of theology, the center of worship, and the center of life.

Luther's theological revolution consisted, in large part, in this new apprehension of the Bible. Despite the risk of reading more into the sources than may actually be there, one needs to distinguish between Luther's doctrine of Scripture and the place and role of the Bible in his thought.[25] Luther had second (and more mature) judgments about his early rejection of parts of the canon, such as the Epistle of James and the Revelation of St. John. In terms of formal doctrine, Luther accepted such traditional beliefs as the scholastic assertion of the infallibility of Scripture, and he may have assumed—as did most of his contemporaries—that the Bible was inerrant.[26]

What was revolutionary in Luther's grasp of Scripture was his shortening of the distance separating the Bible from theology. To be a theologian was to be a citizen of the Biblical world and to use all one's talents and all available resources to make the Word spoken in the Bible meaningful to contemporaries. This was not so much a doctrine of biblical authority as it was an assertion of the supremacy of the Scripture in all ecclesiastical life and thought. Bainton, using Luther's own words, put it simply:

> The Word of God has to be communicated to us and Scripture is the means. "Scripture is Christ's spiritual body," "We must be shown the place where Christ lies. This is the manger where one may find him even though Joseph and Mary are not there. That is to say, that Christ is swaddled in Scripture;

---

[25] See David Lotz, "Sola Scriptura," Interpretation 35 (1981), 258-273.
[26] John D. Woodbridge, *The Authority of Scripture: A Critique of the Rogers/McKim Proposal* (Grand Rapids: Zondervan, 1982) 53 passim.

the manger is the preaching in which he lies and is contained, and from which one can take food and fodder..." it is only a slight and simple word but Christ is in it.[27]

As Lotz observed, christology and the Bible were one and invisible. To quote the Bible was to witness to Christ; to witness to Christ was to quote the Scripture.

The implications of this positions for theology were staggering. The elaborate mechanism of scholastic thought, which had been concerned with the resolution of conflicting authoritative claims to truth and with the use of logic in theological enquiry, was not so much refuted as it was set aside. The traditional quotations, particularly those from St. Augustine, continued to dot Luther's (and Calvin's) work, but their place in the argument was different. The Fathers were to be studied because they reflected Scripture, not because they were Fathers. The ancients had no advantage over the contemporary theologian! Each was to be judged by their faithfulness to the Biblical text and, hence, to Christ and not as authorities in their own right.

Luther's revolution was possible, in large measure, because he did not rely on his own limited ability. At the time that Luther made his discovery of grace in the *cloaca,* the humanists were making significant scholarly advances.[28] Latin, the technical language of a clerical elite, was rediscovered as a means of cultural communication, and young intellectuals, such as John Calvin, were exploring its range of expression. The study of Greek, once esoteric, had become part of the furnishing of a literary man, and Erasmus and Philip Melanchthon (1497-1560) demonstrated the scholarly and practical value of a thorough knowledge of that language. Erasmus' critical edition of the Greek New Testament (one of the most important humanist documents) appeared in 1516. Although the western study of Hebrew was in its infancy, Johannes Reuchlin (1455-1522) had already published his *De rudimentis Hebraicis* (1506) and his *De accentibus et orthographia linguae (1518).*

Despite the hostility of many older humanists (including Erasmus and Reuchlin), Luther combined their scholarly methods with his discovery of the Bible. In appealing to the Scripture, Luther did not ask others to share his spiritual experience; he asked them to share his best understanding of the text. He used the resources of humanistic scholar-

---

[27] Roland Bainton, "The Bible in the Reformation," in the *Cambridge History of the Bible,* ed. by S.L. Greenslade (Cambridge: Cambridge University Press, 1963) III, 20.
[28] See E. Harris Harbison, *The Christian Scholar in the Age of Reformation* (New York: Charles Scribner's Sons, 1956).

ship wherever available, and he encouraged others to follow his example. In his Postscript to *Luther and the Old Testament* (E.T. 1969), Heinrich Bornkamm described Luther's method in striking language:

> Luther's axiom, faith rests upon history, requires the absolute truthfulness of historical research... Exegetical methods Luther had already surmounted have no right to survive in the evangelical interpretation of Scripture. Protestant allegorizing and typologizing or Catholic symbolic interpretation simply throw us back to a pre-Luther level of understanding in the history of exegesis.[29]

Humanism with its collections of critical editions, dictionaries, and ancient manuscripts had been unable singlehandedly to transform theology, but when combined with Luther's passion for Scripture, the new learning acquired revolutionary significance.

The Protestant revolt increased the number of theological students in the university and redefined the nature of theological study. In Germany, the introduction of Protestantism was followed by an almost complete reorientation of education along humanist lines. Melanchthon (1497-1560), Professor of Greek at the University of Wittenberg, was one of the leaders in this endeavor. In 1528 Melanchthon's procedures for the visitation of schools were written into law in Saxony, and eventually more than fifty-six cities and lands adopted his program of elementary education.

Every student, lay or clerical, was to have the tools for serious scriptural study. The wide-spread acceptance of the standards of the German gymnasium—the mastery of spoken and written Latin, the ability to read Greek, and a knowledge of the rudiments of Hebrew—was one product of his tireless advocacy of linguistic study.

Melanchthon also worked with the universities. He contributed to the rewriting of the statues of the Universities of Marburg (1529), the University of Wittenberg (1533, 1545), and the University of Konigberg (1544). His ideas were likewise influential at the Universities of Tuebingen, Leipzig, and Heidelberg.[30] Equally important, German pastors attained the new standards. Within less than one hundred years, the majority of German ministers (perhaps 90 per cent) had received humanistic training.

---

[29] Heinrich Bornkamm, *Luther and the Old Testament*, Trans. Eric and Ruth Gritsch (Philadelphia: Fortress, 1969), 269.

[30] James William Richard, *Philip Melanchthon: The Protestant Preceptor of Germany, 1497-1560* (New York: Putman, 1898), 269.

Similar educational revolutions occurred in other Protestant countries. Humanistic studies became the mark of a the "learned" minister, and England—always somewhat different from the continent—discontinued the professional study of theology in order to promote more classical knowledge. The scholar's gown was the Protestant vestment.

The new theological education enabled the ministers to assume a new role in Protestant societies. Ozment has noted the importance of the interpretation of the clergy as "citizens" of their respective commonwealths.[31] In effect, the clergy exchanged their status as a separate, hierarchical body for the potentially more potent position of learned professionals charged with cultural and religious leadership. The quaint New England term, "public teachers of religion," accurately expressed the meaning of theological existence after Luther's revolution.

IV.

A theologically-trained observer travelling from the University of Berlin to the University of Chicago in 1910 might have had difficulty describing the difference between the two schools. The two institutions were remarkably similar. The faculties of both school were devoted to scientific biblical and historical study, and the theology of Albrecht Ritschl (1822-1889) and his equally brilliant disciple, Adoph Harnack (1851-1930), dominated both institutions. But the ethos of the two schools was different. German liberals, despite such brave journals as the *Christliche Welt*, were at home in the high culture of Wilhelm II's Zion; American liberals, chronically dissatisfied with the present, were generating new institutions, establishing new programs of study, exporting universities to China and elsewhere, and actively (not militantly) supporting programs of social reform.[32]

---

[31] Steven Ozment, *The Reformation in the Cities: The Appeal of Protestantism to Sixteenth Century Germany and Switzerland* (New Haven: Yale, 1975), 84-90. See also Wilhelm Pauck, *The Heritage of the Reformation* (Philadelphia: Fortress Press, 1961), 101-145.

[32] The temptation of American religious historians has been to analyze the American liberal tradition either as part of the progressive era and, thus, to make available paradigms drawn from H. Richard Niebuhr's *Christ and Culture* (1951) or to see liberal Protestantism as an attempt to resolve certain problems in modernity. Kenneth Cauthen's *The Impact of American Religious Liberalism* (New York: Harper and Row, 1962) combined both tendencies. As Pelikan noted in his Foreword:
Repeatedly he shows how uncritically the advocates of the liberal spirit accepted the spirit of their time and incorporated it into their own theology. This illustrates one of the most touching ironies in the liberal movement, Among the permanent results of liberalism none is more important than the discovery that the bible and church are conditioned by history. (ix)
Cauthen in his own "introduction," dealt with such vexing problems as science, autonomy, and biblical studies. In contrast William Hutchison in *The Modernist Impulse in*

After 1870 American theological educators busily transformed their programs. The extent of these modifications can be demonstrated in a partial list of these alterations: the historical survey or introduction to the Old and New Testaments, courses in social (or applied) Christianity, the application of the social sciences—especially sociology, psychology, and education—to pastoral work, the reorganization of theological schools along university lines (deans, registrars, credit courses), the popularization of new standards of achievement (the Ph.D. for teachers, the B.D. for students), and the attempt to use supervised employment in the church to train candidates. Moreover. these institutional changes were permanent. The three great surveys of American theological education (Kelly, 1921; Brown-May, 1934; and Niebuhr-Williams-Gustafson, 1957)[33] assumed that the liberal seminary was the standard by which all theological education was to be measured. Ironically (although perhaps unconsciously), many conservatives accepted the liberal changes when they formed or reformed their own institutions. Other schools, including some Roman Catholic schools, made these transitions when they sought accreditation from the American Association of Theological Schools (ATS).

Where did the impetus for these changes begin? In the rapidly changing intellectual milieu of the late nineteenth century, a period aptly described as the second enlightenment, candidates aplenty vie for the role of revolutionary. In many ways, for instance, the theological future was set by the 1859 publication of *Das Kapital* and *The Origin of Species*. Darwin proved (at least to those who read and understood his work) that the Genesis account of creation could not be historical, and, thus, forced biblical scholars to take the new higher criticism seriously. Strauss was shouted down when he published *Das Leben Jesu* in 1835; after 1859, the anti-critical voices, perforce, were more muted. For if the Bible were not simply the recording of God's words and, hence, part of His divine perfection, theology had to explain what it was, and modern critical investigation gave the most cogent account of Scripture's message and development. A similar [although much weaker case] can be made

---

American Protestantism (Cambridge: Harvard University Press, 1976) saw liberalism (admitted an inaccurate phrase) as an attempt to resolve the question of sacred and secular that had both positive and negative results (pp. 1-11).
  [33] Robert Lincoln Kelly, *Theological Education in America* (New York: George A. Doran, 1924); William Adams Brown and Mark A. May, *The Education of American Ministers*, 4 vols.(New York: Institute of Religious and Social Research, 1934); and Daniel Day Williams, H. Richard Niebuhr, and James M. Gustafson, *The Advancement of Theological Education* (New York: Harper and Row, 1957).

for the impact of socialism on American life as well as for the influence of German historicism.

The problem with locating the liberal revolution in Darwin, Marx, or higher criticism is two-fold. First, the new attitudes antedate the widespread popularity of those movements. In dealing with the new problems of their times, for example, Theodore Munger (1830-1910) and Washington Gladden (1836-1918) used the methods that they had learned early in their ministries to interpret the new thought. Second, the surprising aspect of the American reception of higher criticism and Darwinism was not that these problems required solutions, but that the American liberal theological community surmounted them so easily. By 1890, the most able American theologians (at least, outside of Princeton circles) had moved from a discussion of the problems of modernity to an examination of its possibilities.

William Newton Clarke (1840-1912), one of the most skilled Baptist theologians of his day, left a remarkable record of his own theological development in *Sixty Years with the Bible*, published in 1909.[34] Although Clarke's purpose in writing the volume was to reassure those who believed that modern liberalism had lost some of the values of the Gospel, his intellectual pilgrimage followed a steady, developmental course. The same can be said of other noted liberals, including Shailer Matthews, Charles Briggs, and William Rainey Harper. These thinkers met Darwin and the new biblical study more or less in stride. They behaved like the heirs of a theological revolution, not like its perpetuators.

Cohen's criteria for a scientific revolution provide some useful clues to the name of the thinker who inspired the American liberal theological revolution. When Cohen's criteria are applied to American intellectual history, the trail leads back to Horace Bushnell (1802-1876) and the new directions that he suggested for American theologians.[35] Significantly, many of the elements that made American theological liberalism more creative than European Ritschleanism, including the fascination with religious education, the emphasis on practical religious life and experi-

---

[34] William Newton Clarke, *Sixty Years with the Bible: A Record of Experience* (New York, 1912).

[35] For a detailed discussion of Bushnell's theological method, see Glenn T. Miller "The Character of Christ: Two Nineteenth Century Critics of Classical Christology," *Faith and Mission* 5 (1988) 28-44.

ence, and the willingness to bless political action, were part of his legacy.[36]

Bushnell's theological revolution was carried out in a series of difficult books: *God was in Christ* (1847), *Christian Nurture* (1849), *Nature and the Supernatural* (1859), the *Vicarious Sacrifice* (1866), and *Work and Play* (1884). Although each of these books deals with a separate theme, collectively, they present four ideas crucial to the later development of American theology.

1. The language of theology is not analogous either to the language of physical science nor is it (as Emerson affirmed) the language of poetry. Rather, theological language is a cultural (present-day scholars might use the word, anthropological) development that, like all human attempts to know, is a product of human interaction with the environment. Whatever else religious language may be, it displays the same strengths and weaknesses as other abstract language. The meaning of religious affirmation is, consequently, difficult to discover, and the scholar must be careful not to impute too much precision or concreteness to theological affirmations. Two seemingly contradictory positions—Andover Trinitarianism and Harvard unitarianism—may be affirming a similar religious stance towards the world.

2, The relationship between God and the world is almost infinitely complex. In *Nature and the Supernatural,* Bushnell argued that what makes the theological interpretation of human life difficult is that both the human and the divine must be seen as supernatural (not bound to natural law) and interdependent. The distinction between sacred and secular was not blurred or erased; rather, the impossibility of an episte-

---

[36] Present-day interpreters have difficulty penetrating Bushnell's romanticism and its exuberant forms of religious expression. Anne Douglas (1977) in her tour de force, *The Feminization of American Culture* (New York, Knopf, 1977)—while admitting that Bushnell was "more complex" (p. 128) than her analysis indicates—uses his doctrine of the atonement as one of the showpieces in her argument that Americans abandoned Calvinism (somehow a "masculine" theology) for a "feminine" sentiment:
And in his (Bushnell's) earlier work, God has in a real sense abdicated. Bushnell's deity, like some celebrity dissatisfied with his public existence, has yearned for and found, a private life. It is the fantasy, often not without rationale or validity, of the weak that the strong will spontaneousness give up the pre-eminence which their inferiors would be forever incapable of wrestling from them because they suddenly feel its emptiness. It is a fantasy offering a double compliment to the dreamer, honoring his enforced passivity, vindicating the validity of his position without bettering it.—p 128
Bushnell's discovery of the problem of leisure in *Work and Play* (1884) with its allusions to children and kittens receives more scorn than his doctrine of the atonement (139-140). While Douglas' comments do (albeit indirectly) sustain the interpretation of Bushnell as a revolutionary (but one leading one to vacuity), she has only stayed on the surface of Bushnell's thought.

mological separation of experience into two realms was established. The Bible was the product of both human and divine history. When this insight was combined with Bushnell's understanding of language, liberal Christians were able to combine the practice of biblical criticism with a faith in biblical authority.

3. Bushnell believed that culture (the complex of spiritual forces generated by culture, school, family, and nation) was the atmosphere in which human spirits lived and breathed. The ministry to culture was an important aspect of Christian witness and included the transmission of the best that humankind had achieved. This particular service was not the participation of the minister in the local tea and literature society, but the minister's willingness to be a full participant in his own age.

The sentimentalism in Bushnell's thought was burned away by the Civil War which destroyed so many men and so much property. For Bushnell, the whole nation—not only the South—was responsible for slavery, and both sections had to bear their share of the sin, suffering, and shame caused by the Civil War. Although Bushnell was personally politically conservative (he wrote against women's suffrage), he maintained that Christians had to take positions of leadership in the war against barbarism. Bushnell's doctrine of a vicarious life and of the value of human agency suggested direct Christian involvement in the cure of the world's ills.

4. Bushnell believed that Christianity had to affect all of human life. Bushnells' discovery of the child as an appropriate focus for theological enquiry was to help define a future theological discipline. *Christian Nurture* discovered a new area for critical reflection, research, and practice. After Bushnell, the study of the religion of children became and remained a part of American theological education.

Work and Play should be interpreted in much the same way. The significance of the book was not its application of the model of romantic genius to the problem of labor (although the lines between Bushnell's concept of the dignity of toil and romantic theory are clear)—but *Work and Play's* assertion that authentic theology must deal with the day by day experiences of ordinary people. When Bushnell's successors found new methods of examining ordinary experience, especially those of sociology and psychology, they continued his quest with improved analytical tools.

Bushnell has been compared to Schleiermacher, but Schleiermacher, although he shared many of the same concerns, did not have the same opportunity for action.37 Schleiermacher's *The Brief Outline of Theology*, which argued that all theological work should climax in a reborn practical ministry, remained his private vision. The German study of theology was controlled, alas, not by theologians but by the iron necessity of the state examinations administered by the various state governments. In America, once a new theological style was accepted, the effects on the church and on theological education were allowed to follow naturally. Judged from the standpoint of a pure theological aesthetics, Schleiermacher was the greater theologian, but viewed from the perspective of reflection on theological revolution, Bushnell's work was more supportive of radical institutional change.

V.

Our own time seems ready for a theological revolution. The problems with the present situation are almost too evident to require listing. The professional model of ministry has flourished in our seminaries and divinity schools, but both teachers and students sense that far too much energy has been linked to a goal far too small to justify the schools' existence.

Our world, further, is now infinitely complex. The old problem of Christianity and the world's religions (or of theology and the history of religions) has hardly been addressed, but it is no longer the central problem facing Christianity or other faiths today. In our present world, all religions are confronting secularity, human demands for autonomy, and the acids of modern science. The Christian priest in London and the Buddhist monk in Thailand are more likely to be struggling with the same issues than with each other.

Were that not enough, all religions are being asked to give a meaningful account of our current technological life. We have given the inanimate world more of a human face than it has ever had before, and yet neither we nor the leaders of other world religions have a theological insight into what technology is or how it affects our lives.

It is one thing to note our need of a theological revolution; another to conduct one. The neo-orthodox of the 1930s and 1940s proudly proclaimed their own position to be a revolution, only to continue—with lit-

---

37 The comparison may be particularly apt, since Schleiermacher—a founder of the University of Berlin had the greatest opportunity to effect German theological education since Francke and the University of Halle. His own ideas, however, did not shape the new school as much as the ideal of research that had developed apparently at Göttingen and the general German belief in *Bildung*.

tle or no modification—the earlier professional model of theological education. What we need today is a new way of thinking, a more adequate model, that will make the transformation of our institutions possible. Anything less may be no more than minding the store while we await the return of its owner.

The Study of Religion and the Rise of the American University*

CONRAD CHERRY

Developments in the late nineteenth and early twentieth centuries have afforded theological studies and religious studies many of the restraints and opportunities currently confronting those educational undertakings. During the "age of the American university," roughly 1865 to 1910, all of the major patterns definitive of higher education today took their shape, and those patterns have created the critical context in which the academic and professional studies of religion perform their tasks. Above all, the twin movements of specialization and professionalization, centered in modern American universities that emerged before 1910, have prescribed certain limits for the study; and yet a scholarly attitude lying behind those movements has opened new horizons for the study. Acceptance of the limits set by the modern university can thwart unrealistic and anachronistic reform movements that attempt to "restore" an institution or a field of study to its "unifying ideal." Recognition of strengths yielded by the rise of the modern university, on the other hand, can create genuine possibilities for overcoming the gnostic parochialism often characteristic of modern specialization and professionalization. A detection of both the limits and the possibilities available to the study of religion today is contingent upon an understanding of the decisive influence of the age of the university.

I. The Modern University as Locus of Specialization and Professionalization

"*Vive la specialization!* Go to, let us centrifugate."[1] That exultation, written in a letter to a friend by a graduate student at Johns Hopkins in 1882, captures the mood that animated those engaged in the experiment known as the American university. Specialization of knowledge, manifested in the rapid and widespread diversification of academic fields, was the decisive force of the experiment, driving the institution outward and away from any unifying center. That centrifugal movement was to become a chief mark of institutions of higher education throughout the land in the twentieth century.

Johns Hopkins itself, founded in 1876 under the presidential leadership of Daniel Coit Gilman, began as a graduate school devoted to specialized research and soon became a model for other American universities. Although Gilman sought to prevent the isolation of specialized fields from one another through the introduction of interdepartmental courses, clubs, and newsletters, he encountered considerable opposition and indifference from professors and students to these integrative efforts and he finally stuck by his fundamental conviction that the life-giving air of the university is the free air of specialized knowledge.[2] Even before the establishment of Hopkins and other institutions devoted to graduate specialization, Gilman had been preceded in the conceptualization and (partial) implementation of a university founded on specialization by those determined to reform American higher education. In defending an elective system for undergraduates, President Charles Eliot of Harvard had urged in the 1860s that the university give attention to "the individual traits of different minds," a possibility foreclosed by a uniform curriculum. And in his argument for advanced scientific education, Eliot had insisted that "no subject of human inquiry can be out of place in the programme of a real university. It is only necessary that every subject should be taught at the university on a higher plane than elsewhere." In the 1850s Henry Tappan at Michigan had held that the principle govern-

---

* Portions of this article originally appeared in the *Journal of the American Academy of Religion*, 57.4 (1990), pp. 807-27, under the title "Boundaries and Frontiers for the Study of Religion: The Heritage of the Age of the University."

[1] John Higham, "The Matrix of Specialization," in *The Organization of Knowledge in Modern America, 1860-1920*, eds. Alexandra Oleson and John Voss (Baltimore: The Johns Hopkins University Press, 1979), p. 7.

[2] "G. Stanley Hall Describes Gilman's Policies at the Hopkins in the 1880's," in *American Higher Education: A Documentary History*, eds. Richard Hofstadter and Wilson Smith (Chicago: University of Chicago Press, 1961), II, 650.

ing the true university was a simple one: "That each member as a thinker, investigator, and teacher shall be a law unto himself, in his own department." Such autonomy meant that the university should aim to be a "cyclopedia" of education: "where, in libraries, cabinets, apparatus, and professors, provision is made for studying every branch of knowledge in full...; where study may be extended without limit."[3]

The forebears and founders of the modern university were dissatisfied with the college system of education that held sway through the period of the Civil War. Most of the earliest colleges were established as training schools for ministers, and even as the missions of those schools widened and other colleges emerged to embrace the laity, most American colleges in mid-nineteenth century were still under denominational control and were led by clergy presidents. The colleges were shaped by three closely related aims: to educate "learned gentlemen" into knowledge to be shared with other cultured leaders of the nation; to store the student mind with units of truth, those units gathered together normatively by moral philosophy or Christian natural theology; and to provide "mental discipline," an exercise to be achieved most effectively through the study of the classical languages. The curriculum, an adaptation of the English college system, typically had become by the time of the Civil War a core group of studies in Latin, Greek, mathematics, logic and moral philosophy, with elementary work in Hebrew, physics, and astronomy thrown in.[4]

Many of those who envisioned the modern American university were bothered less by the religious aura of the colleges than by the assumptions about culture, learning, and the mind underlying the curriculum. Henry Tappan, though judging it impossible to unite all denominational views into one university theological faculty, was quite willing to allow lectures in "Christian evidences" at Michigan and thought that the university should exist under the "nurturing wings of Christianity." What Tappan and other reformers found altogether inappropriate to the modern world were the mental gymnastics of the classics as a substitute for expansion into new fields of knowledge, the elitist education of cultured gentlemen in a society committed to democratic values and growing in professional opportunities, and the belief that learning was a

---

[3] "Charles William Eliot, Inaugural Address as President of Harvard, 1869"; "Eliot on the Scientific Schools, 1869"; "Henry P. Tappan on the Idea of the True University, 1858"; "Henry P. Tappan on University Education, 1851," in *American Higher Education*, Hofstadter and Smith, II, 608, 636, 519, 493.

[4] Richard Hofstadter and C. DeWitt Hardy, *The Development and Scope of Higher Education in the United States* (New York: Columbia University Press, 1952), pp. 3-18.

mere collection of units of truth devoid of any method for interpreting those truths. A growing number of educational leaders throughout the last half of the nineteenth century thought that the colleges of America were trying to face the cultural and educational challenges of the times with rigid curricula, narrow elitism, and superficial learning.[5]

Agreement on the limitations of the colleges scarcely spelled agreement on a unifying ideal for the modern American university, however. As Laurence Vesey has shown, three views of the university have found their avid defenders from the mid-nineteenth century to the present.[6] The aim of "practical public service," an attempt to reach the various classes of society and to meet the practical vocational demands of those classes, was embraced both by the Harvards and the Browns and by the newly emerging state universities. "We must carefully survey the wants of the various classes of the community," proclaimed President Wayland of Brown, and build courses of study which will meet the needs of all classes, including those of the "useful arts."[7] "It is not by poring over the dreamy and mystical pages of classical lore" that the student will find a place in the modern age, announced a state senate committee on education in a report to the University of Wisconsin, but by storming nature to unlock her great practical secrets.[8] Alongside the view of the university as public service institution there appeared the notion of the university as a place of "pure research." Proponents of this view were often explicit in their repudiation of any utilitarian ends of a university education. "Truth and right are above utility in all realms of thought and action," said Eliot of Harvard.[9] G. Stanley Hall, professor of psychology at Hopkins and then president of Clark University, believed pure research to be the "native breath" of the university, "its vital air," and he found that air fouled by those who "prate of the duty of bringing the university to the people."[10] Finally, the American university has been defined as the disseminator of "liberal culture," the maintainer of the standards of "cultivated tastes." In a kind of throwback to the old college ideal, cham-

---

[5] See "Henry P. Tappan on University Education, 1851"; "Francis Wayland's Report to the Brown Corporation, 1850"; Charles William Eliot, "Inaugural Address as President of Harvard, 1869"; "Eliot on the Scientific Schools, 1869," in Hofstadter and Smith, *American Higher Education*, II, 490, 506-507, 478-487, 603, 624-625.

[6] Laurence R. Vesey, *The Emergence of the American University* (Chicago: University of Chicago Press, 1965), p. 12.

[7] "Francis Wayland's Report to the Brown Corporation, 1850," in Hofstadter and Smith, *American Higher Education*, II, 478.

[8] Hofstdater and Hardy, Development and Scope, pp. 45-46.

[9] Charles William Eliot, "Inaugural Address as President of Harvard, 1869," in Hofstadter and Smith, *American Higher Education*, II, 602.

[10] Vesey, *Emergence of the University*, pp. 123, 151.

pions of this view have seen the university as a place where good breeding could be cultivated—but through diversity of knowledge rather than through mental gymnastics, and by making a kind of religion of civilization rather than by infusing culture with a generalized Protestant piety.[11] Woodrow Wilson at Princeton and A. Lawrence Lowell of Harvard were articulate spokesmen for the ideal of liberal culture.

The history of the American university has been the story of the coexistence in one place of these largely incompatible views of education. By the end of the nineteenth century, on any given American university campus one could find enclaves of students, faculty and administrators defining the educational task as public service, or liberal culture, or research. And it became commonplace for university presidents to defend all three ideals, their rhetoric sliding "easily from one of them to another without the speakers being conscious of incongruity."[12] Neither the eclectic combination of three incompatible views nor the ardent defense of any one of them could provide a unifying center for the university. The aim of liberal culture, though on occasion the guiding ideal of strong university presidents, has been confined for the most part to the camp of the humanities and, even with the inclusion of the "liberal arts" in a general requirements curriculum, has scarcely unified undergraduate university education, much less graduate and professional study.[13] The ideal of the university as an institution serving the practical needs of the social order and the diverse classes of society has likewise enjoyed no unifying power. Despite the noblest of aims, the modern American university has been slow in attracting a truly representative diversity of social classes. During the last half of the nineteenth century, neither the state universities nor the land-grant colleges, with their explicit mandates to serve the diverse citizens of their states, lured the greatest number of students from the farming and working-class sectors. Rather, black colleges, teacher training institutions, schools of nursing, and regional denominational colleges attracted many more. Not until after the Second World War did the state universities begin to draw the largest increases

---

[11] Ibid., pp. 204-205.
[12] Ibid., pp. 58, 342.
[13] Vesey's conclusions regarding the limited role of the liberal arts in shaping university education as a whole before 1910 are complemented by studies of the superficial treatment accorded the liberal arts in today's university general requirements. See Vesey, *Emergence of the University*, pp. 215, 233; and Thomas J. DeLoughry, "Study of Transcripts Finds Little Structure in the Liberal Arts," *The Chronicle of Higher Education*, XXXV, No. 19 (Jan. 18, 1989), A1, A32.

in enrollment from the various classes of society.[14] Furthermore, with the establishment of such practical disciplines as sanitary science, domestic science, business administration, physical education, and many types of engineering, the "useful arts" have borne no intrinsic relation to one another nor to the other tasks of the university.[15] The ideal of "pure research," though frequently defended in many parts of the university, has been shattered by the hard realities of the teaching task and budgetary restraints. And with increasing monetary support for research coming from outside the university, the research ideal has merged readily into the notion of utilitarian public service.[16] The ideal of pure research has also failed to unify the entire university community.

If, however, none of the ideals taken singly or together has provided structural or curricular *unity*, one of them in particular has contributed a *pervasive attitude* to the university. That attitude may be described as "scientific," the attitude which has energized the movement of specialization. The outlook sprang from the ideal of pure research during the late nineteenth and early twentieth centuries, but it came to permeate the other ideals as well. The scientific spirit was founded on the convictions that nothing in principle could lie outside the purview of the investigating mind, that reality is best discovered through sustained inquiry, and that sustained inquiry is best accomplished by concentration or specialization. The demand for specialized practical education simply complemented the calls for specialized research, and by the early twentieth century few self-respecting departments, including those in the humanities, would want to be deemed "unscientific" or unspecialized.[17]

The scientific spirit of the American university was an adaptation of a German model of learning. Throughout the period of the emergence of the American university, calls were issued by American educators for the adoption of *Wissenschaft* in all branches of learning. Many of those educators made their pilgrimages to the German universities and returned eager to reform their home institutions. The peak phase for Americans studying in Germany was 1895-96, when over five hundred American students were matriculated at German universities. But glowing reports from the visitors even before that peak period usually urged the American university to conform to the German model. James Morgan Hart, a student at Princeton and later a professor of English and philol-

---

[14] Lawrence A. Cremin, *American Education: The Metropolitan Experience 1876-1980* (New York: Harper & Row, 1988), p. 556.
[15] Vesey, *Emergence of the University*, pp. 113-114.
[16] Ibid., pp. 142, 178.
[17] Ibid., p. 142.

ogy at Cincinnati and Cornell, studied at several German universities in the 1860s and 1870s. Hart's narrative of his German experiences faults the American university for its lack of the German virtues of specialization and *Wissenschaft*.[18] By the time Hart's narrative was published in 1874, however, American universities were rallying behind the scientific spirit.

The peculiarly German form of that spirit was embodied institutionally in Berlin University, which throughout the nineteenth and early twentieth centuries served as the exemplar for other German institutions of higher learning. During the decades preceding the founding of Berlin University in 1810, Kant, Schelling, Fichte, Schleiermacher, and Humboldt had argued that the true university should not be a training school for state officers but should serve essentially as a place for *Wissenschaft*—best translated as "organized learning" or "systematic scholarship." The arts faculty (*philosophische Fakultät*), rather than those of law, medicine, or theology should therefore constitute the heart of the university since they represented the interests of non-utilitarian learning. Berlin and other German universities were aided in attaining these scholarly goals by the state's linking examinations for secondary teachers to the disciplines of the university faculties of philosophy, and by state requirements which made the classical education of the *Gymnasium* the training needed for matriculation at the university. By 1870, the arts faculty achieved the commanding role in the German university system.[19]

In the philosophy of education entailed in this German system, *Wissenschaft* was closely aligned with *Weltanschauung* and *Bildung*. *Wissenschaft*, "systematic scholarship," was to serve the purposes of *Bildung*, "education for cultivation" or the development of the unique individuality of the person engaged in the scholarship. And *Wissenschaft*, if it was to avoid positivism and radical relativism—the very antitheses of "cultivation" —should be informed by *Weltanschauung*, or a personal synthesis of observations and values. For that reason, the highest form of *Wissenschaft* for the German intellectual was not the natural sciences but *Geisteswissenschaften*, or the humanistic disciplines. This view of education was clearly governed by the philosophical presuppositions of German Idealism.[20]

---

[18] "James Morgan Hart Compares the German University and the American College during the 1860s," in Hofstadter and Smith, *American Higher Education*, II, 571, 581.

[19] Fritz K. Ringer, *The Decline of the German Mandarins. The German Academic Community, 1890-1933* (Cambridge: Harvard University Press, 1969), pp. 24-25, 412, 416).

[20] Ringer, *Decline of the Mandarins*, pp. 103, 104-106. Also Fritz K. Ringer, "The German Academic Community," in Oleson and Voss, *The Organization of Knowledge*, pp. 411, 425.

The German view of education was not transplanted roots and all onto American soil. Sometimes the American borrowings seem to have been deliberately selective, at other times misinformed. "Science," the translation of *Wissenschaft*, often came to mean in the American university the very ideas which the German word sought to oppose: empiricism and, eventually, positivism. The notions of "cultivation" and "value system" were limited to the American ideal of liberal culture and had nothing to do with public service or pure research. A university education centered in the arts faculty, although widely discussed as a possibility in this country, never found an institutional footing in an American system of higher education busy trying to accommodate itself to several social and educational ideals. Even specific institutional forms allegedly adopted from the German system took on a distinctively American character. The seminar, which so impressed the Americans who studied in Germany, became, in addition to the German method of reporting on and stimulating research, an American potpourri of book reports, long student papers, and lectures by the professor.[21] And in making the PH.D. the highest degree for certifying specialization, Americans overlooked the fact that the degree was not the highest on a scale of several degrees in Germany and that the German doctorate required demonstration of broad learning.[22]

What then was the air that Americans breathed so deeply in Germany, found so exhilarating, and exhaled so fervently into their distinctive educational environment? It was, above all, the spirit of what they called "science." However they may have mistranslated—and misunderstood—*Wissenschaft*, they found in the German atmosphere of pure research the intoxicating freedom to pursue any subject with openminded curiosity and painstaking discipline. It was, in short, the spirit of the Enlightenment that so captivated American educators. In their own fashion Americans caught the meaning of Kant's challenge: "*Sapere aude*! 'Have courage to use your own reason!'—that is the motto of the enlightenment."[23] The motto was stripped of its Idealist habiliments and wrested from the safety of its "cultivated" home. It connoted *Wissenschaft* without *Weltanschauung*. The spirit of the Enlightenment in American universities would dare to throw off the shackles of religious control and the binding rigidities of the college ideal. And it would dare

---

[21] Vesey, *Emergence of the University*, p. 155.

[22] Higham, "Matrix of Specialization," in Oleson and Voss, *The Organization of Knowledge*, pp. 10-11.

[23] Immanuel Kant, "What Is Enlightenment?," *On History*, ed. Lewis White Beck (Indianapolis: Bobbs-Merrill, 1963), p. 3.

even to abandon any unifying center in its university home as it pursued knowledge in its wide diversity through the disciplined concentrations of specialties.

During the closing years of the nineteenth century, American paeans to the scientific spirit supplied the rhetorical accompaniment to institutional specialization. Latinists called for the importance of the "investigating mind" in studies of the classics; professors of art urged application of the "scientific method" to the interpretation of paintings; the director of athletics at Harvard even announced that he aspired to be a "scientific man" with the gymnasium as his laboratory.[24] When in the early twentieth century the great founders of the American universities began to express reservations about a science empty of human values and a specialization spinning out of control, they were treated by the specialists in most fields as old men devoid of power and without the wisdom of their own vision—that is, they were ignored.[25] And despite the frequent extolling of that "historic compromise"[26]—a broad liberal education at the college level, with specialization at the graduate levels—the American version of "science" was working its ways of specialization on the colleges as well. Little wonder, since those who would teach at the college level would be required to attain a mastery of a specialty and would want to teach that specialty.

Instances of specialization abounded on the American scene. Libraries were transformed from "storehouses" into "workshops" for scholars, with the Dewey decimal classification system and the card catalogue emerging to assist the specialist and to provide a map of the specialized fields. The American publishing industry began to diversify and expand the number of its titles (with a sixfold increase in new titles between 1880 and 1910), and university presses were founded to disseminate scholarly works with limited readerships.[27] The social sciences appeared in the late nineteenth century as fields of study with their own specialized integrity, and in the early twentieth century they were self-consciously dissociating themselves from their heritage of "Christian culture."[28] The humanities, though long the stronghold of the ideal of liberal culture and a small fortress erected against the tides of research

---

[24] Vesey, *Emergence of the University*, pp. 173-174.

[25] Ibid., pp. 255-256.

[26] Higham, "Matrix of Specialization," in Oleson and Voss, *The Organization-Knowledge*, p. 6.

[27] John Y. Cole, "Storehouses and Workshops: American Libraries and the Uses of Knowledge," in Oleson and Voss, *The Organization of Knowledge*, pp. 370-374, 367.

[28] Dorothy Ross, "The Development of the Social Sciences," in Oleson and Voss, *The Organization of Knowledge*, pp. 107, 121.

specialization, were also by the early twentieth century yielding to the specialized demands of the university. Like other curricula in the university, the undergraduate curriculum in the humanities was transformed into departmental units, thus serving notice that the several humanistic disciplines were independent fields of inquiry. The departmental organization of the university, first fully implemented by the University of Chicago toward the end of the nineteenth century, was both a recognition of the value of specialization and an acceptance of the need for specialists to engage in self-governance.[29]

The effects of specialization were widespread. Even those colleges which chose to present an alternative to the forces of academic specialization were not immune. The following data cited by Lawrence Cremin regarding developments at Amherst College, which took a strong stand against indiscriminate specialization and for a unified liberal education, are most revealing:

> The number of liberal arts departments in the universities burgeoned, as did the number of courses; and the same phenomenon could be observed in the colleges, despite regroupings from time to time in the interest of integration. To cite but one example, Amherst College offered 83 trimester courses in the mid-1870s and 203 by the turn of the century, then 112 full-year courses by the mid-1920s, after a decade of effort by President Alexander Meiklejohn and Dean (later President) George Daniel Olds to achieve greater synthesis in the curriculum, and then 353 semester courses by the mid-1950s.[30]

At Amherst and other liberal arts colleges, a specialized faculty was increasingly determining what would be taught, and how often.

The drive toward specialization in the American university made that educational institution the spearhead of the accelerating movement of "professionalism" that swept through the nation after the Civil War. As Burton Bledstein has observed, professionalism grew into a middle-class culture, a means of structuring society according to the values of moving up in a career. "Professionalism emerged as more than an institutional event in American life, more than an outward process by which Americans made life more rational. It was a culture—a set of learned values and habitual responses—by which middle-class individuals shaped their emotional needs and measured their powers of intelligence." And the culture was fiercely democratic in principle, appearing to offer every social group the ladder of upward mobility provided by

---

[29] Laurence Vesey, "The Plural Organized Worlds of the Humanities" and Hugh Hawkins, "University Identity: the Teaching and Research Functions," in Oleson and Voss, *The Organization of Knowledge*, pp. 64, 293-294.

[30] Cremin, *American Education*, pp. 562-563.

the specialization of career.³¹ It was only after the Second World War that the careers Americans deemed "professional" would proliferate beyond count, resulting in such title inflation as "sanitation engineer," "tree surgeon," and "financial planner." The course had already been set in the late nineteenth century, however, as the careers of teaching, military service, engineering, dentistry, pharmacy, veterinary medicine, and accountancy were added by surveys to the traditional professions of theology, law, and medicine.³² And during that same period there occurred radically specialized differentiation within the professions, betokened by the formation of numerous professional societies devoted to sub-specialties.³³

For our purposes, special note must be taken of several consequences of the culture of professionalism in America. First, the university as the seat of higher learning has been the logical place to provide training in the specialized knowledge and practices required of many of the emergent professions—at the undergraduate level, but most especially at the graduate professional schools. For all of the frequently noted conflicts between the "practical" and the "theoretical" demands of professional education—as well as the tensions among the students, the faculty, the professions, and the society in defining the goals of professional education³⁴—few American educators or professionals have been willing to suggest that universities should unshoulder the burden of professional education altogether. The ideals of public service and of research, infused by the value of expanding specialized knowledge, have made the American university the willing locus for professional education. Second, since the founding of the American universities, the status of the various professions has changed. Measured by the criteria of endowments and entrance requirements for professional schools, divinity schools far surpassed law schools and medical schools in status into the 1890s. But measured by the criteria of distribution of college graduates, size of enrollments in professional schools, and income levels for careers, trends in the late nineteenth century were already carrying law, medicine and business into their twentieth-century status of far surpassing that of divinity.³⁵ Finally, professional specialization has transformed the iden-

---

³¹ Burton J. Bledstein, *The Culture of Professionalism. The Middle Class and the Development of Higher Education in America*. (New York: W. W. Norton & Co., 1976), pp. x, 38.
³² Bruce A. Kimball, "Review Essay: *Law School* by Robert Stevens and *Learning to Heal* by Kenneth Ludmerer," *Journal of Higher Education*, 59, No. 4 (1988), 458.
³³ Bledstein, *Culture of Professionalism*, p. 86.
³⁴ See, for example, Derek Bok, *Higher Learning* (Cambridge: Harvard University Press, 1986), pp. 73-113.
³⁵ Kimball, "Review Essay," p. 459; Bledstein, *Culture of Professionalism*, p. 198.

tities and tasks of the older professions. The virtual disappearance of the general practitioner in medicine is frequently cited as an example of such a change. But the effects are equally apparent in other vocations that have come to require in one person an impossibly wide assortment of specialized skills and bodies of knowledge. The university or college president, for example, who once could converse intelligently with most of his faculty concerning their areas of expertise, and who could keep tabs on most dimensions of his small corporation, by the close of the nineteenth century was faced with the gargantuan task of running and funding a complex organization and was unable to provide educational leadership for diverse specialized fields that no one person could possibly comprehend.[36] Demands upon the clergy as a profession have been similar. Clergy are expected to perform the specialized roles of administration, preaching, counseling, teaching, and organization, with administration, an activity that they are least trained to carry out, requiring the greatest proportion of their time and energy.[37] The culture of professionalism has not only rendered some generalists obsolete; it has laid on others the unrealistic expectation that several specialties can be stirred smoothly into one large mix.

Internal to the university itself, professionalism has meant the increasing division of labor according to specialty. Structurally, the university became a massive bureaucracy with its managers, middle-managers and clerks, with special expertise in practical knowledge required at every level of administration. Politically, the university became a loose collection of fiefdoms, with power distributed (in varying proportions, depending on the university) among the president, vice-presidents, trustees, schools, and departments. Intellectually, the university became an even looser assemblage of schools and departments, which in turn housed the various disciplines and sub-disciplines representing the diverse fields of specialization. And those disciplines and sub-disciplines have looked increasingly to the burgeoning professional societies for their standards of scholarship and modes of professional certification. From the outset, the American "university," through the complementary movements of specialization and professionalization, was launched in the direction of Clark Kerr's "multiversity," "not one community but

---

[36] Vesey, *Emergence of the University*, pp. 311, 360; Bok, *Higher Learning*, 194-195.
[37] James M. Gustafson, "The Clergy in the United States," in *The Professions in America*, ed. Kenneth S. Lynn (Boston: Houghton Mifflin, 1965), p. 74.

several," not an organism but a mechanism with "a series of processes producing a series of results."[38]

But has anything held this mechanism together? Are we reduced finally to Robert Hutchins' definition of the university as separate schools and departments held together by a central heating system? Or to Clark Kerr's hunch that what holds it all together is a common grievance over parking? Or to Laurence Vesey's only slightly less cynical observation that the only thing that could unite "boys who still played with marbles, men who hid in libraries, and worldly executives" was a "bureaucratic administration" that had no "recourse to specific shared values"?[39] My suggestion is that something *has* pervaded the modern American university—not as an animating principle, to be sure, for the American university is not organic. And not as a centering ideal, certainly, for the American university has always lacked a center and has stood for several incompatible ideals. But the university in its academic tasks, at least, has been driven by the forces of specialization and professionalization and by the Enlightenment value of "daring to know" in all imaginable fields of learning. The paradox which is the modern university is that it is an institution which "holds together," continues to exist, in large measure by its decentering motion springing from the Enlightenment perspective.

II. Boundaries and Frontiers for the Study of Religion

The patterns of specialization and professionalization have left lasting marks on the American university, and there is no evidence that those patterns are disappearing. They continue as unabated forces in American higher education. To be sure, budgetary constraints, joined with administrative fiat, have a way of periodically curtailing or terminating specialized schools, departments, and programs in an increasingly "market driven" educational environment. But the university's resistance to some specialties has scarcely entailed its deterrence of the growth of specialization or professionalized training as such. The study of religion enjoys a much wider and deeper heritage than that bequeathed by the age of the university and its forces of specialization and professionalization. Still, that heritage sets many of the limits and opens many of the prospects for the study of religion in the foreseeable future.

---

[38] Clark Kerr, *The Uses of the University* (Cambridge: Harvard University Press, 1963), pp. 18-20.

[39] Kerr, *Uses of University*, p. 20; Vesey, *Emergence of the University*, pp. 311, 332.

Schools, programs, and departments of religion, and those university-based theological schools that have developed in concert with their larger educational settings, share a common legacy and face a common future by virtue of their lives in the age of the American university. One need not overlook important differences in educational aim and community accountability between university departments of religion and university divinity schools to appreciate that commonality of heritage and future. The education of a citizenry in the roles of religion in its own and in other cultures on the one hand, and the education of a professional ministry in the literature and tasks appropriate to the life of the church on the other, are aims which may overlap at significant points, but they are different. Responsibility to students and citizens of diverse religious preference on the one hand, and responsibility to a church with a specific religious commitment on the other, although not always mutually exclusive, result in different priorities of accountability. For all of these differences, however, religious studies and theological studies in the modern university encounter many of the same boundaries and frontiers in their educational tasks. Those limits and opportunities are obscured by the too-simple distinction between the "non-partisan study of religion" in religious studies and the "advocacy of a religious position" in theological studies. In the terms employed by Joseph Kitagawa in his Introduction to this book, both the "autobiographical" and the "biographical" approaches to religion are equally available to the two enterprises and are quite in keeping with the mission of the modern American university. And the forces of specialization and professionalization, which have shaped that university, have created boundaries equally binding on theological schools and schools and departments of religion.

First of all, it is important to recognize that the study of religion is hampered in finding its appropriate place in the university if it appeals to a better time, if it invokes the "college ideal" or an "ideal of cultured (or civilized) study." The old pre-Civil War college ideal was decisively laid to rest by the American university—and just as well. The college was controlled by sectarian or cultural-Protestant religious interests, limited in its mission to the cultivated gentleman (and later, gentlewoman), and predicated on the conviction that learning occurs through linguistic exercise and the imbibing of discrete units of truth. Only those scholars determined to escape from the modern world of religious pluralism, new frontiers of knowledge, and equality of opportunity could yearn for a return to the college ideal. More tempting—perhaps because a part of the modern university story—is the invocation of the ideal of liberal culture. At a time when professors can assume on the part of students little or no familiarity with basic texts of religion —or with any text, for that matter—it would seem advisable to return to those days of requiring every educated, civilized person to have mastered the fundamental texts constitutive of our culture. The problem with such an outlook is that it was never a requirement of the American university. However much the lower schools, the churches, or university humanities departments may have inculcated a love of and familiarity with certain texts, mastery of those texts has never defined the university-educated person. The ideal of culture, as one of several ideals for the university, has never provided an effective center for university education. Furthermore, university humanists, at one time the most ardent defenders of the ideal, quickly during the age of the university abandoned the basis for any agreement on what the fundamental texts might be as they turned to their specialties and sub-disciplines and to their diverse texts and methods of interpretation. None of this is to gainsay the glaring need today for cultural—and religious—literacy, or the contribution that the academic study of religion might make to that literacy. But it is to insist that if students of religion join those who call for the university to return to a time when it was founded on a fixed canon of texts, they are displaying the classic feature of the jeremiad: the measuring of the present by a past that exists only in the imagination of the present.

The history of the American university has produced another, closely related boundary. The university has shown a stubborn structural resistance to any form of disciplinary or intellectual imperialism. At any given time on any given campus, one of the three views of the nature of the university can prevail in the aims of a president, in monies allocated for programs, in power blocks of faculty, in student demands. Yet for all of the shifts in emphasis that such circumstances occasion, the university has retained its pluralism of purpose. Neither the purpose of liberal culture nor the aim of public service nor the ideal of research has managed to gain the exclusive center. The decentering forces of specialization and professionalization have produced in the university one of the nation's most pluralist of institutions in aim. That fact should serve as notice to those who would hope for too much from the university—for its radical restructuring along the lines of "interdisciplinary studies," for example, or the widespread infusion of "values in higher education"—reforms which would seem to have immense appeal to those in religious or theological studies.

In addition to presenting the study of religion with some firm boundaries, the age of the university has opened for the field some of its most exciting frontiers. Above all, the Enlightenment spirit of the university, the spirit which is the *sine qua non* of specialized learning, has amounted to nothing less than the liberation of the study of religion—liberation from special pleading for religious doctrine, from the religious and cultural dictates of church or society, from the need to measure all religions according to our own preferred sacred texts. The university has provided the open frontier for the ongoing pursuit of understanding religion in its wide diversity of belief and behavior. Kant's maxim, "Dare to know," is so often taken for granted by the contemporary scholar of religion that it is easy to ignore how many intellectual battles historically have been required for its defense or how the modern American university has provided the weapons for its protection. The founders of the American university, dedicated to building an educational institution free from the control of denominational or sectarian interests; the assemblage of university scholars, committed to concentrated study in diverse fields of knowledge; the emergence of academic professional societies, designed to establish and maintain scholarly standards[40]—all created the environment for the liberation of religious and theological studies. As Jonathan Z. Smith has said, with its entrance into the academy, "religion was brought within the realm of common sense, of civil discourse and commerce. Rediscovering the old tag, 'Nothing human is foreign to me,' the Enlightenment impulse was one of tolerance and, as a necessary concomitant, one which refused to leave any human datum, including religion, beyond the pale of understanding, beyond the realm of reason."[41]

Religious and theological studies scarcely have been immune from the suspicions, even the opposition, of their "cultured despisers" in the university. If the free pursuit of knowledge has created the institutional possibility for the academic study of religion, it has also—through

---

[40] Frequent mention is made in the literature on academic professional societies of how the American Philological Association (1869) was the first such society of note on the American scene, the emphasis on philology springing from the German influence on the study of the classics. The early founding of the Society of Biblical Literature and Exegesis (1880), representing an approach equally owing to German notions of *Wissenschaft*, is hardly ever mentioned or is passed over as "religiously oriented." See Vesey, "The Plural Organized Worlds of the Humanities," in Oleson and Voss, *The Organization of Knowledge*, p. 73. The SBL, however, has had a distinguished history of setting standards of scholarship over against the churches which have repeatedly attacked professors of the bible. For a brief history of the SBL see Ernest W. Saunders, *Searching the Scriptures: A History of the Society of Biblical Literature, 1880-1980* (Chico, CA: Scholars Press, 1982).

[41] Jonathan Z. Smith, *Imagining Religion: From Babylon to Jonestown* (Chicago: University of Chicago Press, 1982), p. 104.

departmentalization, narrow specialization, and a glossolalia of academic jargon—created a balkanization of the university community. Small wonder that one cognitive ghetto is suspicious of another, a circumstance exacerbated for the academic study of religion by the widespread assumption in the United States that religion is best viewed as a matter of private opinion. Edward Farley has properly warned against idealizing the university, for that institution has revealed a tendency to ignore the nature of the knowledge to which it is allegedly committed. The university has subjected the Enlightenment courage-to-know to the corrupting assumption that knowledge is a "precious possession" rather than a "responsive activity," that it is "a stamp of a timeless content on the mind" rather than "an ongoing individual and social struggle."[42] In short, the university has not only opened the frontiers of knowledge, including knowledge of religion; it has also, in its compartmentalization of knowledge, created the means for the premature closing of those frontiers.

The consequences of sealing domains of knowledge off from one another through specialization is captured with biting irony by Wayne Booth:

> I ask you who are professors whether we do not have overwhelming daily proof that no one of us can understand more than a fraction of the frontline work of the rest. We are simply shut out of almost all front parlors but our own, permitted only to do a little polite begging at the back door: "Please, sir, give a poor beggar just a slice of nuclear physics to keep me warm, just a tiny portion of paleontology to keep up my illusion of keeping up, just a touch of cosmology—the new anthropic principle, say—to help me survive the next cocktail party[43]

Booth does not exaggerate the university situation of fragmented knowledge or the silliness of some of our attempts to "keep up" with other specialties. But he does hold out the hope that, if recognized and employed, there exist within the university modes of communication and judgment which can reach their lines to the several disciplines.[44] Similarly, I believe that religious and theological studies enjoy within their university settings some modest but notable opportunities for overcoming the most constricted and solipsistic features of specialization and professionalization.

---

[42] Edward Farley, *The Fragility of Knowledge: Theological Education in the Church and the University* (Philadelphia: Fortress Press, 1988), p. 3.

[43] Wayne C. Booth, "The Idea of a University as Seen by a Rhetorician," *The University of Chicago Record*, 23, No. 1 (1988), 2.

[44] Ibid., pp. 4-5.

First of all, rigorous adherence to the Enlightenment principle that nothing human is beyond the pale of understanding not only liberates the scholar from the control of all religious and cultural dogma, it also liberates the field from closed boundaries of knowledge. No religious phenomenon—however traditional or untraditional, familiar or unfamiliar, domestic or foreign—need in principle be excluded from scholarly scrutiny. The only real alternative to this Enlightenment "arrogance of the understanding" is the "arrogance of ignorance" or the disdainful refusal to treat seriously human religiousness in its wide diversity. This pluralist impetus of the Enlightenment principle is not quite captured by today's buzzword "globalization"—which hints too much of a *reaction* to the loss of Western Christianity's and Western culture's world dominance and which contains the ghost of the old, pious dream of "one worldism." The opening of the field for study by the Enlightenment principle is radically pluralist in scholarly *intent*, and not just in its response to a changing political climate. Neither geography nor culture nor race nor sexuality nor time nor doctrine nor behavior shall exclude religion from careful inspection. Such principled academic pluralism is nothing short of what Ruel Tyson, citing the philosopher Vincent Descombes, has called the "decolonization of the mind."[45]

Mental decolonization can lead to even narrower forms of specialization—or it can lead to greater breadth of knowledge. The huge wash of data that is human religiousness invites its damming into small, shallow pools of information easily navigated by specialists expert only in those puddles of knowledge. In the study of religion, we are often reduced to begging our sub-disciplines for cups of information on the Ghost Dance, the cargo cults, or the Wesleyan holiness movement to keep up the illusion of keeping up—or to make it through the next class! Not simply fields, but sub-fields also become ghettoized. Yet sensitivity to the pluralism of religious phenomena can lead, and has led, to *acts of interpretation* that draw the interpreter into the connections between fields and between sub-fields of knowledge. In short, data beg for theories. As William S. Green has put it, "Without theory, we are victims of our data and can barely describe the materials we gather from the archive or the field, much less discern their decisive variables and causal interrelations, or generalize from and about them."[46]

---

[45] Ruel W. Tyson, Jr., "'Live by Comparisons': A New Home for Reason in the University?" The Sixth Annual Memorial Lecture of the Society for Values in Higher Education, 1988, p. 10.

[46] William Scott Green, "Something Strange, Yet Nothing New: Religion in the Secular Curriculum," in *Soundings: An Interdisciplinary Journal*, LXXI, No. 2-3 (1988), 277.

If theories of religion are to be adequately general, theorists must be willing to employ methods and information deriving from the work of diverse scholars inside and outside the field of religion.[47] And if they are to avoid abstraction to a level where they cease to represent the lived experiences of religious people, theories of religion must preserve the particularity, the concrete otherness, of the phenomena studied.[48] The combination of theoretical "reduction" and particularist "otherness," of abstraction and concretion, is attained in the construction of those paradigms of interpretation that draw discriminately but widely from the other disciplines and sub-disciplines while keeping a clear focus upon the concrete phenomenon under examination. The *aim* of such models is to render the unintelligible intelligible, the discrete exemplary, and the general concrete. The *assumption* lying behind the models is the value of communication across disciplinary lines and collaboration among scholars in various fields.

Some of the natural sciences, most conspicuously biochemistry and biophysics, have adopted the aim and assumption of model-building.[49] Something similar is happening in the humanities and the social sciences. There is widening recognition that in our attempt to understand human belief and behavior the rigid disciplinary divisions simply do not obtain. In the words of Clifford Geertz, interpretation in the humanities and the social sciences is leading to "blurred genres." Scientific reports are looking like belles lettres, philosophical investigations like literary criticism, anthropological treatises like travelogues—evident in the work of persons like Loren Eiseley, Stanley Cavell, and Claude Levi-Strauss. Geertz sees in this blurring of disciplinary boundaries a need for neither an "interdisciplinary brotherhood" nor a "highbrow eclecticism." The need, rather, is the recognition of how the "lines grouping scholars together" can run "at some highly eccentric angles."[50] And those eccentric angles are often marks of the effort to discover those models of

---

[47] See Smith, *Imagining Religion*, p. 19.
[48] See Green, "Something Strange, Yet Nothing New," p. 277.
[49] I disagree with Edward Farley's claim that "narrow empiricism" currently dominates the physical and engineering sciences and, by imitation, has come to represent the approaches of the social sciences and the humanities. Farley, *Fragility of Knowledge*, pp. 40-43. If anything, the model-building in the physical and engineering sciences is dominated by mathematics, and that is increasingly the case in some of the social sciences as well—e.g., in economics. As I indicate in my following paragraphs, however, many of the humanities and social sciences are moving in interpretive directions which certainly could not be characterized as either empirical or mathematical.
[50] Clifford Geertz, *Local Knowledge: Further Essays in Interpretive Anthropology* (New York: Basic Books, 1983), pp. 19-20, 23-24.

understanding which will simultaneously make sense of, and preserve the otherness of, human beliefs and practices.

The opportunity for religious and theological study created by this situation of blurred genres is some intrepid poaching among the disciplines and subdisciplines inside and outside the field—not in order to gather bits of information, but to construct those theories of religion that simultaneously lift a human phenomenon to the level of intelligibility and preserve its vital concreteness.[51] Within the larger university context, the consequences of the pursuit of this opportunity are modest. There is no evidence that the blurring of the lines between disciplines constitutes, or can constitute, a unifying structural force within the university. Rather, it is as if in flying off in their own directions some of the specialties have collided and formed intellectual alliances. Scholars of religion may cross disciplinary boundaries and join scholars from other fields in their ventures, but the university maintains its stubborn refusal to be governed by any one ideal, and it continues to organize itself into departments and schools.[52] One should not hope for too much from an institution formed by a long history of the forces of specialization and professionalization and the well-ensconced interest groups those forces have created. But one can delight in the fact that the institution affords opportunities in research and teaching for crossing narrow disciplinary lines.

Finally, in its provision of those opportunities the university has created the space for acts of interpreting religion that transcend the distinctions between advocacy and objectivity, indoctrination and description. It may well be true, as Edward Farley claims, that on the one hand the university has been suspicious of the objectivity of the study of religion and, on the other, has been hospitable to advocacy in other fields.[53] Neither pole, however, defines the university-provided occasions for headlong plunges into interpretation of religion when the interpreter is required to manifest the deepest empathy for and the most careful dis-

---

[51] Any number of studies of religion which have undertaken this course could be cited, but two which strike me as particularly imaginative and which deal with the same familiar/strange phenomenon in my own specialty of American religion—Jim Jones and the Peoples Temple—are those by Jonathan Z. Smith, *Imagining Religion*, pp. 102-120 and David Chidester, *Salvation and Suicide: An Interpretation of Jim Jones, The Peoples Temple, and Jonestown* (Bloomington and Indianapolis: Indiana University Press, 1988).

[52] For a report on one failed attempt to reorganize a graduate program along lines other than departments within the humanities and the social sciences see Jonathan Z. Smith, "'Religion' and 'Religious Studies': No Difference at All," in *Soundings*, LXXI, No. 2-3 (1988), pp. 241-242.

[53] Farley, *Fragility of Knowledge*, pp. 71, 78.

tance from a subject. Whether it be in the study of a doctrine, a founding figure, an event, a text, or a ritual, the scholar equally committed to illumination of the particular and explanation through the general cannot fail to take the attitudes both of empathetic participation and of critical distance. In this twofoldness of attitude, the scholar of religion simply manifests what Philip Rieff has deemed the mark of any good university teacher: a kind of "dancing distance" from the subject matter.[54] Too close, and we commit the act of ideology on the dancefloor. Too far, and we lose the rhythms of our partner. The environment of the American university can doubtless be faulted for many problems besetting the academic study of religion, but the unfortunate choice between positivism and indoctrination is not one of them.

The Hopkins graduate student who in the late nineteenth century celebrated the powerful force of specialization in the American university need not be joined in his youthful enthusiasm in order to be congratulated for his wise foresight. Religious and theological studies that have found their home in the university have been subjected to the disciplining limits and the liberating outlets of the homelife. In its failure to attain a unifying vision for education, the university provided no field a sense of centered security. But in its disencumbering higher education of sectarian interests and its replacement of the rigidities of the old college ideal, the university freed students of religion to dare to know. In its organization of knowledge into fields and sub-fields and in its compartmentalization of learning, the university cut off communications between fields and rendered impossible one person's acquaintance with the full intellectual life of the institution. But in its unrestricted endorsement of "science" and its encouragement of acts of interpretation, the university created opportunities for the crossing of disciplinary boundaries. One could imagine worse limits and less exciting frontiers.

---

[54] Philip Rieff, *Fellow Teachers: Of Culture and Its Second Death* (Chicago: University of Chicago Press, 1973), p. 5.

A Common Ancestor:
Theology and Religious Studies
CHARLES H. LONG

I. Cultural Protestantism as Presupposition for
the Theological Enterprise

In the strict sense of the word, theology may be understood as a discourse and study within a narrowly limited context. Such a context would be restricted to the doctrines, teachings, liturgical practices, and historical formulations of a particular religious tradition. The aims of theology within this context are to clarify, enhance, and extend through serious thought, reflection, and practice the meaning and the ministry of the specific religious tradition.

Theology as understood in this discussion is not limited to this more restricted definition. We are not ruling out theological understanding or tradition, nor are we defining ourselves over against it. Rather, we are attempting to come to terms with a wider discourse about the nature and meaning of theological traditions in the United States, both in their implicit and explicit formulations. One of the most effective strategies for beginning this discussion is to focus on the university-related theology and divinity schools. Schools of this kind have been more aware of the meaning of their institutions as aspects 1) of a broader meaning of American culture in general and 2) of a certain form of American Christianity in particular.

The student bodies of such schools, more often than not, come from a variety of American religious traditions. This is equally true of their faculties. Thus, the organization of these schools on both the administrative and curricular levels expresses another meaning of theology. The other important element in such schools is their location in university communities as part of the regular structures of the university. Therefore, the structures of the university have a profound effect upon their life and thought. This situation has been accepted as a resource. Such universities live with the extra apologetic issue concerning the role of theology as a form of intellectual activity within the university.

For the most part, the study of religion within the context of university-related theological and divinity schools is a product of the American Protestant Christian Tradition. Beyond the fact that such schools tended to be Protestant themselves, it is equally important to note that the universities of which they are a part are also heirs to Protestant traditions, having originally been organized to train a learned clergy and to present a Protestant view of the organization of knowledge that would lead to a proper understanding and practice of the moral and ethical life. The general assumption of the theology and divinity schools in particular and the universities in general was that America was a Protestant nation.

Max Weber's classic, *The Protestant Ethic and the Spirit of Capitalism* [1] gives an initial definition of this meaning and the curricular structure that emphasized the beginnings of American religion with the New England Puritans as an unquestioned assumption. Paul Tillich's essays published in 1948, *The Protestant Era*,[2] foreshadow the present discussion. Since Weber put forth his thesis regarding the almost necessary relationship of Protestantism to capital formation in the modern period, it has not ceased to evoke discussion both pro and con. The very fact that it still evokes lively debate does not mean that the thesis is correct in all of its parts. The issue under discussion is not simply the origin of an economic theory, but the interrelationship of a theory of *praxis* (economics and culture) to a definition and justification of the human that was formative for the United States of America.

One of the most trenchant and effective critiques of Weber was that of Benjamin Nelson in his *The Idea of Usury, From Tribal Brotherhood to Universal Otherhood*.[3] The emphasis in Nelson's work is the relationship between the notion of usury and community. One cannot exact usury from those in one's community. The early Christian view was that the revelation of God in Jesus Christ made all humans actually or potentially

---

[1] New York: Scribner's Sons, trans. by Talcott Parsons, 1958.
[2] Chicago: University of Chicago Press, trans. by James Luther Adams, 1948.
[3] Chicago: University of Chicago Press, 1969.

a part of the same community; therefore, usury should not be practiced at all. This was affirmed in the subsequent history of Christian theology, though not in practice. With the Reformation and especially in Calvinism the doctrine and practice of universal usury is affirmed. The theological and practical question—"who is my sister and my brother and what is my community?"— becomes a central issue in the religious formation of the United States, a nation composed of a wide variety of religious, ethnic, and national groups. The triumph of Protestantism in the United States and its influence in the creation of an American ethos expressed the apologetic and ameliorative stylistics of this problematic. For the most part universities that had their origin within the Protestant tradition sooner or later became open to persons from all religious traditions. Their theology and divinity schools followed suit.

The Protestant principle as a mode of the American national character was conducive to the founding principles of the Republic and, while not perfect, helped to institutionalize a meaning of liberalism within the culture at-large. In Paul Tillich's *The Protestant Era*, there is a chapter entitled, "The End of the Protestant Era?" in which we find:

> Protestantism now faces the most difficult struggle of all the occidental religions and denominations in the present world situation. It arose with that era which today is either coming to an end or else undergoing fundamental structural changes. Therefore, the question as to whether Protestantism can face the present situation in a manner enabling it to survive the present historical period is unavoidable. It is true, of course, that all religions are threatened today by secularism and paganism. But this threat, at least as far as pure secularism is concerned, has perhaps reached its culminating point. The insecurity which is increasingly felt by nations and individuals, the expectations of catastrophes in all civilized countries, the vanishing belief in progress—all have aroused a new searching for a transcendent security and perfection.[4]

Paul Tillich's *Protestant Era* first appeared in English translation in 1948. Its appearance almost immediately after the end of World War II and just before the 1950s is significant. By this time Tillich had become a major force on the American theological scene and held a chair in Christian theology at Union Theological Seminary in New York. It was during the 1950s that the university-related theological school was in the midst of sweeping changes in both institutional organization and intellectual orientation.

---

[4] Tillich, op.cit, p.222.

The Federated Theological Faculty in Chicago came into being during this period, as did the Interdenominational Theological Consortium in Atlanta and the Fund for Theological Education, a national foundation for the promotion of theological education. On the intellectual level, theological curricula followed what has come to be called a "theology of culture," following Tillich's method of correlation which stated that culture poses the questions and issues to which theology then responds.

"Theology of culture" expressed a critical and apologetic meaning for the theological enterprise. In other words, in a rather mild, yet critical sense, the unquestioned acceptance of the dominance of the Protestant ethos was placed under scrutiny. This critical scrutiny included the recognition of other religious traditions on the American scene than those of the Protestant liberal traditions, but for the most part it was a recognition that the cultural and religious assumptions of the Protestant era were either lost or had become hidden and obscured in the general culture. It was during this period that "religion and ..." courses and areas appeared in the theological curriculum. Areas and courses such as "religion and literature," and "religion and personality," made their appearance in the curriculum. In other words, the essential meanings of the Protestant traditions now were deciphered from their obscurity using appropriate methodologies acquired from theological and non-theological disciplines. Graduate students in "religion and literature" at Chicago were required to take courses in the English Department of the University almost to the equivalent of the A.M. degree.

A critical stance was taken *vis-à-vis* those Protestant traditions that assumed that this deciphering process was unnecessary and that the Protestant orientation could be regained through a disciplined theological will and assertion. Given the university context for the "theology of culture," the university context became a necessary meaning of the theological enterprise and thus was intensified. The study of theology in alliance with the non-theological disciplines of the university meant that theology was becoming a "secular" discipline, albeit under Protestant auspices.

II. Conjunctions and Disjunctions:
Residues and Returns

The dire warnings and descriptive pronouncements that Tillich had set forth as a result of the end of the Protestant era were received in the form of a challenge. The actualities of the realities to which he referred did not express an existential meaning in the culture at large. During the

the 1950s and early 1960s a genuine mood of robust creative activity characterized the theological and divinity schools related to universities. This period covered the 1954 Supreme Court decision outlawing segregation, the discovery of the Dead Sea Scrolls, the first Roman Catholic president of the United States, and Vatican II. From this perspective, the end of the Protestant era seemed to have the possibility of ushering in new culture- creating elements within American culture, thus opening the theological enterprise to newer and wider dimensions.

The Protestant principle which is the basis for the critical attitude and mood of Protestantism is, from Tillich's perspective, based upon the Protestant doctrine of justification by faith alone which implies that no individual or human group can claim divine dignity for its moral achievement, sacramental power, sanctity, or doctrine. This principle, allied with the Enlightenment traditions of modern Western culture, made for an easy amalgam with the Protestant secular universities. The tension between Protestant theological schools in the university and the university disciplines was lessened because of this fact. Robert Bellah's programmatic essay on "civil religion" which appeared in 1967 seemed to underscore what was happening in universities and their theological schools as a general discernment of America as a religious culture.[5] The end of the Protestant era in the United States signalled the beginnings of a theological renaissance.

There were, however, other realities, shadows, and specters contained within and surrounding the events and meanings of the 1950s and the early 1960s. It was in the early years of the 1960s that the term 'WASP', first coined by sociologists, appeared. As an acronym for White-Anglo-Saxon-Protestant, it appeared as a recognition and critique of the normativity and naturalness of Protestantism as the American cultural reality. Given the end of the Protestant era, there was the discovery that the Protestant reality was not necessarily the will of God but a construction like all other human realities. The decision actively to engage in the war in Viet Nam was made about this time. The Civil Rights movement began to take on power and become a threat to the Protestant cultural establishment. The specificity and uniqueness of the Roman Catholic tradition of Christian Faith as a distinct form of American religiosity was inspiring an American theological discourse about its traditions. The Jewish tradition, in light of the formation of the state of Israel, was becoming more self-conscious regarding its relationship with Christianity under the old rubric of Judeo-Christian faith.

---

[5] Robert Bellah, "Civil Religion in America," *Daedalus*, (Winter, 1967), pp. 1-21.

All of these developments were not directly related to the end of the Protestant era. However, with the end of the Protestant era, the attempt to make sense of them became more difficult. Even more, the very occurrence of these events and their discourses threatened the meaning of the Protestant principle as it was allied with and amalgamated within the university traditions of Enlightenment reason.

In the midst of these congeries of meanings and events, a religious professional society, the National Association of Biblical Instructors (NABI, an organization that had its beginnings in 1909) met in 1963. After assessing its history and goals, it decided to change its name and form.[6] The Self Study Committee of the National Association of Biblical Instructors proposed a change of name to the American Academy of Religion. It is interesting to note that NABI was the only national professional organization of teachers of religion at the time, though there were many regional and local "theological societies."

In 1963, the Self Study Committee assessed the history of the Association as the basis for change and renewal. They summarized the original intentions for the creation of NABI in terms of four goals: 1) to encourage members to share the results of their scholarly work; 2) to establish professional standards in teaching and study; 3) to increase the spirit of fellowship among themselves and to promote the practical development of the religious life of their students; and, 4) to promote publication of important papers and reviews of literature relevant to their fields of study. The Committee acknowledged that for the first twenty-five years of the existence of NABI the goals had matched the intention of the founders, but that over the last thirty years, with the increase in membership and the growth of regional societies, NABI was now composed of a large membership expressing a wide variety of concerns. Thus, effective operation could no longer be construed under the original intentions of the founders. This led them to a reconsideration of the name, form, and function of the organization.

The name, National Association of Biblical Instructors, implied that the organization was limited to those whose special field of competence was Biblical Studies. The designation, "Instructors," implied that the organization was limited to those who held this junior academic rank in the academy, and "National," seemed to limit membership to those in the United States. The Committee proposed a new name, "American

---

[6] See my article, "The Bible and the Study of Religion in America," in *Justice and the Holy: Essays in Honor of Walter Harrelson*, edited by Douglas A. Knight and Peter Paris, (Atlanta: Scholars Press, 1989).

Academy of Religion;" *American*, to include scholars in Canada and Mexico; *Academy*, to suggest a society of learned persons united in the advance of an art or science; and *Religion*, because the Committee agreed that it had a wider set of possible applications to the various concerns of its membership than any other term. In this new proposal, NABI seemed to be moving from a certain clarity about the study and teaching of religion that was defined by the book, *Bible*, to a less clear and more ambiguous discourse about *religion*.

In these changes, the National Association of Biblical Instructors was confronting in an institutional manner the "end of the Protestant era," but in a characteristic Protestant manner. Instead of asking more fundamental questions regarding the nature of the phenomenon of religion in the life of humankind, the study of religion under the aegis of the change led to more apologetic and liberal approaches to the meaning and adaptation of religion to the American scene. The "interdisciplinary" approaches to religion led to various interpretations and meanings of religion that can be characterized as the "religion and..." orientation to the study of religion. Studies of this kind seemed to suit both the university religion faculties—for they involved their colleagues in other disciplines of the human sciences—as well as the church congregations served by the students of university-related theological schools by offering a sophisticated and therapeutic meaning of religion. In a paradoxical manner, the theology of Tillich and his assertion of the end of the Protestant era proved to be the harbinger of a creative theological renaissance for university-related theological schools.

The apologetic and secularizing tendencies that came into being with the Protestant renaissance in the theological schools of the 1950s and 1960s did not reflect the inability of Protestantism, at least in the form of its liberal university divinity schools, to serve as the "container" of the American cultural reality. The Protestant discourse could no longer serve as the proper arena for discussion of these realities. Robert Bellah's article, "Civil Religion in America," represents the attempt to bring about a new discourse for the understanding of American cultural religion. This essay is reminiscent of Sidney Mead's earlier essay on the "Religion of the Republic." These programmatic essays seem to move the problem of the meaning of American religion from the churches to the public arena expressed by and through the founding documents of the Republic and the rhetorical and ritualistic language of American presidents. While this was a significant move in the discussion of religion in the United States, it still did not touch many cultural and historical aspects of the meaning of religion in America. Though its appeal was to "secular" documents and pronouncements, it failed to touch upon the difference and alterity of many religions and aspects of religious life that had not been promulgated by Protestantism in either its religious or secular forms.

This new discourse about religion in America did enable scholars to acknowledge the plurality of religious groups within the country, e.g., Jewish, Roman Catholic, and even some Eastern religions, and Islam. The discussion about religion was extended, and some cultural legitimacy was given to these religions as authentic expressions of the religious life. In spite of this, the normative discourse about religion tended to stay within the framework of a Jewish-Christian-Enlightenment meaning of its fundamental nature. In a word, this new descriptive meaning of religion was at the same time programmatic in that it limited in a new way the possible meanings of religion on the American scene.

The organization of the American Academy of Religion presented a similar dilemma. Precisely at a moment when it was possible to raise the issue of meaning and the fundamental nature of religion from a scholarly point of view, the American Academy of Religion, in taking over from its predecessor, the National Association of Biblical Instructors, stayed within the limited arenas already defined by religious and secular Protestantism. When the change was made from NABI, very few of those involved in making the transition knew anything of the scholarly study of religion that had been inaugurated in the early part of this century by Professor Morris Jastrow, Jr.[7] This was the tradition of *Religionswissenschaft*. While this orientation might not have solved the American dilemma of the study of religion, it would have placed its problem and meaning within a wider historical and comparative context.

But there were genuine cultural reasons for the decision made at the formation of the American Academy of Religion. Its constituency was the many university divinity schools and free-standing seminaries, most of them confronting the issues of American and world culture from a Protestant orientation.

III. Pluralism, Protestantism, and Religion

Pluralism is the term most often used to define the religious scene in American culture today. This term is not descriptive of recent historical

---

[7] See the "Introduction" by William Clebsch and Charles H. Long to the reprint of Morris Jastrow Jr.'s, *The Study of Religion* (Chico, Ca.: Scholars Press 1981). See also chapter one, "The Study of Religion: Its Nature and Discourse," in *Significations* (Philadelphia: Fortress Press, 1986).

cultural events which have taken place in the United States. It is, rather, the recognition on the part of the scholarly community of a new discourse about religion in America. America has possessed a plural religious culture from the beginnings of European settlement. At the beginnings of European settlement, there were various and many forms of European religion, some brought over from Europe and others developing out of the American experience itself. But there has been almost from the beginning another modality of pluralism. That pluralism is represented by the musings of Alexis de Tocqueville in his chapter in *Democracy in America*, entitled, "Some Considerations Concerning the Present State and Probable Future of the Three Races That Inhabit the Territory of the United States."[8] This is the oldest and most radical form of American pluralism.

This older form of pluralism has much to do with many of the factors and events that have brought on the discussion of the newer meaning of pluralism. In both cases, a new and different meaning of religion in the United States is evoked. Sidney Mead's essay, "The American People: Their Space, Time, and Religion,"[9] is probably the only statement by a student of American religion that seems to parallel de Tocqueville's insight. The meaning of American religion must be placed within the broader understanding of religion itself. The self-justifying meaning of American religion and its distinctiveness should be tested within the framework of a new discourse about the meaning of religion. Too much has been said about the difference between European and American religion, but hardly anything is ever mentioned regarding the structural differences and similarities with other religions of humankind. In other words, the study and meaning of religion in the United States could be enhanced if we examined it from the perspective of the History of Religions (*Religionswissenschaft*). Such a perspective has several advantages. In the first instance, it would allow us to open the range of our historical and cultural data for an understanding of American religion. We would be able to include the "older pluralism" of de Tocqueville's three races that inhabit the continent, The Aborigines, the Europeans, and the African Americans. These traditions could be seen as embodiments of specific religious orientations in their differences, but could also define another meaning of religion in their influence, contact, and rela-

---

[8] Alexis de Tocuqeville, *Democracy in America*, edited by J.P. Mayer and trans. by George Lawrence, Part II., chapter 10 (New York: Harper and Row, 1969).
[9] Sidney E. Mead, *The Lively Experiment: The Shaping of Christianity in America* (New York: Harper and Row, 1963) chapter one.

tionships with each other. New meaning might emerge from an understanding of the transplanted European traditions and "civil religion" or, in Sidney Mead's terms, "the religion of the Republic." Furthermore, the contemporary understanding of the American religious scene as pluralistic would have a historical basis for its standpoint and critique.

At the beginning of the last decade of the twentieth century, it is clear beyond the shadow of a doubt that we are at the end of the Protestant Era. While this has had different meanings for all the Protestant formations throughout the world, it must have a very profound meaning for the United States of America. The Protestant tradition has so dominated the life of American culture that it is often difficult for the ordinary citizen to separate the meaning of American religion from the meaning of Protestantism, or for that matter, to separate a moral legal meaning of American culture from a Protestant inspired understanding.

As Sacvan Bercovitch put it,

> History has been making it clear for some time that the hazards of living out the dream outweigh the advantages...Who knows, the errand may come to rest, where it always belonged, in the realms of the imagination; and the United States recognized for what it is, not a beacon of mankind, as Winthrop proclaimed in his *Arbella* address of 1630, not the political Messiah, as the young Melville hymned in *White Jacket*—not even a covenanted people robbed by the un-American predators of their sacred trust—but simply *goy b' goyim*, just one more profane nation in the wilderness of this world.[10]

While this statement diffuses the triumphalism of destiny and millenarian hopes endemic to American religion and American nationalism, it yet leaves open the possibility for a new discourse about American religion—a discourse that requires both those in the theological traditions and in Religious Studies.

In a recent article, Van Harvey laments what he calls the "intellectual marginalization of American theology."[11] While some of the blame for this situation may be placed at the door of secular intellectuals, Van Harvey thinks that the major cause for this state of affairs is the theologians themselves.

---

[10] Sacvan Bercovitch, "The Rites of Assent: Rhetoric, Ritual, and the Ideology of American Consensus," in Sam B. Girgus, ed., *The American Self: Myth, Ideology, and Popular Culture* (Albuquerque: The University of New Mexico Press, 1981). pp. 5-42.

[11] Van A. Harvey, "On the Intellectual Marginality of American Theology," in Michael J. Lacey, ed., *Religion and Twentieth-Century American Intellectual Life* (Cambridge: Cambridge University Press, 1989) pp. 172-192.

It could plausibly be argued that the blame for the marginality of theology in our time should be placed not on the doorstep of secular intellectuals, but rather on that of the theologians themselves. It could be argued that, particularly in the past two decades, Protestant theology has been characterized by narcissism and faddism that have virtually destroyed it as a serious intellectual discipline and deprived it of any respect it might thus claim. The slightest breezes that have stirred the trees of the groves of academe have been frantically harnessed for the purpose of generating energy for some new theological 'movement'—a 'theology of the death of God,' a 'theology of play,' a theology of hope,' a 'theology of liberation,' a 'theology of polytheism,' a 'theology of deconstruction,' and even redundantly, a 'theology of God.'[12]

I think that this statement says at once too much and too little. He observes later in the article that several sociologists of American religion point to the fact that while theology seems to be irrelevant, church and church activities seem to be burgeoning. Theologians, according to Harvey, here following the sociologist Peter L. Berger, have spent a great deal of their time responding to the several discrepant social worlds of our culture, each of which challenges the cognitive and normative claims of the other. At this point Harvey takes up the meaning of the professionalization of theology within divinity schools and accepts the analysis of Edward Farley in his *Theologia: The Fragmentation and Unity of Theological Education in America.* One of the issues raised is that of the legitimacy of theological studies in the university. He thinks that the American university-related divinity schools accepted the four-fold curricular structure (biblical studies, church history, dogmatics, or Christian doctrine, and practical theology) of the older German universities as the basis for American theological education.

The justification for the existence of theology within the university with its curriculum created an ambiguity. Although theology is defended as a legitimate academic discipline because its subject matter is the Christian religion, this justification is based on the premise that the university exists to provide leadership in the churches. While this created an ambiguity for German culture, it is a special and intense dilemma for American culture and its principle of the separation of church and state. Moreover, this meaning of theology as a specialized discipline and training, in the same manner that the study of law is for lawyers, separates, rather than establishes, a relationship between the theologian and the laity or with the life of the world itself.

---

[12] Van Harvey, op. cit., p. 173.

At the end of his article, Van Harvey points to Reinhold Niebuhr as one of the last non-marginal American theologians along with Paul Tillich. They were theologians who spoke to the laity and into the public arena about matters related to the public. Van Harvey makes clear that he feels that Niebuhr was able to do this precisely because *he did not possess* a doctoral degree from one of the preeminent university-related schools. He implies that it is the education in these schools that thwarts the possibilities for a new form of discourse since the curriculum is so specialized, almost esoteric. Van Harvey's article ends on this plaintive note, "Oh Reinhold Niebuhr, where are you now that we need you.?"

Van Harvey's article highlights some of the basic issues in the relationship of theology to culture. Some of these issues echo major themes foreshadowed by Sidney Mead, Robert Bellah, and Sacvan Berkovitch. All of these scholars have raised the issue of what one may call a public theology. This public theology can no longer be defined in the terms of the singularity of a Protestant discourse. In addition, the situation of America, both in terms of its older and newly understood pluralism, is different. Further, the situation of the United States in the world has changed drastically.

While Sacvan Berkovitch has critically defined the United States as just another profane nation in the wilderness of this world, this critique is more toward the notion of the United States and the Protestant tradition as the normative center for a discourse about religion in the United States. Even with the decentering of this tradition, there is still a creative role for both theology and religious studies. While Bellah's "civil religion" and Sidney Mead's "religion of the Republic" are basic ingredients in this new orientation, they should not occupy the center abandoned by the dominance of the Protestant discourse. The Enlightenment heritage of these positions has fallen under severe critique from both practical and theoretical points of view.

The range of what is meant by "the public" must be extended, and this extension needs the resources both of the study of religion from theology and from religious studies. Religious studies could extend the range by placing the meaning of American religion within the problem of religion. From a historical and cultural point of view, this could be done first of all by contextualizing the religions of the United States within the Western Hemisphere. After all, the cultures and nations in this hemisphere grew out of similar colonizing processes, and the dominance of the United States within this hemisphere was often justified by the presumed sacrality of the Protestant tradition. Many of the internal problems of the United States are related to their relationship and connections with the cultures and nations of this hemisphere.

The field of study defined by Religious Studies is still vague. From a practical point of view, it means the teaching of religion without advocacy or without the aim of proselytizing. This means that it can be taught in public universities. From a curricular point of view, this has meant the inclusion of "other" or non-Western religions as a part of curricular structure.

Religious Studies from this perspective often ends up being a secular form of the older Protestant theological curriculum. Most of the teachers in departments and programs of religious studies received their training in Protestant university divinity schools and are often unable to define the difference between religious studies and theological studies except for their locale and setting in another academic arena. In other words, the difference defined by the emergence of religious studies is a difference that does not make a difference.

The seeming chaos in the academic study of religion has been caused in part by "the end of the Protestant era." This "end" not only destroyed a discourse and paradigm about the nature of religion, it equally brought into view new and different forms of religio-cultural data. The notions of "pluralism," "public theology," and "civil religion" are indicative of this range of new data. Even with this opening to a new range of data, the basic structural paradigm is still couched in the language of a Protestant stylistic convention.

In my opinion, theology needs an even wider range of data to redefine its meaning. These data could be forthcoming from a Religious Studies informed by *Religionswissenschaft*. Such a study could relocate the meaning of Protestantism within a proper and new situation, and thus its relativity and relationship to a wider humanity would be established. This is one way of understanding it as a "profane" religion, in the words of Bercovitch. We are all aware, given Said's, *Orientalism* and the various studies in post-modernism, that "religion" as an object of study is a construction of the academy. It is time for a new construction of religion based upon another understanding of the nature of our world.

On the other hand, Religious Studies needs the critique of theology to save it from the illusions of objectivity and to point out the ethical and teleological nature of all intellectual endeavors. University-related theological schools could take the lead in this reconstruction of the meaning and study of religion for the next century. Such a clarification would define real differences but not antagonistically, and would enable the study of religion, with the cooperation of theology and Religious Studies, to become an authentic Human Science.

Between Church and Academy: The Dilemma of American Catholic Theology

WILLIAM C. SPOHN

Roman Catholic theological education presents distinct issues in relating the academic study of religion and the American university. University-related divinity schools struggle for credibility in academic communities often indifferent to their subject and for support from denominations that they have traditionally served. Their Roman Catholic counterparts face the added challenge of maintaining academic freedom while being responsible to a teaching church with definite doctrinal commitments. If divinity schools currently fear being orphaned, Catholic theology departments fear being smothered.

Theological education among Catholics in the United States takes place in three different settings: free-standing seminaries which primarily train diocesan priests, clusters of theology schools run by religious congregations attended by clerical and lay students, and Catholic colleges and universities that primarily instruct undergraduates but also offer graduate programs for non-ordained ministry. A handful of Catholic universities offer graduate theology programs, such as Notre Dame, Boston College, Marquette, St. Louis University, and Catholic University of America (most of these specialize in certain areas of theology). With the exception of certain departments at the latter, the university programs are affiliated with the hierarchical church but not controlled by bishops or the Vatican.

In the past thirty years the primary social location of Catholic theology has shifted from seminaries to universities. Its ethos has moved from a clerical preserve dominated by ecclesiastical superiors and concerns to the ethos of the American university. With its fundamental commitment to open inquiry, the university often regards with suspicion scholarship done in the service of other institutions, particularly churches. Church authorities are not always sanguine about the climate of debate and questioning of official positions which is necessary in the university context. The recent removal of Rev. Charles Curran from the theological faculty of Catholic University highlights the tension between a magisterial church and the academy (although we shall see below that the faculty of theology at C.U. operates under a pontifical charter unlike other American Catholic universities.)

We shall examine the effects of this shift of location in American Catholic theology on three points: 1) the development of the role of theology in the university since the Second Vatican Council; 2) the unique set of tensions between academic freedom and ecclesiastical supervision of doctrine, particularly in light of current Vatican initiatives; and 3) the question of method in theology done in the Catholic context and some examples of constructive dialogue between academy and church.

I. Catholic Theology in 1959 and 1989

The generation following the Second Vatican Council ushered in profound changes in every dimension of Roman Catholicism, including American Catholic higher education. In 1989 there are 235 United States Catholic colleges and universities, which enroll over six hundred thousand students. The study of religion in these institutions contrasts sharply with the approach of thirty years ago. The Catholic university of that era took a frankly custodial view toward its mission, as Michael J. Buckley wrote in 1969:

> It transmitted a teaching, the common teaching of the magisterium [i.e., official church]. This body of doctrine afforded a criterion by which faculty was selected, curriculum chosen, morals enforced. Counter-positions within the university were permitted more as a token, as a stimulus to study and refutation, rather than as a serious presence...[1]

---

[1] Michael J. Buckley, S.J., "The Function of a Catholic University," *U.S. Catholic and Jubilee* (Sept. 1969) 47.

For example, the typical undergraduate attending one of the 28 Jesuit colleges and universities in 1959 faced a requirement of at least four semester courses of "religion" and at least eight courses in neo-Thomist philosophy. The latter was the main vehicle of intellectual formation: every student minored in philosophy, taking courses in a sequence which progressed from logic to ethics. The students were overwhelmingly Catholic and products of a unitary Catholic culture which placed considerable emphasis on obedience to moral directives. It was not a culture rife with self-criticism or outstanding intellectual accomplishment, as the historian John Tracy Ellis pointed out in his famous essay of 1955, "American Catholics and the Intellectual Life." [2]

These schools had departments of "religion" rather than "theology," since the latter referred to a more technical discipline reserved for the training of clerics and research. "Religion" meant the fundamentals of official Roman Catholic dogma, presented in apologetic fashion with little reference to Scripture or experience, let alone other Christian traditions or world religions. Standard textbooks by approved authors presented the teachings of a church that tolerated few dissenting voices.

This parochial form of religious education usually duplicated the seminary training of the clerics and members of religious orders who staffed the department. So clerical was the profession that the rare non-ordained theologians were hailed as "lay theologians." Only a fraction of this decided minority were women. The ordinary theological training required for ordination was deemed sufficient preparation for instructing undergraduates. Some seminary professors had doctorates from ecclesiastical faculties in Europe, particularly the Roman universities, or from the Catholic University of America whose graduate theology program for clerics dated back to 1889. Most of the religion faculty would not have been involved in professional societies outside the Catholic ambit and would have few publications to their credit. This lack of professionalism did not go unnoticed by their colleagues in other departments where academic standards were being upgraded as Catholic higher education expanded in the fifties.

University administration was firmly in the hands of the men's or women's religious community that sponsored the institution. In most cases, the religious superior could assign a member of the community to teach in a school under his or her jurisdiction, and the college administration had no choice but to accept the appointment. Boards of trustees

---

[2] John Tracy Ellis, "American Catholics and the Intellectual Life," *Thought* 30 (Fall, 1955) 351-388.

were almost always composed exclusively of clerics or members of the religious order. Public funding was beginning to become available for dormitories and classroom buildings not used for religious instruction. As it did, the question of academic freedom began to arise more frequently. Catholic primary and secondary schools were excluded from state aid because they explicitly inculcated church doctrines—did Catholic universities and colleges have a different educational rationale? If they encouraged the free examination of all traditions, how could they justify departments of religion which were more catechetical than critical?

Seminary education in 1959 was still in the form mandated by the Council of Trent. Undergraduate and graduate seminaries for both regular diocesan clergy and religious orders were carefully isolated from university campuses. They offered tightly organized curriculums long on philosophy and theology done in the neoscholastic mode which Pope Leo XIII had mandated in his encyclical *Aeterni Patris* in 1879.[3] The lectures and recitations were often held in Latin, with little encouragement for wide reading or critical inquiry. Gustave Weigel, S.J. the noted ecumenist, said that he had been raised in a church where theology was reduced to ecclesiology. Others opined that ecclesiology in turn had been reduced to the study of papal authority.

A visitor returning to the same departments in 1989 would scarcely recognize them. In the space of thirty years, many have changed their title from "Religion" to "Theology" and then to "Religious Studies" to reflect the changing nature of their enterprise. (Some have changed from "Religious Studies" back to "Theology" to stress their Catholic heritage.) Philosophy has largely disappeared from the general education requirements and two or three courses satisfy the theology requirement. Students can study Eastern religions, the Reformation, or "God in Modern Literature" and avoid Roman Catholic dogma entirely if they choose to do so.[4] Modern exegetical methods address Scripture while history of religions and sociology of religion approaches complement the more traditional theological methods. Given the low state of theological literacy engendered by prior schooling, courses in Roman Catholicism are often well subscribed by young Catholics previously unacquainted

---

[3] See Gerald A. McCool *Catholic Theology in the Nineteenth Century: The Quest for a Unitary Method* (New York: Seabury Press, 1977) for a comprehensive treatment of the effects of this imposition of neoThomist thought on Catholic scholarship.

[4] At the University of San Francisco, where the author taught philosophy from 1969 to 1971, only Roman Catholics were required to take theology courses. This led to a number of timely apostasies so students could expand their electives.

with any intellectual rationale for believing, for example, in the resurrection of Christ or the personal character of God.

The department likely includes Protestant and Jewish members and is predominantly non-ordained. New women faculty are actively recruited. The fulltime faculty appointed since the early sixties hold earned doctorates. Their advancement and tenure would be judged by the same standards as the members of any department in the university. While some have graduated from Notre Dame or Fordham, many would come from university-related divinity schools such as Chicago, Union Theological, Vanderbilt, etc. The explosion of interest in theological questions among American Catholics following Vatican II markedly increased their attendance at such divinity schools. In several of them, Catholic students have constituted the largest Christian denomination for some time.

The university administration and board of trustees are no longer controlled by the sponsoring religious community. Most have "separately incorporated" the institution so that it is under the control of the board of trustees rather than religious authorities. Although some top administrators in the university would be religious community members, the board of trustees and the majority of deans and vice-presidents would be lay, often Catholic, often not. The numbers of religious community members who taught or administered could not accommodate the growth Catholic colleges experienced during the fifties and sixties. An increasing number of lay faculty serve the expanding student bodies, and many such faculty bring with them the ethos of the first-rate American universities where they have matriculated.[5]

In thirty years the university would most likely have evolved from a custodial institution to the open forum model which is characteristic of a genuine university. As Buckley notes, "There was, then, in the earlier conceptualization of the Catholic university, a fatal conjunction of ingredients mutually contradictory." An institution could not have a faculty and curriculum that represented the scope of the universe of knowledge and simultaneously have "its most important conclusions... already determined" and bend its energies "only upon their defense, or their presentation or their inculcation."[6]

---

[5] Catholic schools recruited from a rapidly expanding pool, as Andrew Greeley notes: "In 1960, 25 percent of the college graduates in the United Sates were Catholic; now 45 percent are Catholic. Half of the Catholics in the United States have attended college." from "Is There an American Catholic Elite?" *America* May 6, 1989 160/17, p.429.

[6] Michael J. Buckley, S.J. "The Catholic University as Pluralistic Forum" *Thought* (Spring, 1971) 204-205.

Seminary education has changed as well. Dwindling numbers of candidates and interest in a broader education led many free-standing seminaries to become "collaborative college seminaries," residences whose students attend a nearby Catholic college or university. Only 42% of the total seminary college priesthood student population study in the nineteen remaining free-standing institutions.[7] At the graduate level, where four years of theology are required for ordination, diocesan seminarians still have minimal contact with universities. However, the composition of faculty and students has changed considerably. Many of the desks emptied by declining candidates for priesthood are filled by lay persons, mostly women, preparing for church ministry. The number of women faculty in member schools of the Association of Theological Schools rose from 14 in 1971 to 106 (11.9% of the faculty) ten years later. The percentage of doctorates rose 37.6% in the same ten years.

Prior to the Council almost all seminary faculty had been trained in Catholic institutions, with Rome's Gregorian University and Catholic University of America being the main sources of degrees. Although the ATS did not record the figures for 1962 (when the Vatican Council started), they show that in 1971 there were 102 doctorates from the Gregorian and 71 from Catholic University, and only 69 from other North American Schools, while in 1981 there were only 56 from the Gregorian and 56 from Catholic University, while 236 were from other North American schools. Although we should not conclude that "other North American schools" were all Protestant or nondenominational, a large percentage of the degrees were taken in such institutions.[8] Bishops, especially those whose dioceses have graduate seminaries, may still exercise some scrutiny over the teaching of those faculties; however, faculties that train religious order candidates for ordination enjoy greater freedom.

Religious orders have pooled their graduate resources in Catholic clusters such as the Chicago Theological Union or ecumenical ones such as the Graduate Theological Union in Berkeley. Their identity has changed with the shift of social location to the university. Local bishops rarely exercise any control over the seminaries of religious orders, although they were included in the recent Vatican investigation of American seminaries and earned generally favorable reviews. The con-

---

[7] "A Commentary on Seminary Priesthood Enrollment Statistics for 1989—Part I" CARA Seminary Forum 16: 3-4, p. 11

[8] T. Howland Sanks, S.J. "Education for Ministry since Vatican II" Theological Studies 45:3 (September 1984) 487.

tribution of university-related divinity schools to such faculties is very significant. To take one example, in the author's area of Religion and Society at the GTU, of the eleven faculty (drawn from the six Protestant and three Catholic schools which comprise the Union) four hold doctorates from Chicago, three from Yale, one from Harvard, and one from Boston University.

In sum, current Roman Catholic theological education in universities and religious order seminaries draws heavily upon the resources of university-related divinity schools for faculty. An examination of course syllabi would show a comparable dependence on these institutions for scholarly publications. The training of American Catholic theologians in major private institutions and their increasing professionalization has heightened their awareness of academic freedom, a value not always respected by ecclesiastical authorities.

II. *Academic Freedom and Official Church Teaching Theology Responsible to the Academy*

Academic freedom is a relatively recent ideal in Roman Catholic colleges and universities in the United States. Other essays in this volume have traced the emergence of the modern university from Enlightenment liberalism and nineteenth century German universities that placed the highest premium on unfettered research. Colonial colleges and most nineteenth century American higher education arose from churches and became more secular when the influence of the sponsoring denomination waned. Up until the twentieth century most American colleges were publicly committed to the religious and moral formation of their students. Religiously affiliated institutions have continued that tradition, although not always in ways harmonious with free inquiry and critical examination.

Catholic higher education gradually became more professional and less clerical after the Second World War. Prior to the 1950s, it was commonly assumed that the ideal of academic freedom did not pertain to Catholic colleges. Since they saw themselves as extensions of the teaching mission of the Church, these institutions were committed to inculcate its doctrinal and moral teaching. They became more like other universities as a new generation of teachers and administrators reshaped them along the lines of their secular counterparts. Numerous factors helped accommodate Catholic faith to a more American identity: the increasing integration of Catholics into American professions and economic affluence, the election of John F. Kennedy that laid to rest most of the remnants of American nativism, the first full endorsement of human rights in Pope John XXIII's encyclical *Pacem in Terris* in 1963, and the availability of federal funds for nonsectarian aspects of university education. All these trends were encouraged by the new openness towards the modern world, other world religions and human experience in general ratified in the documents of Vatican II. In its final year the Council endorsed, after considerable debate, the American experience of religious liberty and the rights of conscience in the face of civil and ecclesiastical authority. Conservatives realized this endorsement for what it was: a complete reversal of the Church's traditional position on the establishment of religion. The American John Courtney Murray, S.J., who had been silenced for the previous decade for arguing against the anti-democratic bias that had dominated official Church teaching since the French Revolution, co-authored the "Declaration on Religious Freedom" with Pietro Pavan. It states, "The truth cannot impose itself except by virtue of its own truth, as it makes its entrance into the mind at once quietly and with power."[9] The document concentrated on the duty of civil authority to respect religious freedom and, unfortunately, did not specify the responsibility of ecclesiastical authorities to safeguard it within the Church.

In 1967, one year after the close of the Council, twenty six Catholic educators and church leaders met at Land O'Lakes, Wisconsin, to discuss the nature of the contemporary Catholic university. They produced a strong declaration on academic freedom: "To perform its teaching and research functions effectively, the Catholic university must have a true autonomy and academic freedom in the face of authority of whatever kind, lay or clerical, external to the academic community itself."[10]

That same year the College Theology Society, an association of theology teachers from Catholic undergraduate institutions, endorsed the American Association of University Professors' 1940 statement on academic freedom and tenure. While these actions were not binding on administrative policy, they pointed the way toward further professionalization of the system. Like most changes that hit American institutions during the turbulent era of the sixties, the trend towards greater auton-

---

[9] *Dignitatis Humanae* in *The Sixteen Documents of Vatican II* National Catholic Welfare Conference translation (Boston: St. Paul Editions, no date) par 1., 398.

[10] Land O'Lakes Statement in *The Catholic University: A Modern Appraisal*, edited by Neil G. McCluskey (Notre Dame: University of Notre Dame Press, 1970) p. 336. See Charles E. Curran "Academic Freedom and Catholic Institutions of Higher Learning" in *Readings in Moral Theology No. 6 : Dissent in the Church* edited by Charles E. Curran and Richard A. McCormick, S.J. (New York: Paulist Press, 1988) 253-270; also James John Annarelli, *Academic Freedom and Catholic Higher Education* (New York: Greenwood Press, 1987)

omy for Catholic colleges and universities did not occur without fierce resistance. Traditionalists lamented that the schools were selling out their birthright for a mess of state funding.

What rationale for academic freedom can be offered by universities identified with a particular religious tradition? At the outset we should note that the free pursuit of truth is a complicated matter in American higher education. Although freedom of inquiry may be the central value that holds together the academic community, American universities have multiple social functions. Because they are so dependent on outside funding for their research efforts, they rarely qualify as ivory towers. At the same time, covert forms of orthodoxy, such as free market capitalist views in economics or deconstructionism in literature, can influence hiring and promotion in some departments of secular and private universities.

Abstract conceptions of the nature of the university, Catholic or otherwise, offer little help in deciding how to safeguard the pursuit of truth. Like most values, academic freedom has a functional foundation: it is essential for the practical purposes of the university. It contributes indispensably to its common life and flourishing. The larger society needs the university to have an autonomous voice and a free hand in pursuing the truth.

A Catholic university has a dual responsibility since it contributes both to the larger secular society and the Church. The Land O'Lakes Statement stated that a Catholic university provides "critical reflective intelligence" for the Church, a service which would be undermined by ecclesiastical interference in its inquiry and internal procedures. Quentin L. Quade, former executive vice-president of Marquette University in Milwaukee, writes that Catholic universities need to guarantee freedom of inquiry in order to attract first-rate scholars." [Such] guarantees simply mean that scholars, in pursuing truth in evidence and analysis, are free—nay, *expected*—to go where their minds take them. If their minds in fact take them toward error, the expectation is that other scholarship will correct them in the natural dialectic of intellectual inquiry." He argues that there is only an apparent incongruity when a scholar at a Catholic university questions some church teaching because "these people do not speak for the church, or in its name, or under its mandate..."[11]

---

[11] Quentin L. Quade "A University Perspective on the 'Oath of Fidelity' *America* April 15, 1898, 160/14, 348.

The Catholic university constitutes a legitimate academic alternative on the American scene: to pursue the truth within a given religious tradition while subjecting that tradition to critical examination. The university has an obligation to make this commitment clear to prospective faculty members and they should be willing to respect it; at the same time, the institution must respect the integrity of their academic disciplines. It should not require that they be Catholics themselves. Constraints should be kept to a minimum even where sensitive doctrines are discussed: dissent should not be equated with incompetence. The professor of geography who asserts that the world is flat can be dismissed for cause; his or her academic freedom is not absolute. The Catholic (or indeed the non-Catholic or non-believing) theologian who misrepresents official Church teaching can be dismissed for cause—but not if, in addition to an honest presentation of integral official doctrine, he or she offers legitimate critique and dissent.[12]

If all the faculty held the same viewpoints it would discourage the dialogue characteristic of a university in a pluralistic culture. A department of theology or religious studies should have some members well versed in the Church's doctrines, as well as those competent to represent other traditions and ways of studying religion. Student services, campus ministry and administrative policies can reflect the priority of Christian values without impinging on the freedom of students who have elected to attend such a university.

In sum, the emerging consensus holds that the Church is best served by Catholic universities that are genuine universities rather than sectarian bible colleges. They should not indoctrinate their students but present Christian values and beliefs as credible options which can withstand critical scrutiny. Academic freedom and open discussion of alternatives is indispensable for that to occur.

Theology Responsible to the Church

What responsibility do Catholic university theologians have to the official Church? Is it a personal responsibility or one which is institutional? While Catholic theology has changed its social location in the past generation, its practitioners remain members of a worldwide church that traditionally has been concerned for unity in profession and practice of the faith.

---

[12] Frederick R. McManus, "Academic Freedom and The Catholic University of America" *America* May 27, 1989, 169/20, 507.

The autonomous American Catholic university, religiously affiliated but neither ecclesiastically chartered nor episcopally controlled, has no counterpart in Europe, Latin America, Africa or Asia. Recent Vatican initiatives toward Catholic universities and theologians have shown little comprehension of the value of academic freedom that defines American higher education.

In order to appreciate the conflict that Catholic theologians experience between the demands of church and academy, it will be helpful to grant for argument's sake two principles that would require more extensive elaboration than is possible in this essay.

a. Theological assertions can be both meaningful and true (whether or not one adds the caveat "within a certain religious perspective and community of discourse").

b. Church authorities have the responsibility to proclaim the Gospel and to safeguard the core of the Christian message in the community. They do this as pastors rather than as scholars, although scholarship is necessary to determine what is central to Christian belief and what is peripheral or heterodox. As such, bishops have a ministry of "judgment" in regard to theological opinions current in the community. (This responsibility takes different forms—from Paul admonishing the "Judaizers" to the Council of Chalcedon rejecting Arianism to Luther rebuking Melanchthon or condemning peasant revolts.)[13]

Most Catholic theologians see their scholarship as participating in the life of the Church as well as the academy. They strive to articulate the self-understanding of the community as it relates the Gospel to modern culture and not primarily their private insights. Most would share Paul's position in First Corinthians that the Spirit of Jesus inspires the whole Church through the converging testimony of all the charisms, from prophecy to teaching to administration and ordinary service.

The different disciplines of theology approach this responsibility in their own way. Exegetes exercise their skills on an ancient text which is simultaneously the revelation and authoritative document of the com-

---

[13] See Avery Dulles, S.J. *A Church to Believe In: Discipleship and the Dynamics of Freedom* (New York: Crossroad, 1982); Thomas P. Rausch, S.J. *Authority and Leadership in the Church: Past Directions and Future Possibilities* (Wilmington, Delaware: Michael Glazier, 1989). Also essays of bishops from various points of the spectrum in *Readings in Moral Theology No.3: The Magisterium and Morality* edited by Charles E. Curran and Richard A. McCormick, S.J. (New York: Paulist, 1982) 171-222, 271-76.

munity of faith.¹⁴ Historians are less bound to examine the truth-value of creeds and conciliar documents than are systematic theologians. Moral theologians have to take into account the numerous declarations on moral questions that Popes and the Vatican have made since the middle of the nineteenth century. Sociologists of religion, comparativists and phenomenologists of religion appropriately adopt a more distanced perspective on Catholic practices and beliefs since their disciplines take a "biographical" rather than an "autobiographical" stance, to follow the terminology used by Joseph Kitagawa earlier in this volume.

The proper role of theology in the Church depends to a great extent on one's ecclesiology, or theology of the church—which is precisely the area of greatest development and change since Vatican II. Presumably all Catholics would agree that the Church ought to teach with authority. However, who teaches, what form of teaching is appropriate and what limits there are on authoritative claims are all matters of intense debate.

Avery Dulles and Yves Congar have shown that the *magisterium* or teaching function of the church has been exercised in a variety of ways in the course of twenty centuries—only recently has it been monopolized by official Vatican teaching. In the patristic era, bishops were usually theologians and scholars. With the rise of the great medieval universities, the doctrinal functions of the church were distributed between the *prelatio* of bishops and the *magisterium* of university professors. Theological faculties, such as that of the University of Paris, were called upon by Popes and prelates to judge disputed questions. Theologians played important roles in the papal and reform councils after the Fourth Lateran Council in 1215. From the time of the Council of Florence (1439-45) when the great medieval universities were in decline, the hierarchy and papacy assumed greater doctrinal leadership. Even at the Council of Trent (1545-1563), which reaffirmed papal primacy in the face of the Reformation, theologians and prelates were present in equal numbers. Dulles sums up this history: "The notion that theologians have authority is well grounded in the tradition."¹⁵

---

¹⁴ The freedom of exegesis to employ modern approaches is endorsed in Pius XII's encyclical *Divino Afflante Spiritu* (1943), which reversed the long-standing opposition of the Pontifical Biblical Commission to modern critical methods.
¹⁵ Dulles, *Church to Believe In* 110. See Yves Congar, O.P., "A Semantic History of the Term *Magisterium*" 297-314 and "A Brief History of the Forms of the Magisterium and Its Relations with Scholars"in *Readings in Moral Theology No. 3* 314-31 Also Congar's "Theologian and the Magisterium in the West: From the Gregorian Reform to the Council of Trent" *Chicago Studies* #17-18, (1978-79) 210-224; Michael D. Place, "From Solicitude to Magisterium: Theologians and Magisterium from the Council of Trent to the First Vatican Council" Ibid.

After Trent, however, the teaching function begins to be identified with the hierarchy alone. The "teaching church" (hierarchical and increasingly papal) is distinguished from the "learning church" (mostly lay). As the model of the church becomes more juridical and centralized, the role of theologians becomes more subservient. This development accelerated in the nineteenth century until it reached a climax of sorts in Pius XII's encyclical *Humanae Generis* (1950) which asserted that the task of the theologian is to search Scripture and tradition to support the declarations of *the* magisterium. The multiple sources of teaching in the community had become so monopolized by the hierarchy, particularly the Vatican, that the term became singular.[16]

The experience of Vatican II ushered in a quite different model of the Church. The *schema* prepared by the Vatican were repudiated by the assembled bishops. With close collaboration by major theologians such as Murray, Congar and Karl Rahner, documents were developed that contained a vision of the Church as a pilgrim community that had to be attentive to the signs of the times, willing to learn from the whole range of contemporary experience, needing the insights of all its members, reversing its suspicions of modern democracy and religious freedom, and acknowledging that the hierarchy does not have all the answers to contemporary problems. In effect, the "teaching church" acknowledged that it also had to learn and that the "learning church" had much to teach it.

Bernard J. F. Lonergan, describes this change in theology as the shift from a classical consciousness to a historical one. A realist epistemology which confidently defined faith and morals in unchanging terms is giving way to a hermeneutically informed theology which recognizes that any formulation of faith is culturally conditioned.[17] If exegetes apply critical historical analysis to the Word of God, should not other theologians employ similar approaches to the words of councils and Popes? Reaction from the right to such boldness is producing a uniquely

---

225-241; T. Howland Sanks, S.J. "Co-operation, Co-optation, Condemnation: Theologians and the Magisterium 1870-1978" Ibid. 242-263.

[16] Dulles notes the effects such juridicism had on the understanding of faith: "They spoke as though faith terminates in the words of hierarchical teachers. In a deeper theology it becomes apparent that ecclesiastical teaching, however authoritative, is at best a sign permitting the believer to receive or recognize the word of God, to which alone the assent of faith is due." *Church to Believe In* 115.

[17] Bernard J. F. Lonergan, S.J. *Method in Theology* (New York: Herder and Herder, 1972) ch 9; 326-339. also "The Transition from a Classicist World-View to Historical Mindedness" and "Theology in its New Context" in *A Second Collection* edited by William F. J. Ryan, S.J. and Bernard J. Tyrrell, S.J. (Philadelphia: Westminster Press, 1974) 1-10, 55-68.

Catholic variety of fundamentalism that demands unquestioning submission to Holy Writ—in this case, the declarations of "the magisterium."

During the pontificate of Pope John Paul II many detect a conscious attempt at "restoration" of the primacy of centralized teaching authority. Under the leadership of Cardinal Joseph Ratzinger, head of the Congregation for the Doctrine of the Faith (formerly the Holy Office) several initiatives have been taken to assert hierarchical control over theologians in the Church.[18] These developments threaten the ethos of academic freedom that characterizes Catholic universities in America:

a. In 1979 the Vatican issued the apostolic constitution *Sapientia Christiana* that outlined the mission of pontifically chartered universities and seminaries that included prescriptions concerning curriculum and ecclesiastical review of faculty hiring and promotions. Canon lawyer Ladislas Orsy contrasts the approach of *Sapientia Christiana* with that of Gratian and Thomas Aquinas: "Neither of the two medieval authors speaks of the authority of the Church being somehow vested in the teacher; both make it clear that the authority a teacher must invoke is that of reason (meaning reason informed and enlightened by faith)."[19]

b. In the 1983 revision of Canon Law Canon 812 states: "It is necessary that those who teach theological disciplines in any institute of higher studies have a mandate from the competent ecclesiastical authority."[20] This canon has not been enforced by the American bishops, who seem quite reluctant to interfere in the life of the university; nevertheless, they are under considerable pressure to implement the canon. It is doubtful that the requirement of episcopal approval applies to civilly chartered universities. The only canonically established pontifical faculties at an American university are found at Catholic University of America. The institutional conflicts which arise from being civilly and canonically chartered became obvious in the recent dismissal of Rev. Charles Curran from Catholic University. The Faculty Senate insists that academic free-

---

[18] See Richard A. McCormick, S.J. *The Critical Calling* (Washington, D.C.: Georgetown University Press, 1989) esp. chapter 4 "The Chill Factor in Contemporary Moral Theology" 71-94.

[19] Ladislas Orsy, S.J. *The Church: Learning and Teaching* (Wilmington, Delaware: Michael Glazier, 1987) 146.

[20] Code of Canon Law trans. by Canon Law Soeiety of America (Washington, D.C.: Canon Law Society of America, 1983) 305.

dom must be an integral part of that university's life; the bishops who compose the board have yet to be heard from.[21]

c. Since 1979, the Vatican Congregation for Catholic Education has been attempting to impose a set of norms on Catholic colleges and universities which are civilly chartered. American academic leaders objected strongly to the initial drafts of the document that prescribed that the local bishop would exercise authority over matters pertaining to Catholic doctrine in the university. The U.S. pattern of civil charters, academic freedom and public funding would be threatened by such an imposition. Rev. Theodore Hesburgh, C.S.C., then president of Notre Dame, flatly stated that if the proposed directives were implemented either Notre Dame would cease to be Catholic or cease to be a university.[22]

III. Academy and Church in Complementary Dialogue

It is impossible to define the role of academic theology and episcopal responsibility in final fashion. History testifies to the diversity of their relation. One should be cautious about any attempt at finality in the present moment that sees Catholic higher education redefining itself more along the lines of American universities and the Church in the midst of an epochal transformation. There will always be a tension between church and academy, but it remains a necessary one.[23] A few suggestions follow and then some examples of fruitful and respectful interaction between the two sources of authority.

---

[21] Orsy interprets Canon 812 in the traditionally restrictive sense: civilly chartered Catholic universities "have not, however, petitioned for an ecclesiastical charter, hence they have not become 'persons' in canon law; they are not (as an institution) under the jurisdiction of the Holy See or the local ordinary [bishop]...Unless an institution obtains legal personality in the church, it cannot have legal rights and duties in the church." *Church* 116, 117. He insightfully discusses the relation of magisterium, theological assent, dissent and academic freedom. For the current faculty debate at Catholic University see James H. Provost, "Hard Cases Make Bad Law," Raymond H. Potvin, "Setting the Record Straight" and Mary Collins, "Where Do We Go From Here?" *Commonweal* May 5 1989 116/9, 270-275.

[22] See Congregation for Catholic Education "Proposed Schema for a Pontifical Document on Catholic Universities" *Origins* 15:43 (April 10, 1986) 707-11; "Catholic College and University Presidents Respond to Proposed Vatican Schema" Ibid. 698-704; Congregation for Catholic Education, "Summary of Responses to Draft Schema on Catholic Universities" *Origins* 17:41 (March 24, 1988) 694-705; "A Draft Document on Catholic Higher Education" *Origins* 18:28 (December 22, 1988) 445-464. Recently, it would appear that the Vatican has responded by recasting the document in an inspirational rather than a prescriptive tone. See the article by Joseph A. O'Hare, S.J., president of Fordham University, "The Vatican and Catholic Universities" *America* (May 27, 1989) 160/20, 503-05.

[23] This was the conclusion of the International Theological Commission held in 1975. See International Theological Commission, "The Ecclesiastical Magisterium and Theology" and Otto Semmelroth, S.J., and Karl Lehman "Commentary on the Theses" in *Readings in Moral Theology No. 3* 151-170.

a. There is no substitute for competence. When an archbishop recently visited a Catholic university and proclaimed to the assembled faculty, "I am the chief teacher in this archdiocese," his claim was puzzling. The prelate holds a Master's in Social Work but no advanced degree in theology. He cannot be claiming professional teaching competence, even though bishops do have responsibility to safeguard the essentials of the Gospel.[24]

The episcopal charism does not convey professional competence. Bishops rely on theologians for critical investigation and interpretation of past formulations of faith in order to determine what is central and what is peripheral to the Gospel. John XXIII opened Vatican II by reminding the Church that there is a difference between the truth of faith and the historically limited formulations that inevitably must articulate it. Since most Church leaders were educated in a theology that did not recognize pluralism of method or the varying authority of the "hierarchy of truths" in church belief, they are in danger of canonizing formulae which cannot exhaust the mysteries they seek to express.[25] Although the Church has never adopted a uniform philosophical system for its theology, in the heyday of "magisterial theology" the formulations were articulated in the language of a single camp, the Roman School of neoscholasticism. It would be more accurate to say that present disputes are less between bishops and theologians than between the last representatives of the Roman theology and more contemporary theological methods.[26]

Hierarchical teaching must arise from broad consultation if it is to become authoritative. In an educated and pluralistic church, respect for ordinary teaching has to be earned by argument and evidence drawn from the entire range of charisms and constituencies in the community. Magisterial statements that come from the top down assume a one-way flow of inspiration that is neither credible nor true to Catholic tradition. An initial respect and willingness to give community leaders the benefit of the doubt must be complemented by sound evidence and persuasive argument in their assertions. In a democratic society, public consultation, debate and reformulation earn church documents credibility and

---

[24] See *Lumen Gentium* Dogmatic Constitution on the Church in *The Documents of Vatican II* ch 3.
[25] See William Henn, O.F.M.Cap., "The Hierarchy of Truths Ten Years Later" *Theological Studies* 48:3 (September 1987) 439-471.
[26] See T. Howland Sanks, S.J. *Authority in the Church: A study in Changing Paradigms* Dissertation Series, 2 (Missoula, Montana: American Academy of Religion & Scholars Press, 1974)

authority, as the reception of the recent pastoral letters on the nuclear threat and the U.S. economy testify.[27]

b. Catholic universities are the places where the Church does her critical thinking. This service would be impossible if they became official instruments of evangelization and indoctrination. They serve the Church as genuine universities, open forums of discussion ranging over the entire universe of knowledge. What makes them Catholic is not necessarily the presence of a theology or religious studies department with a number of Catholic faculty. Rather, the basic problems which a university addresses sets its priorities in terms of resources, curriculum and faculty. The Massachusetts Institute of Technology has priorities different from those of the University of Iowa as they each have purposes which are to some extent distinct. A technological community produces a university different from one produced by a state with strong agricultural interests. Michael J. Buckley argues the analogy for a university that comes from the Church community: "Thus the dogmatic posture of the Church tells upon the universities which she fosters—not in terms of conclusions to be defended or positions to be excluded, but in terms of the subjects and questions she thinks most important: God, Christ, Man, Community, Love, and so on." These questions require the freedom that John Henry Newman espoused in his *Idea of the University*: "Certainly the name of university is inconsistent with restrictions of any kind."[28]

Without the stimulus of theologians whose loyalty demands that they question, probe and dissent at times, the Church's teaching would become stagnant and disengaged from the contemporary culture it seeks to address. At the same time, theologians should carefully investigate the level of authority enjoyed by the doctrines they discuss. They should also make it clear when they are expressing their personal views in distinction from general church teaching. They need to be candid in assessing their colleagues' work if the academy is to live up to its claim of being self-correcting. (Heavy-handed use of ecclesiastical power does not invite

---

[27] On the assent which a Catholic ought to give to the teachings of the "ordinary magisterium" (i.e., teachings not proposed as infallible—which means the vast majority) see Bruno Schuller, S.J. "Remarks on the Authentic Teaching of the Magisterium of the Church" in *Readings in Moral Theology No. 3* 14-33; Karl Rahner, "The Dispute Concerning the Teaching Office of the Church" Ibid. 113-128 and "Open Questions in Dogma Considered by the Institutional Church as Definitively Answered," Ibid. 129-150.

[28] Michael J. Buckley, S.J. "The Catholic University as Pluralistic Forum," 207; John Henry Cardinal Newman, *The Idea of a University* Discourse ii (Garden City, New York: Image Books, 1959) 61.

such candor. As one theologian described his review of a work by Hans Kung: "I'm going to be critical, but I'll be damned if I'm going to give Rome any ammunition!") Finally, a new virtue for theologians may be required in our time: resistance to the temptation to reduce complex theological arguments to "sound bites" suitable for instant media exposure.

c. The sources of religious authority are plural and complementary. Whether it has acknowledged it or not, the teaching church always has learned from a variety of sources in the community: councils, theology, prophetic testimony, pastoral practice and the *sensus fidelium*.[29] The interplay among the sources can no more be fixed in the community than in the experience of the individual believer.

Baron Friedrich von Hugel distinguished three elements in religion: the historical-traditional, the reasoning-argumentative, and the experiential-actional-mystical element. These complement one another and are mutually corrective.

Without reasoning, institutional religion becomes superstition; without proper affective response and action, systematic religion becomes sterile rationalism; and without criticism, the actional-mystical element lapses into fanaticism. When a single element of religious experience dominates, faith is skewed, whether in the individual or in the community as a whole. Mature theological reflection requires religious experience, criticism and moral commitment.

Intellectual integrity does not demand that the theologian bracket his or her personal assent to God's existence any more than it demands that a philosopher who analyzes the meaning of the principles of justice suspend personal commitment to fairness. In any genuine intellectual quest, appreciation of values guides rational inquiry and ought to issue in action consonant with felt convictions. The sources of religious insight are complementary, dialectical, mutually corrective and equally necessary.

Von Hugel proposed this model in his *The Mystical Element of Religion* during the Modernist crisis in Catholicism at the turn of this century. He intended to remind the officials who were pursuing a theological McCarthyism that an interplay of elements was necessary for a vital Church. His words could not be more timely today. They reflect a model of human experience that is consonant with the Catholic tradition which

---

[29] See John Mahoney, S.J. *The Making of Moral Theology: A Study of the Roman Catholic Tradition* (Oxford: Clarendon Press, 1987) ch 4.

posits the entire community as the subject of inspiration and its safest test.[30]

Examples of Complementary Dialogue

Since examples help us discern appropriate conduct more concretely than principles, we shall conclude by citing three recent instances where the interplay of academy and church has been more respectful and fruitful than in the lamentable outcome of the Curran case at Catholic University.

a. Archbishop Rembert G. Weakland of Milwaukee addressed himself to the views of moral theologian Daniel Maguire of Marquette University, which is in Weakland's diocese. He stated in the diocesan newspaper that Dr. Maguire's teaching "on the question of abortion is not consonant with the official teaching of the Catholic Church..." His criticism of the theologian, however, "is not meant as a criticism of the university providing for his work." American Catholic universities have adopted the standard guarantees of academic freedom "not as a compromise of ideals to secular reality, but as a way to make those institutions more effective in their service to the church." He acknowledged that the open pursuit of truth had its risks, however, "to apply to a Catholic university any tactics that would resemble those of a totalitarian state and that would deprive it of its academic freedom would be indeed an even more dangerous process in the long run." One hopes Weakland's action sets a precedent: bishops should deal with dissenting theologians as individuals rather than through any formal assertion of jurisdiction over the university in which they work.[31]

b. At the Jesuit Loyola University of Chicago, a member of the philosophy department, Thomas Sheehan, published a book that raised serious challenges concerning the resurrection of Christ and traditional claims for his divinity. Neither Cardinal Joseph Bernardin nor the university administration censured the author or his work, although the book provoked no little outcry from the Catholic right. In February, 1987, the book was debated before four hundred students and faculty in an open panel discussion which featured two members of the theology department and one from philosophy. They voiced some of the same reservations that

---

[30] Friedrich von Hugel, *The Mystical Element of Religion* (London: James Clark and Co., 1923) chapter 2. Compare the interplay of moral, intellectual and religious conversion in doing theology as described by Bernard Lonergan in his *Method in Theology*, particularly chapter 11.

[31] Archbishop Rembert G. Weakland, O.S.B. *Catholic Herald* March 21, 1985) 3.

reviewers in professional journals had concerning the author's dismissal of twentieth century discussions in Christology. Professor Sheehan responded to their objections and a lively debate ensued. Rather than yielding to censorship or ignoring a challenging voice, the university provided a forum that turned the matter into a learning experience for the whole community.

c. At the inauguration of Santa Clara University's new president in November 1988, Bishop Pierre DuMaine remarked that Santa Clara and similar institutions are being challenged more frequently on their Catholic character. He endorsed the university's commitment to academic freedom and the Catholic heritage: "And if vigilance is offered to a Catholic university, it should not be primarily an ecclesial vigilance, which by itself can prevent and cure nothing in the pursuit of truth and the avoidance of error. The only preventative and the only cure for error in the pursuit of truth are the integrity of the academic enterprise itself; strict adherence to the canons of scholarship, free inquiry, and free and mutual criticism among scholars. The process is slow, the process is hazardous. Although it makes some people impatient, it is the essential guide for the pursuit of truth, religious or secular, in our time." [32]

The parameters of discussion of theology alter in the Catholic context where ecclesiology, tradition, official magisterium and awareness of the *sensus fidelium* in practice nuance a strictly academic approach to topics. Theological inquiry feeds on the community's religious experience even while it purifies it. Although Catholic higher education has benefitted considerably from the graduates of the major United States university-related divinity schools who increasingly staff its departments of religious studies, those divinity schools have not infrequently left such graduates unequipped for the church context in which they will do theology. It is certainly challenging to reflect critically on matters of faith without "a willing suspension of belief" or bracketing insights that come from participating in a community of faith. Whether mainstream American theology can be both *in the academy* and also *for the life of the believing community* remains an open question. Both church and academy will be the poorer if the answer is negative.

---

[32] Bishop Pierre DuMaine, "Inaugural Message" *Santa Clara Magazine* (Winter, 1989) 31/2, 46.

Theological Consortia: The Creative Space Between Church and University

JUDITH A. BERLING

In his introduction to this volume, Joseph Kitagawa makes a distinction between free-standing seminaries and the divinity schools (or theological schools) related to graduate universities. Although in a number of significant respects this is a valuable basis on which to pursue the questions central to this volume, the distinction oversimplifies the rather complex continuum of theological institutions with some sort of relation to a major university. The so-called university-related divinity schools have found it difficult to see themselves as a unique and distinctive group; they see differences among themselves which are at least as great as those which distinguish them from free-standing seminaries. Their relationship to their various denominational constituencies (past and present), the relative priorities given to the training of religious professionals or of doctoral students, the institutional relationships to their respective universities all vary widely and make generalizations difficult.[1]

There are also a number of institutions which are in some ways like university-related divinity schools in having respected doctoral pro-

---

[1] The difficulty in finding the common ground for the university-related divinity schools has been evident in a project to study this group of institutions funded by the Lilly Endowment and directed by James L. Waits of Candler School of Theology. The Waits project will produce several volumes and conferences on the future of theological education in such institutions.

grams which are integrally related to a university, but whose structural relationships to the university are quite different from the divinity schools. Obvious examples are the Claremont School of Theology, various Roman Catholic schools or departments discussed by William Spohn in this volume, and theological consortia, esp. the Graduate Theological Union and the Toronto School of Theology. This essay will explore theological consortia as an alternative paradigm for understanding the place of theological scholarship in relationship to the university and the church.

I. The Development of Theological Consortia

Other essays in this volume have traced the origins of the American University and the evolution of the place of theology within it from the middle ages in Europe through the course of American history. That story is a long and complex one.

The historical roots of theological consortia, by contrast, are relatively recent, so much so that consortia are still in the process of discovering their potential. The decline of a number of consortia has suggested to some that this arrangement was a passing fad not destined to survive the test of time, but it is perhaps too early to tell. The structural and governance problems of consortia are extremely complex. If they are not resolved, at least to some degree, consortia will suffer the long-term fate of most enterprises that rest on voluntary cooperation; they will persist only as long as the immediate motivations and issues for cooperation last. They will be an example of "loose coupling" (intentionally temporary cooperative ventures) rather than a permanent, more routinized form of affiliation.[2] However, where consortia find some enduring institutional "glue" to ensure the durability of arrangements, they provide opportunities for an approach to research and teaching which other institutions would be hard pressed to replicate.

As early as 1963, the American Association of Theological Schools was formed to encourage cooperative ventures in theological education, but it was some time before instances of large-scale academic cooperation began to emerge. The earliest attempt to form a consortium was the so-called Chicago cluster, or the Federated Theological Faculty of the University of Chicago. Formed in 1943, it had a rocky history which ended officially in 1959. The concept of the Federation was that faculty in

---

[2] "Loose coupling" was language used in the Draft of Cheswick Center/Lilly Conference report on "Cooperative Ventures in Theological Education," Thomas J. Savage, S.J., (1986) pp. 2-7.

seminaries and Divinity houses within the Chicago area would be appointed to a single faculty related to the University of Chicago Divinity School and participate in its joint programs. There were problems from the outset. The plans for the cluster did not take into account the radically different educational philosophies and missions of the various schools, and thus there were inevitable fights over faculty appointments. Second, the radical differences in the size and prestige of the participating institutions, and in particular the dominance of the University of Chicago and its Divinity School, created major obstacles to forging "peer" relationships among the institutions. Consequently, the exact power relationships and common mission of the Federation remained unclear, and it foundered. In its wake a series of limited bilateral agreements were formed among the various seminaries and the university, some of which work very well indeed. However, there is no larger consortium or venture with a distinctive mission or purpose.[3]

A second early example was more successful, but quite different in history and approach. In 1955 a number of historically Black seminaries in Atlanta formalized nearly twenty years of cooperation to create a cluster. The immediate impetus for their move to a formal association was the failure of one of the seminaries to win a foundation grant because of its denominational character; the cluster created an interdenominational umbrella under which they could apply more successfully for external support. After several years of planning and negotiations the Interdenominational Theological Center was chartered in 1958. The schools included Gammon Theological Seminary (Methodist Episcopal), Morehouse School of Religion (National Baptist Churches of the South); Philips School of Theology (Christian Methodist Church); and Turner Theological Seminary (A.M.E.). The consortium sought to provide fuller financial resources, improve the quality of education, enhance facilities and equipment, take advantage of the broader academic resources of Atlanta, create student bodies and faculties of optimum size for a sound education, and give some of the smaller schools access to resources which might lead to their accreditation. ITC was successful whereas Chicago had not been for three primary reasons: a shared purpose (education of Black ministers); lack of domination by any one school or

---

[3] Aute L. Carr, "The Federated Theological Faculty of the University of Chicago: An Analysis of Agreements, Structures, and Relationships, 1943-60," *Theological Education* 4 (Summer 1968, Supplement 1): 61-79.

university; and the strong sense of mutual self-interest in seeking much-needed financial support from foundations.4

The 1960s saw the beginning of several other major consortia which, although quite different, have dominated the history of the enterprise. The Graduate Theological Union was founded in Berkeley in 1962 originally as a union of four Protestant schools. Roman Catholic schools joined two years later, and the union grew to include nine member schools by the end of the 1960s: American Baptist Seminary of the West, Church Divinity School of the Pacific (Episcopalian), Dominican School of Philosophy and Theology, Franciscan School of Theology, Jesuit School of Theology at Berkeley; Pacific Lutheran Theological Seminary; Pacific School of Religion (interdenominational, with covenants with U.C.C., Disciples, Methodists); San Francisco Theological Seminary (Presbyterian); Starr King School for the Ministry (Unitarian-Universalist). The GTU also established a set of complex relationships with the University of California, Berkeley.

The Toronto Graduate School of Theological Studies was incorporated in 1964 by four protestant seminaries and joined two years later by a Roman Catholic school. The Toronto School of Theology, (TST), as the consortium is now known, has established a complex and intimate relationship with the University of Toronto Graduate School. The original members were Emmanuel College (United Church), Knox College (Presbyterian), Trinity College (Anglican), and Wycliffe College (Anglican). They were joined in 1966 by St. Michael's, the first Roman Catholic member. TST does not confer degrees, and instruction is offered by the faculty of the five colleges. Doctoral degrees are granted through the University of Toronto, and qualified TST faculty are appointed to the Graduate Faculties of the University.5

The Association of Theological Faculties in Iowa was begun as a series of common lectures in 1962; by 1967 the schools had adopted a common schedule of courses. It originated in Dubuque with the cooperation of Dominican, Lutheran, and Presbyterian Seminaries, and was joined later by the School of Religion at the University of Iowa. The schools established a certain level of cooperation in programmatic areas,

---

4 Aute L. Carr, "The Interdenominational Theological Center: A Descriptive-Evaluative Study," *Theological Education* 4 (Summer 1968, Supplement 1): 33-45.
5 David S. Schuller, "The Toronto Graduate School of Theological Studies: A Descriptive Evaluative Study," *Theological Education* 4 (Summer 1968, Supplement 1): 47-60.

but in part because of geographical separation did not evolve into a formalized consortium offering joint degrees.[6]

The Boston Theological Institute (BTI) began in spring of 1967, originally as a cooperative venture in the area of field education with an emphasis on training for ministry in urban areas, but later expanded to include cross-registration and other formal arrangements. It was established as a venture of faculties at Harvard, Boston University, Boston College, Andover Newton Theological School, Episcopal Theological School, Weston College School of Theology, and St. John's Seminary. In this consortium, the individual schools offer degrees, and use the consortium as a mechanism for cooperation and cross-registration.

The histories of the consortia founded in the 1960s have in many respects defined the possibilities and limitations for more recent efforts at cooperation such as the Washington Theological Union in Washington, D.C. What was it in the sixties that gave such impetus to large-scale and ambitious cooperative ventures in theological education?

The decade of the 1960s was in a number of respects a turning point in higher education in the United States, not merely in theological education. One of the initial and most fundamental changes was social and demographic; this basic change helped to set the stage for the other more dramatic changes which marked the 60s. The first and fundamental change was the opening of higher education to a much broader base of students. Joseph Hough has discussed the spectacular technological advances in research during and after the World War II, which led to a public celebration of the progress which university research could underwrite. Connected with these gains was the professionalization of many fields, particularly science-related fields such as nursing, agriculture, and business. As Hough writes, . . "the university is not only a professional education center. It has become the single most powerful arbiter of social status, and thus, indirectly, the chief dispenser of economic benefits in the society."[7] The dramatic rise in the prestige of the university and the attractive job opportunities for the university-educated reinforced the hopes and dreams of millions of Americans that college would be the road to success and opportunity for their children. Moreover, the post-war economic boom and generous government and foundation support for students in a host of high priority fields opened the doors of a university education for the first time to students from a

---

[6] David S. Schuller, "The Association of Theological Faculties in Iowa (Dubuque): A Descriptive Evaluative Study," *Theological Education* 4 (Summer 1968, Supplement 1): 22-32.

[7] Joseph C. Hough, Jr., "Theology and the University," unpublished paper, p.2.

broad range of social backgrounds. The university had become a powerful dispenser of social status, and it was no longer educating only the children of privilege.

As this broader student population moved into the front ranks of the professions and the academy, they brought with them issues and questions that reflected their broader backgrounds. This expansion of issues and perspectives was also fuelled by the faith in the late 50s and early 60s in the ability of university research—in the sciences, the social sciences, and even perhaps the humanities—to improve society and better the human condition. Thus the simple demographic change did not simply mean larger classes, dramatic growth of campuses and faculties, and a challenge to the traditional mores, pedagogical methods, and social assumptions of universities; it also began slowly but inevitably to expand the fields of inquiry, to raise different issues of justice and interpretation, to question models which had reigned unchallenged for decades. The university not only had a larger role in society; it had changed in a number of fundamental ways.

This decade which saw the first effects of a new and more open society (or at least education system) also produced two social movements which had profound impacts on students in higher education and particularly in theological education. The first was the civil rights movement, which while begun in the streets, buses, cafes, churches, and schools of the South, was eventually felt in virtually every corner of American society, including the campuses. Not only were many students involved in marches, signing petitions, or other aspects of the movement, but students of color gaining entrance to mostly white campuses confronted their white colleagues with how alien and uncomfortable the ethos of those campuses felt to someone from an African-American background. If the colleges and universities felt the impact of this movement, however, it was even more intense in seminaries and theological schools. The movement in the South was courageously led and inspired by pastors and church leaders, and many seminary students felt inspired, challenged, and called to put their bodies on the line in this righteous cause. As a major march in Alabama approached in 1965, many seminaries, including the Episcopal Theological School in Boston, were alive with the excitement of students.

> It appealed to their sense of social justice, and a number immediately responded. The questions "Are you going?" and "Are you coming with us?"

were repeatedly asked as students passed one another in the halls or visited in dormitories.[8]

For many seminary students in the mid-60s, their commitment to civil rights was one of the ways in which their scholarship was connected to the hope of changing the world.

The second major social movement of the 60s was the growing criticism of the Vietnam War, particularly among students and faculty of universities. The peace movement also had powerful spokespersons from among theological circles (the Berrigan brothers, William Sloan Coffin, and others) who were among the first to denounce publicly the U.S. commitment to the war. Although anti-war sentiment provoked waves of upheaval in colleges and universities across the country, once again the seminaries and theological education had a special relationship to this movement, for seminary study was a prime deferment for those who felt they could not in conscience fight in a war which they opposed. Thus during this period a number of seminaries and divinity schools attracted populations of students for whom resistance to the Vietnam War was a central part of their motivation for choosing seminary. Many of these students saw no gap between theological studies and scholarship which engaged pressing social issues. This generation of students committed to and inspired by civil rights and peace issues narrowed the gap between theological studies and the research of the human sciences and the "concerned" humanities. Many of them wanted training in sociology, economics, other cultures, Black studies, feminism and the like to give them the background for understanding and speaking to the social issues of the day, and they pressed theological schools to provide such opportunities.

Thus the forces bringing together theological education and university research had at least three dimensions: a) the increasing luster of and cultural faith in the ability of university research to better the world; b) the concomitant professionalization of many fields, including ministerial studies; c) a lively interest in contemporary social issues and social justice issues which seemed to require a background in academic training beyond the aegis of traditional theological disciplines.

A quite separate but extremely powerful historical base for the possibility of large-scale consortia was the impetus which Vatican II gave for a much broader level of ecumenical exchange and cooperation, which now for the first time could encompass both Catholics and Protestants.

---

[8] William J. Schneider, ed., *The Jon Daniels Story* (New York: The Seabury Press, 1967), pp. 25-26.

Ecumenical cooperation among some Protestant seminaries had existed for a long time; most of the consortia formed in the 1950s and 1960s were built on a base of ten or twenty years of cooperation among the Protestant schools. However, the opening of gates in the walls between Catholics and Protestants gave new energy and hope to the ecumenical movement. The entry of the first Roman Catholic schools into the ATS in 1966 represented a dramatic turning point in the opportunities for and scope of theological cooperation in this country. The removal of a barrier of several centuries made progress on other hard issues seem realizable; it would be hard to underestimate the symbolic import of that historical moment. As William Spohn's paper demonstrates, there were motivations from both the Protestant and Catholic sides to take advantage of this new openness in order to enrich, strengthen, and further theological education. However, as is always the case in cooperation, the specific motivations and process for each cooperative venture were determined in many ways by contextual and local considerations.

Finally, although it may at first seem tangential to theological education, the Supreme Court decision on the Schempp case in 1963 also had its effects on the possibilities of and motivations for theological consortia. The Schempp case opened the door for teaching about religion in public institutions, and led to the establishment of Religious Studies departments and programs in many state universities in which the separation of church and state had kept them from involvement in the field of religion. On the one hand, the establishment of Religious Studies departments created a form of competition with seminaries and Divinity Schools, particularly the latter, since such Divinity schools had previously enjoyed a virtual monopoly of graduate level training in topics pertaining to religion. On the other hand, however, they opened a door of opportunity; now in many if not most universities there were faculties and departments engaged in teaching and research about religion. Not only were graduates of Divinity schools becoming faculty in these departments, but there were suddenly more paths of entry into the university for research pertaining to religion. In addition to the general prestige of university research, more of that research could be seen as directly pertinent to issues which theological students and faculty were raising.

The Schempp decision also gave rise to cultural rhetoric justifying public support of non-denominational and non-sectarian approaches to religion that also was adopted by many foundations. Ironically the court's decision did not provide a firm legal basis for all of this rhetoric,[9] but it did engender a set of governmental and cultural understandings in defense of public support of non-sectarian study of religion, and thus provided the possibilities for funding for theological schools who were in cooperation with a non-sectarian, non-denominational ecumenical cluster. This new language of public support for "religion" created an extra incentive to formalize the inter-denominational cooperation which was beginning to flower.

Thus a convergence of a set of social ideals, a confidence in university research as a way of finding solutions to social ills, the prestige of the university, ecumenical idealism, and opportunities for broader cooperation and for funding all combined to support impulses for theological cooperation and the establishment of consortia. The convergence of factors and motivations is important, for it helps to explain how very different sorts of consortia could arise in different settings with distinctive motivations and still see themselves, at least in part, as involved in a trend or movement within theological education. However, the confluence of motives and factors also complicates an understanding of the success or failure of such ventures.

The euphoric vision of the promise of ecumenical consortia is perhaps best represented in the 1968 report of the Resources Planning Commission of ATS.[10] The Commission's concern was planning for the next decade of theological education, taking into account changes in enrollment patterns and student demography, directions of the church and ministry, needed improvements in theological education, and the financial condition of seminaries. They built their recommendations and analysis in part on a report called "Theological Education in the 1970s," which had been prepared by a Task Force of ATS.[11] Without endorsing all the details of that Task Force's recommendations, they noted that the Task Force had strongly recommended that seminary course work be offered in "a major theological center set in a university environment" in order to provide the range of courses and electives necessary for a seminary education adequate for ministry in the contemporary world.[12] They also noted that in order to staff their model curriculum an average

---

[9] W. Royce Clark, "Legal Status of Religious Studies Programs in Higher Education," *Beyond the Classics? Essays in Relikgious Studies and Liberal Education,* Frank E. Reynolds and Sheryl L. Burkhalter, ed. (Atlanta: Scholars Press, 1990, pp. 109-140).
[10] "Resources Planning in Theological Education," *Theological Education* 4 (Summer 1968), 751-845.
[11] Ibid, pp. 757-763.
[12] "Resources Planning," p. 788.

of 92 faculty would be required (as compared with an average of 18 at an independent seminary), and an average student enrollment of 775, as compared with the 220 average in seminaries.¹³ Hence, the Resource Planning Commission concluded,

> The landscape of theological education in North America a decade hence is likely to be characterized by a small number of major clusters. These will be in proximity to large universities in the major metropolitan areas in which most of the nation's great public and private universities are now located. We believe that these clusters will be ecumenical in character; they will be groupings of confessionally-based seminaries.¹⁴

A number of aspects of the Commission's view are noteworthy for the present study. First, although they noted the ecumenical nature of the clusters and their need for diverse faculty resources, university proximity and urban location were singled out as the two salient characteristics of a consortium. Thus access to university resources was central to their concerns. Second, their conclusions were based primarily on the needs of M.DIV. education, not doctoral education. Their report explored the possibilities of having a more unified M.DIV. curriculum within each cluster. They cite reports of Presidents and Deans in one metropolitan area that 75% of their courses were virtually identical, and thus might be consolidated or regrouped to allow for more experimental use of faculty resources.¹⁵ Third, although they wisely foresaw that costs of seminary education, given all the new demands, would continue to rise, they felt that cooperation could lead to some cost savings which would make the rates of increase somewhat more gradual.¹⁶ Finally, they were concerned with increased competition among seminaries for a declining student population, and argued that the clusters were more likely to attract students and find resources for those programs which would give them the competitive edge.

Not quite twenty years later The Cheswick Center was funded by the Lilly Endowment to do a study on theological cooperation, assessing the success and achievements of the consortia founded in the 1960s as well as other less formal approaches to theological cooperation. Their study was based on extensive questionnaires sent to theological faculty and on interviews with Presidents and Deans of theological schools. Their report noted, first, that the Resource Planning Commission's premise that such

---

[13] Ibid., p. 790; note that these figures are as of 1968.
[14] Ibid., p. 791.
[15] Ibid., p. 778.
[16] Ibid., p. 812.

clusters would change the face of M.DIV. education had not been borne out by history; no cluster had successfully adopted the notion of the "curriculum for the 70s," in part because of the resistance of schools to give up their M.DIV. curriculum. In fact, the report noted, "other cooperative ventures succeeded, in part, because they avoided this difficult issue and focussed on graduate education and library cooperation, not the major goals of the RPC."[17] The report goes on to note that given the history of intra- and inter-denominational rivalry in the U.S., seminaries are often seen as the source of identity of a particular denomination, and thus the M.DIV. program is closely guarded as a symbol of the school's denominational identity.[18] A key factor in the success of cooperative ventures, then, is the agreement not to tamper with M.DIV. curricula.

While the Resources Planning Commission was careful not to promise that consortial cooperation would lessen costs, their references to some possible cost savings through economies of scale has in the decades of the 1970s and 80s been an attractive motivation for cooperation. Unfortunately, when that is the sole or primary motivation of cooperation it is extremely difficult to establish enduring relationships, since the cost of administering such ventures, given their complexities and built-in ambiguities, are often high. Moreover, ongoing success requires strong leadership. Too often as the ecumenical impetus waned, the costs of continued formal cooperation were seen to outweigh the benefits, and ventures foundered on this.

Thus, of the factors listed by the Resources Planning Commission it is the relationship to a major university with its rich resources and the diversity of faculty resources not only for instruction but for the sake of faculty development which are among the major benefits of consortia. Moreover, because of the intimate relationship between M.DIV. programs and identity astutely analyzed by the Cheswick report, it is usually doctoral level cooperation or the coordination of special enrichment programs (overseas studies opportunities, centers for specialized ministries, or special library collections) which can sustain enduring cooperative ventures. Of particular interest to the theme of this essay is the importance of relationships with a university in many theological consortia; it is this aspect of consortia which can help clarify the issues raised in this volume.

---

[17] "Cooperative Ventures," p. 30.
[18] Ibid., pp. 42-43.

II. An Example: Graduate Theological Union

The GTU in Berkeley, now entering its 30th year, is one of the oldest and most tightly knit examples of a theological consortium. It represents both the positive and negative aspects of cooperative ventures noted above, and thus provides an interesting example of how the consortial model provides a different angle on the relationship of theological institutions to the university.

The GTU, it is fair to say, was inspired by the ecumenical ethos and opportunities of the early 1960s, and was given great impetus by the participation of the Roman Catholic Schools; their entry signalled an historic accomplishment. However, the immediate motivation for the formation of the Union was the desire to offer a doctorate which would be sounder than that which any of the institutions could offer individually and for which the students would also have access to the outstanding resources of the University of California at Berkeley. The GTU was from the outset differentiated from the unhappy Chicago Federated Faculty model in two respects: 1) none of the schools was part of the university per se, and thus none could dominate the Union at the expense of the others, and 2) each of the schools agreed from the outset that the PH.D/TH.D. would be offered only through the Consortium; none of the schools offers an independent PH.D. or TH.D. The establishment of the doctoral program, it should be noted, had many levels of motivation. First, schools felt that the opportunity to teach first-rate doctoral students and to have access to university colleagues and research resources would help the schools to attract and retain outstanding faculty. Second, in light of the increasing competition for students among seminaries, it was felt that such strong faculties plus the rich resources of both the university and ecumenical atmosphere would help attract students to all programs, not simply the doctoral program. Third, it was hoped that the doctoral program and the relationship with a world-class university would give more visibility to the West coast as a center for theological education.

There have been at points in GTU's history some exploration of coordinating the M.DIV. curriculum, but they never went very far. There have been team-taught courses in church history or other fields, with shared large lectures and denominationally based small-group discussions,[19] but none of these has endured the test of time. Beyond such experiments, the

---

[19] Note that these were rather optimistically described in David Schuller's 1968 article on the GTU; that optimism was not justified. David S. Schuller, "Graduate Theological Union: A Descriptive-Evaluative Study" *Theological Education* 4 (Summer 1968, Supplement 1): 3-21.

schools have always reserved the right to design their own M.DIV. curricula, and in the 1980s denominational pressures have made these curricula more and not less distinctive. On the other hand, all of the M.DIV. students have full cross-registration privileges with other schools; the schools share a common course schedule and calendar, and a Common Registrar; even the classroom space is pooled. Moreover, since six of the nine seminaries are within easy walking distance of each other and the university, and transportation is provided to and from the outlying schools, cross-registration is relatively unhindered by geographical separation. The M.DIV. programs enrich each other to a greater or lesser extent (the cross-registration patterns vary considerably from school to school), but the consortium does not administer or proscribe anything about M.DIV. education. The Council of Presidents has long recognized that more coordination at the M.DIV. level would be cost-effective. The consortium as a whole has around 135 full-time faculty; however because of the autonomous M.DIV. programs the course offerings are highly repetitive in many areas and enrollments are often quite low. This was recognized as early as 1976 in a study on faculty deployment.[20] More coordinated deployment of faculty would free resources for more electives in the M.DIV. programs and for doctoral education, but progress in this area has been slow. The Council of Deans has recently begun to review three-year course projections to determine whether some of the duplication can be eased and some gaps caused by sabbaticals filled, but that is a small first step.

The strong desire for a relationship with the University established the groundwork for the most important move in creating a truly permanent consortial relationship. The University was open to cooperation with GTU libraries, but did not feel it was feasible to deal with nine separate libraries. Thus the seminaries moved beyond their initial coordination of purchasing and cataloging to create a common library agreement which consolidated all of the libraries into one. The common library provides a much deeper and broader collection than would be possible with individual libraries, and there are also considerable cost savings although the seminaries still groan under rising library costs. The Flora Lamsen Hewlett Library, both as a building and as an academic reality, is often cited as both the symbol and institutional "glue" of the GTU. Because of their participation in the common library it is not realistically possible for any of the schools to leave the consortium although they

---

[20] Michael R. Rion, "Graduate Theological Union: Background Data on Faculty Deployment," January 6, 1976; report written on request of the President.

have the legal right to do so. If they were to leave, they would no longer have a viable library.

One of the tensions in the GTU has been the cost of administering the consortium and the common library. In the course of the past two decades, as the individual schools have developed a plethora of programs beyond the classic M.DIV., they have relied on the GTU central administration to administer the common programs and some common services. However, the cost of that administration has grown faster than some of the schools had anticipated, particularly when they feel pressures on their own budgets. At times there has also been some tension about the fact that the doctoral program is taught almost entirely by faculty hired by the member schools (the GTU rostered faculty is 6.5 FTE), so that faculty time is seen as yet another "donation" to the GTU. A second tension has to do with governance and authority. While the Deans and Presidents of the member schools do not have the time to administer the central programs or common services, they still legitimately view the GTU consortium as their creation and thus want to be able to shape its directions. At its worst, this can degenerate into a sort of "veto" mentality in which the GTU can do nothing unless all of the schools agree—and given the diversity of schools there are very few things on which they can agree. Usually, however, GTU initiatives require extensive consultation and discussion; there is a popular saying at the GTU, "Nothing at the GTU is ever decided until it has been decided seven times."

If this sounds complex and chaotic, it is; such is the nature of consortial enterprises. In a very real sense the member schools are the GTU; in other senses the GTU operates as if it were a "tenth" school. The issues of identity and authority are so complex as to bear resemblance to the subtleties of trinitarian doctrine. Yet the enterprise works remarkably well.

The Cheswick Center report on cooperative ventures noted: a) the high level of ambiguity and complexity with which administrators of consortia must cope; b) the importance of strong leadership to inspire and negotiate continued cooperation; and c) the deep idealism about and commitment to cooperation beneath the patina of criticism and complaints that accompany any cooperative venture. The report referred to the latter as "an untapped level of commitment to a future of cooperation which should be fostered."[21] The layer of deep commitment to cooperation beneath a surface of tensions and complaints is very much evident at

---

[21] "Cooperative Ventures," p. 56

the GTU, and the central administration works to deal with the tensions while tapping that level of commitment.

III. GTU and the University

The consortium movement highlights some interesting aspects of the relationship of theological education to the university. First, establishing closer relations with the university was an important factor in virtually all instances of the formation of theological consortia. Because of the prestige of university research, at least in the early 1960s, and the interest of seminary students and faculty in issues of social justice and reform, a number of seminaries sought to enrich their programs, attract students and faculty through establishing relationships with a university.

However, the relationship between the seminaries and the university is definitely asymmetrical. While the divinity schools within some major universities experience a degree of marginalization, the attempt to negotiate a relationship between external theological schools or seminaries and a major university serves to highlight the complex and problematic relationship between university and theological education. That it can be done at all, however, is an important fact that also merits attention.

The relationship between the GTU and the University of California at Berkeley is almost a paradigm of a "hard case." The University of California is not only a publicly funded state institution, but one at which to this day there is faculty resistance to the establishment of a Religious Studies Department. In all of the history of political turmoil of the 60s and 70s at Berkeley, there also has been fierce resistance on the part of some faculty to the establishment of religion as a field of study. There has been an undergraduate interdisciplinary program or major in Religious Studies for about fifteen years, but a proposal to establish a graduate program and department has failed within the last five years.

The GTU has a long-standing relationship with the university which, it must be admitted, is more central and vital to the GTU than it is to the university. There are two areas in which the relationship is not only formally symmetrical but also based squarely on mutual self-interest. One is library cooperation. UCB and GTU libraries have healthy and mutually important agreements about collection priorities which allows the joint libraries to offer richer collections in a number of areas than they otherwise could. The faculty and students of the GTU consortium and UCB have mutual borrowing privileges. The GTU library has terminals for the GLADYS on-line catalog of the UCB libraries. Another is the joint degree program in Near Eastern Studies. This program is administered by a joint faculty committee under the joint supervision of UCB and GTU deans; students are admitted to both institutions and pay tuition to UCB and GTU in alternate years. The joint degree program is successful because neither institution alone has the depth of faculty resources to mount it, but together they are in a strong competitive position. The two institutions are currently exploring a second joint degree in Jewish Studies. The one disadvantage of a joint degree program is that unless the chair of the faculty committee provides leadership for recruiting students and advertising, the program can drift toward the margins of the priorities of both participating institutions.

If library cooperation and the joint degree program are characterized by symmetrical relationships, in general the relations of GTU and UCB are characterized by asymmetry. There is a cross-registration agreement in which students of either campus may enroll in courses in either institution with no tuition adjustment, but the reality is that the vast majority of cross-registration goes from GTU to UCB. All PH.D. students at the GTU must be admitted "to coursework" at UCB by having the university's registrar's office approve GTU admissions, but this general admission does not guarantee students entrance into courses in a specific department; in high demand fields, such as clinical psychology, departments are loathe to let "external" graduate students into their courses. The GTU underscores the importance of the UCB connection and of the secular disciplines of research by requiring that all comprehensive and dissertation committees include an "external" member who is ordinarily to be a member of the UC faculty; other external members require special approval of the GTU Dean. Thus the GTU has built UCB into the structure of its programs in a way in which the University does not reciprocate. A number of GTU faculty in history, Jewish Studies, and philosophy sit regularly on graduate student committees at UCB, but the pattern is still very asymmetrical.

The general lesson is that while theological disciplines have enthusiastically turned toward their conversation partners in the human sciences, literature, and philosophy, it is much less common that the other disciplines have as a general trend found themselves turning toward theology. Theological education and Religious Studies are both interdisciplinary enterprises which tend to ask broad and synthetic questions, while many other disciplines have turned inward and become increasingly specialized. In order to remedy this asymmetry, theological studies will have to take more leadership in establishing an intellectual agenda which can inspire the interest of colleagues in other disciplines.

With all of the obstacles and asymmetries, why was the GTU successful in establishing a relationship with the state university? The most crucial factor was the dedication and vision of a number of administrators and faculty in both institutions who were able to see the possibilities and build on them. However, there were a number of other forces on which they were able to build.

One was the strong advisability of library cooperation. The GTU was established at precisely the moment when library administrators began to perceive the kinds of budgetary pressures which would come from automation, rising costs in books and periodicals, and the explosion of knowledge. The library was a significant factor in the success of the GTU. It was noted above that the library is in many ways the institutional glue which, as one of the Presidents describes it, "joins the schools at the hip." The combining of the member school libraries was precipitated by pressure from the university, which was open to cooperation but could not deal with nine separate libraries. For both the University and the GTU schools, library collaboration provided a relatively non-controversial front on which to push cooperation forward.

The second is the more elusive "untapped level of commitment to a future of cooperation" which was cited in the Cheswick Center report. One has only to read the Chronicle of Higher Education to note that for the past ten or twenty years university administrators have been trying to encourage institutional cooperation and exchanges, on the one hand, and to revive some sense of the unity of learning on the other. There are, to be sure, powerful countervailing forces. Nevertheless the ideal of strengthening theological education by giving its students access to the critical inquiry and discourse of the university was inspiring to leaders of the university as well as those in the consortium.

The third is perhaps related. GTU faculty have at times wondered why extremely busy and eminent UCB faculty agree to serve on committees of a consortium which is structurally "external" to the university. What we hear from the university faculty who do so is that the kinds of questions which GTU doctoral students pursue are so bold and interesting, particularly in the sense that they are related to issues that matter, that they find working with them refreshing and fascinating; it involves them in research which is rarely if ever pursued at the university. One or two university faculty have claimed that working with GTU students has been a critical factor in shaping their own research. The structure of the GTU program which requires doctoral students to persuade outside faculty to serve gratis on their committees certainly encourages students to be able to "sell" their ideas to faculty. What the GTU structure may also have inadvertently done is to ask our doctoral students to do that which theological faculties have not been entirely successful in doing: define a research agenda which can help to rebuild ties to other disciplines. I will return presently to the notion that the very structure of a consortium independent of and yet related to a university creates a base for an approach to research which is both independent of and in conversation with both university and church.

The GTU benefits greatly from its relationship to the university. Many GTU faculty enjoy the prestige of participating in a doctoral program related to the university and enjoy the privileges of access to world-class library resources, and they are delighted that their students have access to the intellectual resources. On the other hand, the relationship with the university has sometimes been a source of contention within the GTU.

For many years GTU by-laws stipulated that the major governing councils of the doctoral program were to include UCB faculty representatives. Occasionally, when a student's doctoral dissertation proposal was rejected or a faculty member was not approved for service on the doctoral faculty, there was a tendency to blame the "university." Recently, the doctoral faculty decided on the urging of the GTU Dean that the principle of peer governance of faculty requires that GTU faculty set and enforce the academic standards of the doctoral program. The GTU doctoral faculty have collectively set rigorous standards of academic scholarship; they need to own them as their own.

Second, despite the importance of the cross-registration agreement and the requirement that students include UCB faculty on their committees, the consortium has never been able to bring itself to align its academic calendar with that of the university. Whenever that issue is raised there is rhetoric about the "university's tail wagging the consortium's dog." One practical argument against the university calendar is that it would complicate summer internship placements for M.DIV. students, but to a large degree the issue is symbolic. The consortium wants the relationship with the university, but somehow feels that it introduces an alien set of standards and agendas. The most thoughtful version of this issue or tension is doubts about whether the model of the modern research university sets the paradigm for the sort of research which is needed in the humanities and human sciences, including theology. I will return to this issue below.

The issues, small and large, only serve to underscore the patterns of tension between theological studies and the so-called secular university in the late twentieth century. Because the GTU is structurally external to the university both sides are somewhat freer to express these tensions over a range of issues; there is no historic or structural connection to soften the differences.

IV. GTU and the Denominations

If being external to the university exacerbates certain tensions, being structurally external to the churches frees the consortium from certain constraints. The GTU central administration and programs are governed by their own Board of Trustees, which includes representatives from the member school boards, but also a large percentage of "at-large" members. The Board also includes a significant contingent of Jewish members who have been generous in their support of the GTU and its Center for Jewish Studies. The Jewish presence serves to deepen the GTU Board's transcendence of a denominational focus. The GTU's "non-denominational" nature has been a key factor in procuring grants from the NEH and some other foundations, and has at some moments been a critical factor in discussions with the UCB faculty senate and its committees. Internally, it also has its advantages. As one of the member school's Presidents likes to put it, "The GTU provides a creative free space in which we can do things or offer opportunities which the individual schools do not have to endorse specifically, thus avoiding negative pressure from the denominations." There are, of course, very real limits to that freedom; consistent flouting of a denomination's sensibilities by the GTU would eventually threaten that member school board's willingness to continue supporting the consortium. Nonetheless, the "separateness" of the GTU can provide some limited freedom of action and movement for the schools.

The non-denominational center of the GTU, however, lives in creative relationship to the denominationally-based member schools. This mitigates a problem some students feel at interdenominational schools or historically denominational schools which now have a broad mixture of students and faculty. Within the rich ecumenical and interreligious diversity of the GTU (Pure Land Buddhist, Jewish, and Eastern Orthodox Institutes or Centers add to the natural denominational mix), the denominationally-based member schools provide havens of relatively clear religious community and identity. That is to say, the GTU is structurally inter-denominational in a way that does not efface or confuse denominational bases. Each of the schools is strongly linked to its denominational base, and is committed to offering a denominationally coherent curriculum and maintaining a liturgical and social community. In the cross-registration and common programs of the consortium, this denominational identity is brought into creative conversation with a broad ecumenical mix. The structure of the consortium continually underlines this dialogue between and among communities, and helps to sort out individual differences as opposed to differences among denominations and communities.

Many theological schools are today wrestling with the issues of pluralism: cultural, global, racial-ethnic, and ecumenical. On the latter issue the GTU by its structure lives with a pattern of daily ecumenical interchange which is both clear and diverse. The denominational structures of the schools helps to reassure students and faculty (and denominational constituencies) that the variety of the GTU does not undermine identity. Students and faculty virtually unanimously report that the ecumenical mix helps to clarify identity; the ecumenical conversations require that unexamined assumptions be brought to light and clarified, and thus students and faculty are challenged to be very clear on where their communities stand.

V. The GTU's Creative Space Between the University and the Church

The GTU, then, is structurally a space between the university and the denominations, belonging to neither and yet intimately engaged with both. On the negative side, this means that the case for the GTU needs to be continually and articulately made to both university and church. On the positive side, the GTU has, quite literally, the space to define theological education and scholarship in new and positive ways which can contribute to both environments. The GTU's structural location between the two poles of church and university has to some extent built that creative space into the structure of its programs, but it has only begun the process of articulating and intentionally nurturing the new pattern of research and scholarship which that space makes possible. Ironically, the rhetoric of the mission statement of the GTU and its catalog do not define this particularly well or specifically. That is another example of the problems of consortia. The single most difficult thing for a consortium to agree upon is a mission statement or set of specific common goals. Such a mission statement is useless if all of the participating institutions do not endorse it, but if the institutions are truly diverse they will find it difficult to agree on common rhetoric, since the single institutions each have distinctive missions and purposes. The purposes which can be universally endorsed are usually limited and specific (a common doctorate; a common library; a few common services), but these are not adequate to support an institutional mission statement. The common statements of such consortia tend to very general purposes and values. It is more helpful to observe what the consortium actually does and to deduce its mission and philosophy from its actions. A hard look at the doctoral program speaks eloquently, I believe, about the GTU's philosophy of education and its distinctive location between church and university.

First, the GTU doctoral program is not based on a set of core courses either universally or within any of the Areas of study. Students at the GTU are given very broad freedom to design their own courses of study in consultation with the faculty; the rigorous evaluation of students is focussed on the comprehensive examinations and an elaborate procedure for review of the dissertation proposal. The latter is approved first by the student's committee, then by the faculty of the Area, and finally by the Doctoral Council composed of Area Conveners, the Dean, and student representatives. Each of these review processes is exacting; most students undergo a long and elaborate process of developing, refining, and presenting the proposal for the dissertation. While there are plans to develop a common intellectual experience for all GTU doctoral students and to develop regular Area seminars, the flexibility of the program reflects a recognition that the size and diversity of the consortium precludes a standard curriculum. If one tries to imagine Jesuits, Unitarian-Universalists, and American Baptists trying to agree on a standard core curriculum in, say, theology or liturgy, one begins to grasp the scope of the problem.

The Doctoral Areas are not organized along denominational lines, but rather reconfigure the faculty of the consortium under the general rubrics of: 1) Biblical Studies; 2) Systematic Theology and Philosophy; 3) History of Christianity; 4) Ethics and Society; 5) Religion and Personality Sciences; 6) The Arts, Worship, and Proclamation; 7) History of Religions, and 8) Christian Spirituality.

Second, the doctoral faculty have built an ecumenical or interreligious dimension into the program. If the doctoral program rests primarily on the comprehensives and dissertations, the committees overseeing these two in fact structure and oversee the student's work. These committees must include representatives of "more than one school" of the GTU; in this case the GTU is treated as a tenth school, and its faculty is expanded to include those faculty from the Institute for Buddhist Studies who participate in the doctoral program. The impact is to ensure that no dissertation or comprehensive is narrowly sectarian. Comprehensive examinations or the dissertation proposals receive the critical scrutiny of scholars from more than one religious community.

As noted above, the doctoral program also structurally requires significant exposure to and dialogue with the "secular" disciplines of the research university through the requirement of an external reader, who is normally expected to be on the university faculty. The Council on Graduate Studies in Religion has traditionally listed familiarity with other university disciplines as one of the hallmarks of a sound doctoral program in "religion." The GTU has institutionalized this component through its committee structures.

Finally, the freedom of the program combined with the necessity for students to "sell" their project to outside readers has produced an approach to research which I think is highly suggestive of how "university-related divinity schools" might contribute to redefining or broadening the research agenda. Again, this has been more of a happy product of the structures of the program than a consciously developed philosophy of theological research, and yet it arguably is the best exemplar of the values on which the GTU doctoral program is based.

It is difficult to find the appropriate vocabulary to talk about this distinctive sort of research. The doctoral faculty tried to name it at a meeting in which they sought to define for planning purposes what is "distinctive" about the GTU's program. One faculty member called it "research for advocacy," although others thought that phrase carried political baggage from the 1960s, which they felt was misleading. Others referred more colloquially to "research that matters."

The elusiveness of the language was reinforced by a study of recent dissertation topics and proposals; while many proposals were indeed motivated by issues which "made a difference" in the current world, the approaches and methodologies were not by any means preeminently practical. Given the elaborate procedure for the approval of dissertation proposals, GTU proposals must cover scholarly bases and methodological bases very thoroughly: after all, the proposal may be voted upon by as many as 35 faculty before it is finally approved. Yet as one coming from more than a dozen years in a Religious Studies department at a state institution, the proposals I have seen in four and one-half years at the GTU have convinced me more directly than any other evidence of the distinctive and special character of this program. They are sound scholastically, but they also engage bold and significant issues.

The GTU, then, because of its location between the university and the church has come to foster a sort of scholarship which profoundly engaged both precisely because it is free from excessive constraints of either the university or the church. Yet the GTU has not succeeded in naming or defining this distinctive research nor in helping the world of theological education to define its future directions. Like most consortia, it is still groping for its full potential.

Conclusion: Making the Space Between a Positive Space

There is a tendency on the part of divinity schools or university-related theological schools to see themselves as caught between the poles of the church and the university, answerable to both and fully supported by neither. In the worst cases they feel marginalized and under suspicion from two directions. University faculty and administrators sometimes doubt that divinity school faculty are as hard-headed and critically rigorous as faculty in more traditional departments, while church leaders fear that the divinity school faculty have "sold out" to intellectual elitism and forgotten the practical needs of the churches. This double marginalization is particularly ironic since both the church and the university are facing internal challenges which sound theological scholarship is well situated to address.

The challenges facing the church are basically the same as those outlined in the curriculum for the 1970s by the ATS task force: demographic shifts in society radically changing the needs of both urban and rural parishes; the increasing importance of racial-ethnic populations within U.S. churches who want their religious life to affirm their cultural heritages; the increasing recognition of the global nature of the churches and the variety of contextualized theologies which must be produced; the emergence of the voices of women, the differently abled, homosexuals and others who have felt invisible or ignored within the church; the pressing social issues of the homeless, AIDS, ecological crisis, global peace. As in the 1970s these issues require both pastors and scholars/teachers educated broadly not only in the traditions of their denominations but in the emerging issues facing the churches. The resources of the university are as vital as ever, as is scholarship and teaching which engages and seeks solutions for a host of contemporary challenges to the church.

The university is still an important institution in our society, but its prestige and luster have faded somewhat since its heyday, in part because there is today a clearer recognition of the complexities of social problems such as the underclass, racism, multicultural education, and arms control. After nearly three decades of research and projects, it is not possible to be rosily optimistic about "solutions."

There is, however, a deeper problem in the waning of cultural faith in the university. The prestige of the post-war research model and the dramatic growth of universities produced an explosion in the size and number of departments which rapidly accelerated the specialization and fragmentation of disciplines. The technical vocabulary of many disciplines have become so arcane that faculty feel cut off from the broad multidisciplinary conversation which was once characteristic of the university, and from which evolved the university's approach to liberal education. There has been a collapse of faith in the general education curriculum and its canon which has led to very heated and controversial curricular debates both locally and nationally. At the level of research, however, the review structures of the university, which are based in the ever more specialized professional guilds, have reinforced the tendency toward specialized and arcane scholarship. Whereas once scholarship in the humanities was about human issues and values, today it is too often a highly technical exercise of no interest to anyone but another specialist.

There are powerful counter-forces at work, perhaps best symbolized in the proliferation of humanities centers on campuses around the country with the express purpose of fostering interdisciplinary research and conversations in the human sciences. University administrators are seeking creative ways to revive the common discourse and to recreate links between research and undergraduate teaching. Moreover, a number of institutions are consciously seeking to reintroduce "value education" into the core curriculum of the college and the professional schools.

If theological education was once out of step in its distrust of the scientific model as the only appropriate paradigm for research, the cadence of the academic parade is seeking to lock step again with values and human concerns. This is something which theological education never lost. The moment is ripe for theological scholars once again to exert some leadership in defining the research agenda of the university. The problem is that theological scholarship is still undergoing its own redefinitions; what is the distinctive core of theological scholarship? What defines and unites it even as it develops in a dozen different directions?

At the ATS Summer Seminar on Basic Issues in Theological Education held at New Harmony, Indiana, July, 1989, there were two proposals about the distinctive nature of research (or theological research) which suggested how theological institutions might be able to help redefine and broaden the research agenda of the university. First, John Cobb presented a paper which argued, among other things, that research should flow from the "passions" and "existential issues" of the researcher; he believes that those issues which matter in a deeply personal way will in fact express and define issues of import to the broader community and the world. I am not entirely comfortable with the "existential" language of his proposal, but the basic issue is profound. Theological studies can lead the university into its rediscovery that research can and should be about issues of consequence, issues that matter in human terms.[22] There are some in the university who might be embarrassed to admit that they study what they do because the issues matter deeply to them. However, the time may be right once more to stress the significance of the research agenda of faculty, to ask the question "so what?" not just in theoretical terms, but in terms of the human significance of the research projects. This is a point at which theology may legitimately raise some critical questions about the appropriateness of an uncritical scientific paradigm for research; what has happened to the human and humane motivations for learning?

At that same meeting Schubert Ogden in discussions advanced an intriguing definition of authentic research as "that which pushes the boundaries of the guild or field." His point was that all too often research productivity is quantified into "numbers of pages" in highly specialized and arcane journals, but that such definitions all too often lead to formulaic research and overspecialized discourse. He made a distinction between scholarship, which is based on the accepted critical methods and literature of the academy, and research, which has the purpose of pushing the boundaries and moving things forward. Excellent research is of course attentive to scholarly methods and literature, but it should not stop there. Although Ogden offered his definition as a general definition of research and scholarship, it is arguable that the interdisciplinary nature of theological studies, and its connection to living communities through professional education, may naturally lead to questions and issues that push the boundaries.

The GTU is located in a space between the university and the church, and thus is to a greater extent than most university-related divinity schools independent of both. It has because of this structural freedom been able to produce a program which gives students both the freedom

---

[22] John J. Cobb, Jr. "Research for a Theological Faculty," *Theological Education* 26:2 (Spring, 1990): 86-105..

and the impetus to structure their research agenda along the lines of Cobb and Ogden. The relative independence from specific denominational constraints allows and encourages students to push the boundaries of theological research, giving their scholarship a "prophetic" edge. Their location structurally external to the university gives them the freedom to engage large issues of human significance which are seldom tackled within university departments. Such consortia suggest a paradigm of the location of theological research which is enriched by an intimate relation with both church and university, but which can speak vitally and prophetically to both.

The space between need not become a mire in which theological scholarship sinks into oblivion; it can become a positive space if theologians are able to articulate a foundation of sound scholarship which takes advantage of all of the intellectual resources of the academy to engage issues which will challenge the church and help the university to recover a sense of connection to human value and meaning. That space can be a creative space when it is used not only to listen to the demands of both church and university, but to engage them in a critical and creative way.

The space defined in this article is not solely open to consortia; in a sense any theological school related to a university shares that space to some degree. However, since the structural space of consortia is as much a matter of neither/nor as of both/and, their very location tends to create approaches to scholarship which implicitly transcend and speak to both poles of relationship. Theological scholarship has had trouble finding its distinctive voice in the past two decades. If the location of a school to university and/or church is perceived as being mired in or overwhelmed by either, then that creative voice can be lost. The creativity of the "space between" is to experience the freedom of a distinctive location from which the school and its scholarship can contribute to conversations in both the academy and the church, and in that way regain its role as a shaper of inquiry.

Biographical Notes

JUDITH BERLING earned her B.A. in Religion from Carleton College, Northfield, Minnesota, and her PH.D. from Columbia University in New York in Chinese thought, with a research interest in interaction among religious communities. She taught for twelve years in the Department of Religious Studies at Indiana University, Bloomington, and has also taught on a visiting basis at Stanford University and the University of Chicago Divinity School. She has been active in the American Academy of Religion and in NEH-funded projects assessing the role of Religious Studies in the liberal arts. Since she became Dean of the Graduate Theological Union in Berkeley in 1987, she has been exploring the role of ecumenism and religious diversity in theological education, and the relationship of theological education to public universities.

CONRAD CHERRY is Professor of Religious Studies and American Studies and Director of the Center for the Study of Religion and American Culture at Indiana University-Purdue University at Indianapolis. He was previously Professor of Religious Studies and American Studies at the Pennsylvania State University, and for seven years was Director of Scholars Press and Research Professor of American Religious History at Emory University. His publications include the books *The Theology of Jonathan Edwards, God's New Israel,* and *Nature and Religious Imagination.* He is currently working on a history of university-related divinity schools since the rise of the modern American university.

B. A. GERRISH is John Nuveen Professor in the Divinity School, the University of Chicago, and a Fellow of the American Academy of Arts and Sciences. He holds degrees from Cambridge (M.A. in classics), Union Theological Seminary, New York (S.T.M. in systematic theology), Columbia (PH.D. in philosophy of religion), and St. Andrews (D.D. honoris causa). He has written widely on European religious thought since the Protestant Reformation and has served as President of the American Theological Society (Midwest Division) and the American Society of Church History. Among his publications are *Grace and Reason* (1962), *Tradition and the Modern World* (1978), and *The Old Protestantism and the New* (1982).

JOSEPH C. HOUGH, JR. became Dean of The Divinity School at Vanderbilt on January 1, 1990. Prior to his move to Vanderbilt, he had been Dean at the School of Theology at Claremont for fourteen years. He had also served as Professor of Ethics and Public Policy at the Claremont Graduate School's Center for Politics and Policy and Professor of Social Ethics at the School of Theology in Claremont. During 1988-89 he was director of the Humanities Planning Task force for the Claremont Graduate School. Hough has been an educational consultant to a number of divinity schools and seminaries and has co-chaired the Issues Research Program for the Association of Theological Schools for five years. His most recent publications are *Beyond Clericalism* (with Barbara Wheeler) and *Christian Identity and Theological Education* (with John B. Cobb, Jr.). His essay *The University and the Common Good* will appear next year in a volume of essays on theology and the university.

JOSEPH MITSUO KITAGAWA studied at Rikkyo University, SeaburyWestern Theological Seminary, and the University of Chicago. He spent three and a half years during World II at camps for persons of Japanese ancestry in New Mexico and Idaho. He taught the history of religions 1951-85 at the University of Chicago, and he was Dean of its Divinity School, 1970-80. He served as President (1969-72) of the American Society for the Study of Religion, is a past chairman of ACLS's Committee on the History of Religions, and was formerly vice-president of Conseil International Philosophie Sciences Humaines. His publications include *The History of Religions: Understanding Human Experience* (Scholars Press, 1987), *On Understanding Japanese Religion* (Princeton, 1987), and *The Quest for Human Unity: A Religious History* (Fortress, forthcoming).

CHARLES H. LONG is the Jeannette K. Watson Professor of History of Religions at Syracuse University. He has taught at the University of Chicago where, with Joseph Kitagawa and Mircea Eliade, the *History of Religions* journal was founded. He is the Editor of the series, *Studies in*

Religion, at the University of North Carolina Press, where he taught for twelve years. His publications include *Alpha: The Myths of Creation, Myths and Symbols* (coedited with Joseph Kitagawa) and *Significations, Signs, Symbols, and Images in the Interpretation of Religion*. Professor Long's major interests have been the History of Religions, African and African American Religions, Religion in the New World, and the methodological and interpretive problems in the study of religion.

ROBERT WOOD LYNN is now Scholar in Residence at Bangor Theological Seminary. Between 1976 and 1989 he served the Lilly Endowment in various capacities, most recently as Senior Vice-President, Religion. Prior to his work at the Lilly Endowment, Mr. Lynn was the Dean of Auburn Theological Seminary and a member of the faculty of Union Theological Seminary (New York). In the course of his time at Auburn, he served on the visiting committees at Harvard and Yale Divinity Schools as well as a member of a special review committee for the Divinity School at the University of Chicago. His published works include several works on the history of Protestant education. He is currently engaged in writing a social history of the notion of stewardship in American culture.

GLENN T. MILLER is Professor of Church History at Southeastern Baptist Theological Seminary in Wake Forest, North Carolina. After receiving his doctorate from Union Theological Seminary (New York City), he taught at St. Mary's Seminary and Hamilton College beofre accepting the post at Southeastern in 1976. During the last sixteen years, Professor Miller has devoted much of his time as a scholar to the study of American theological education. His most recent work along this line is *Piety and Intellect: The Aim and Purpose of Antebellum Theological Education* (Atlanta: Scholars Press, 1990). His other scholarly interests include the topic of church and state relations in the United States and eighteenth century American religion.

WILLIAM C. SPOHN, S.J. is Associate Professor of Theological Ethics at the Jesuit School of Theology at Berkeley, Graduate Theological Union. He holds degrees from the Jesuit School of Theology at Berkeley (M.DIV. 1974, S.T.L. 1980) and the Divinity School of the University of Chicago (PH.D. 1978). From 1982-3 he was the Bannan Professor of Christian Values at Santa Clara University. He entered the Society of Jesus in September 1962, and was ordained as a priest on March 23, 1974. He is the author of *What Are They Saying About Scripture and Ethics?* (Paulist Press, 1984), and a regular contributor to "Notes in Moral Theology" for

Theological Studies (1984-). Currently he is writing a book on religion and morality in the American philosophical tradition entitled, *The American Ethics of "the Fitting."* He will be a Research Fellow at Woodstock Theological Center at Georgetown University 1990-91.